MW01595841

Internationally Known
Locally Disrespected

This is Book # 110 *(handwritten)*

As a self-published author and independent creator,
I can't thank you enough for supporting this project.

(signature)

ake Driver Ed *(handwritten)*

Internationally Known, Locally Disrespected

The Unbelievable Stories of Driving Uber

Eddie Doyle

Copyright © 2023 by Eddie Doyle

Published 2023 in Philadelphia, Pennsylvania, by Prince Street Publishing. Prince Street Publishing and colophon are a registered trademark of Prince Street Publishing, LLC.

This book may be purchased for educational, business, or sales promotional use. For information please visit eddiepdoyle.com and click the business inquiries tab.

Editing contributions by:
Edward Vogner
ChatGPT
Michael Sandlin

This book is printed on acid free paper by DiggyPOD, Inc., a small business located in Tecumseh Michigan.

The text type used in the body of the book is Garamond.

ISBN : 978-1-7320713-2-2

Author's Note/Disclaimer: This is a work of creative nonfiction depicting actual events as truthfully as recollection and research permitted. Many of these rides were video and audio recorded on a dash camera, so even details down to the actual conversations are entirely accurate. That said, first names have been changed in the name of Rider-Driver Confidentiality.*

*Not actually a legally protected relationship. I'm just not in the business of embarrassing people who were simply looking to get a ride.

For my dad

who always said he didn't care if I grew up to be a trashman, as long as I was the one driving the truck.

I think I finally realized what you meant—to always strive to be the best I could be at whatever it is I choose to do, to always work towards something better, to take control of my own life.

All this time, I thought you just wanted me to be a driver. Oh well. Classic mix-up.

"

Think of how stupid the average person is,
and realize half of them are stupider than that.
- George Carlin

It would be a good idea to drive them around.
-Every Uber Driver Ever

"

Internationally Known, Locally Disrespected
is a collection of stand alone, true short stories.

Introduction

I am an Uber driver. And I'm not as dumb as you think I am.

I don't mean in the sense of intelligence, although if I told you my IQ, you might be reminded that unrewarded genius is almost a proverb.

I don't mean in the sense of education, although if I showed you my transcript, you might be reminded that the world is full of educated derelicts.

And I don't mean in the sense of trivial facts and knowledge, although it should be noted that I have come away victorious not once, not twice, but thrice at my local bar's trivia night. Could have been more if it wasn't for that damn round where you have to name TV theme songs.

Now, I've learned the hard way what people assume about Uber drivers, so I figure it's a low bar to begin with. But when I say I'm smarter than you think, I mean I have one hell of a perspective on the human condition—a perspective I am all but certain is broader than most.

At this point you may very well be thinking, *This guy is a pompous asshole with delusions of grandeur he cooked up during all the idle time he has at his low-class job. If he was so smart, he wouldn't be a fucking Uber driver.*

The sentiment of that last sentence, in some shape or form, has been expressed to me by my Uber riders, and by the strangers who ask what I do for a living, and even by friends and family at times, typically when passions are high and they are trying to cut deep, as friends and family do. So forgive me for such a brash introduction, but it has been my experience that if I don't assert my qualifications, people associate my status as an Uber driver with my intelligence, value, and potential.

I'm not going to claim I grew up poor, especially after what I've seen driving Uber in Philadelphia. I've come across destitution in my own city that most people don't even know exists. By America's standards, I grew up very middle class. But unlike the typical middle-class standard of keeping up with the Joneses, I grew up with parents that believed frugality was next to Godliness. They worked for every red cent they had and wanted to instill in me the same values. I think I was the only kid on the high school football team that had to buy his own cleats. On a very related note, I was also the only kid on the high school football team with the cheap rubber cleats, instead of the screw-ins. I lost my starting position the first game it rained.

Point is, I grew up with the mindset of you do what it takes to handle your responsibilities. In the household I grew up in, the only judgment on the janitor was that he was doing the right thing.

As embarrassing as it is to admit, I had no idea how much stock people put into social status until I became an Uber driver. Here I was thinking my value as a person was found in things like loyalty, reliability, and my status as three-time trivia night champion. I didn't know that being an Uber driver would strain and even end relationships with certain "friends" that looked at it as a step down for me. The crazy thing is, I wasn't even making much more money at the "real job" I had left; it was just that my "real job" seemed more professional.

I'm smart enough to know that their comments are more of a projection rather than anything personal. When I'm working on a Saturday night, and the drunk in the back seat tells me to "get a real job," instead of taking offense, I ask them what they do for a living. Almost every time, the person who criticizes my job shares how they can't stand their own. I once even had a passenger tell me she was hospitalized for having panic attacks every Sunday when she would prep for her work week.

But what I find so fascinating is how these people are so blind to their own source of misery that they are encouraging me drink the Kool-Aid with them, to work a job I hate from Monday to Friday, wash reality away with alcohol every Friday and Saturday, and then spend my Sunday hungover and dreading the week ahead.

Call me crazy, but I'd rather chase after something I enjoy Monday through Friday, and if that means having to work Uber all weekend and the occasional weekday to make ends meet, sign me up.

You should know, I was normal once. I wore khaki pants and shirts with buttons to a job that came with my own office, a long commute, and a weekend that was the highlight of my schedule. But when a pay raise made me take a step back and evaluate the way the rest of my life was being mapped out, I didn't like what I saw. So I quit. As my peers advanced in their careers, and started getting married and buying houses, I started driving for Uber.

Why? Because after I quit my job, I had committed the next three months of my life to something on my bucket list: writing a book. I self-published that first book and it was not what you would call "commercially successful" (read: I am still in the hole from it), but what I found being my own boss was a freedom I never wanted to lose. It wasn't long before I promised myself that I was going to do everything in my power to avoid going back to the grind of the nine-to-five.

Right around the time I had finished writing that book, I realized I had burned through all of my savings. At that time, Uber wasn't new, but it was just becoming mainstream. The freedom and flexibility it offered was enough for me to give it a shot.

When I first started driving, I was able to clear enough on the weekends to support my lifestyle, while working on my creative endeavors during the week. And despite being such a "low-class" job, Uber was what people were interested in at the holiday parties. I was the Kerouac with a story to tell, and driving in a city known for its bad attitude and affinity for alcohol, there was never a shortage of material.

I can think of no other profession that allows you to interact with people from every socioeconomic status in such a private, intimate, and anonymous environment that naturally encourages strangers to share their truth without judgment or consequence. After all, I'm just an Uber driver. Who cares what I think of them?

And if that isn't enough for people to show their true selves, the alcohol usually involved is. Unlike a therapist, who gets clientele constrained to their pay range and learns about the issues in a sober, thought-out retelling on a comfortable couch, I get a glimpse of their real character, raw and in the moment, often as the problem they are dealing with is unfolding, or the wound that needs healing is still fresh.

Point is, my experience as an Uber driver has allowed me to break out of the matrix. We live our lives more and more dictated by the design of the platforms we use. Netflix picks the next movie we watch, Spotify cues up the next song we listen to, and TikTok, YouTube, and Instagram feed us media that manipulates our emotions in a way to hold our attention as long as possible. These platforms mirror our preferences and then, be it by design or unintended consequence, mold us, providing a personalized, endless stream of content full of viewpoints we already agree with. The only time allowed for other perspectives is when they are being mocked, misrepresented, or demonized.

My stories, however, are as random, honest, and unengineered as you can get in the 21st century. Rich or poor, black or white, male or female, and everything in between, the people I meet and the situations I encounter are based on nothing but where me and my rider happened to be at any given point in time.

It seems like everything I need to know about life I learned from driving Uber, and the following is a compilation of the most impactful rides I have ever given. Some of them are funny, some of them are scary, and some of them have changed the way I look at the world so drastically I feel obligated to share. After all, the most recurring question I get from passengers is *has anything crazy ever happened?*

With over five thousand rides in a major metropolitan area where the only barrier to entry into my vehicle is a smartphone and $7 to spend, never mind the fact that alcohol is usually involved, the only reasonable answer to that question is *how much time do you have?*

1
The Wildest Ride

"You got here faster than the cops," was the first thing Jerry said to me when he got into my car. It was 10:30 on a Wednesday night. Thirty minutes prior I was lying in bed, unable to sleep, so I figured I'd turn the Uber app on and see if there were any rides to be had. This would turn out to be the first, and only, request I got that night. It is still to this day the wildest, most unexpected single ride I've ever given in my driving career.

The pickup was in a modest development of townhomes in a wealthy suburb, the kind of place older people move to when they are looking to downsize. In a neighborhood like that, you can imagine my surprise when I pulled up to a middle-aged woman, wearing a robe, using all her might to underhand toss a medium-sized suitcase onto the front lawn.

I couldn't make out exactly what she was yelling about, but I have never seen an adult woman act so much like a six-year-old in my entire life. And the man was essentially ignoring her, moving about as if the tantrum she was throwing was part of his daily routine.

As he walked past her and through the door, she gave a couple open-handed swings onto his shoulder and back. He kept walking as if he didn't feel it, and she screamed after him, "If you get in that car, don't bother coming back!"

When I saw him pick up his bag from the lawn, I got out of my car and opened the trunk, giving him a greeting that went unanswered.

"By the time I come back, you'll be in jail," he calmly answered her. He tossed his suitcase into the trunk. "Let's get the fuck out of here," he said, to no one in particular.

From the context clues I gathered, it seemed like Jerry was the one who called the cops on the girl, and I was half expecting to pass by a cop car arriving on the scene as we left the neighborhood. I didn't know the legality of calling the cops to a scene and then quite literally fleeing from it, and I didn't want to find out, especially given the fact that I'm the one facilitating the fleeing. And while I recognize that it was simply a matter of chance, I did feel a weird sense of pride that I arrived faster than the police, as if my immaculate Uber driver rating had to do, at least in part, with my ability to arrive on scene faster than first responders. That said, it did not escape me that this seemed to be an occurrence that was not uncommon in Jerry's household, so that could have been partly why the police were dragging their feet to the scene. As curious as I was, I knew better than to ask. I've always found that common pleasantries are enough of an invitation for someone who wants to share. And much to my curiosity's delight, Jerry wanted to share.

It was barely two minutes after I confirmed he was heading to the airport that he got into it, still as cool as a cucumber. "She can yell and scream and throw things all she wants. The second she puts her hands on me is when I get the fuck out of there. I called the cops, then I called you. Still can't believe you beat them there."

"What can I say, I'm a professional."

"Hopefully if the cops show up that will scare her enough. Knowing her she'll turn on the water works, and they'll think she's the victim."

"Probably for the best you got out of there." I don't like to insert myself into a situation any more than I have to. Generic lines and agreeing with my passenger is usually the route I take. I think people realize what I'm doing, and appreciate it; not for the words I'm saying, but for staying out of their business.

"You seem alright. How late are you working tonight?"

"Not sure. I'll see how the night goes."

"Well look, I got this flight later... it's private so it's leaving at a weird time, I think a little after three in the morning. You could drop me off at the airport now, and you'll get the fare on the app. Or you can hang with me until the flight. There's a bar I'd like to stop at, and I might want to run to my office downtown."

"Til three in the morning?" I said out loud, as I looked at the clock. What I was really saying was *How much you planning on paying me?*

"I'll make it worth your time, I promise. You'll make more money tonight than you will all week."

At this, I agreed. Sometimes I wonder if I am leaving money on the table by not negotiating up front, but I've always found that the people who make propositions based on convenience will always value the convenience more than I value the service I am providing. At the very crux of it, financially speaking, their time is more valuable than mine. So far, it's proven to be a very effective approach.

He reiterated that he might want to stop by his office later but told me to head to a dive bar located right off 95. I had never been inside, but passed by it many times and knew it as a local spot that served as the stop off for workers leaving the surrounding plants and warehouses in the very blue-collar area.

"So what do you for work?" Being that we might be stopping by his office later, I thought it was a friendly question to pass the time. I had no idea that of all things, including recently seeing his significant other assault him, this question would be what finally cracked his calm demeanor. His tone shifted on a dime.

"Now look, if you have anything recording in here…"

"I don't," I tried to squeeze in, but he continued as if he didn't hear me.

"I don't consent. Let me say that again to be perfectly clear, I do not consent to any recording that is taking place. Pennsylvania is a two-party consent state and if you record me without my knowledge, it's a felony."

He wasn't speaking with a tone of paranoia, but with an unvarnished motive to protect himself. I had recently considered getting a dash camera, and while he was not entirely correct about it being a felony to record in my own my own car, I was impressed that he knew we were in a two-party consent state, and even more impressed with the confidence he had in his own approach to answer my question after he protected himself with his little speech. That said, it was a little concerning that he felt the need to preface whatever he was about to say with all of that.

"I own an adult entertainment establishment you probably heard of. As you can imagine, it's not the most reputable business to be involved in and the club I own has a reputation for being one of the worst."

Ah, that explains his disclaimer.

"Which club is that?"

He proceeded to tell me that he owns and operates the absolute raunchiest club in Philadelphia. It's the kind of strip club that even strippers would be embarrassed* to admit they danced there. Unlike most gentleman's clubs that operate with a liquor license and require you to be 21, this particular club is BYOB, meaning you only have to be 18 to enter. When my best friend turned 18 (coincidentally,

---

* That's not hyperbole, either. I learn that the hard way in chapter 15

also on a Wednesday), per his birthday request, we took a drive down to this very establishment. What my young, innocent eyes saw forever shaped my perspective on strip clubs. Forever burned in my brain is the image of two needle-marked women utilizing the same adult toy, hands free, while a mustached, middle-aged man with glasses, a wedding ring, and an outfit that said he just stepped out of a cubicle, gawked on. I know it's cliche to say those two girls are somebody's daughters, but what really stuck with me that night was that guy. I wondered it then and I wonder it now: what were the circumstances that brought this Ned Flanders impersonator out of his whitebread lifestyle and into a place like this? Even more concerning was the look on his face, transfixed by these very rough-looking women engaged in a very rough-looking activity, in a very rough manner, staring at them as if they were the drug he needed to feed his addiction. I don't know if I've ever seen a man look more pathetic. It was one of those moments where I decided that however my life turned out, as long as I wasn't that guy, I'd be doing alright.

"I bet that is a hell of a business to be in." I tried to play it cool, but I felt like I was with underworld royalty. I couldn't imagine the level of debauchery my passenger dealt with on a daily basis. I mean, he's responsible for managing the aforementioned women performing with double-sided dildos for a living. It's no wonder he can handle a domestic assault like a walk in the park.

We get to the bar, and though I had never been inside before, it was exactly what I expected. I was the youngest person in there by at least twenty years, and one of the only people not in a work uniform. Within moments of stepping through the door, the bartender greets him by name, and Jerry tells her a round of drinks is on him… for the entire bar. I looked around and did a quick count of about fifty. He pulled out a wad of cash as thick as my fist and peeled off a few hundreds onto the bar as the bartender started to pass out drink chips. Despite this apparent generosity, it became very obvious very quickly that part of the reason this guy wanted me to stick around, as opposed to just calling another Uber, was because he was in need of a companion. Nobody seemed to like him, and it didn't take detective skills to figure out why.

Throughout the night, he would point out random people in the bar and share with me his relationship with them, which usually involved him having sex with someone he should not have had sex with:

"That guy won't look me in the eye because he knows I fucked his wife."

"That guy doesn't know it, but I fucked his girlfriend."

"That lady hates my guts because I stopped talking to her... after I fucked her."

I didn't say much to these claims, because after all, what is there to say? Plus, I know a guy like that enjoys the shock value of those stories, so my speechlessness was sufficient. What was most shocking, though, was how all of those people were still very respectful to him. These same people he pointed out, sharing with me explicit and intimate details of his relations with their spouses or significant others, would come up to him and have that kind of conversation you have out of obligation with someone that it would be rude if you ignored, like if you got stuck standing in line at the grocery store next to your boss.

Over the course of these obligated conversations, it would always seem to come out that Jerry was employing the guy, or lent him money, or put her up an in apartment. Basically, in some way shape or form, he had these people by the purse strings, and because of that, they were willing to put up with just about anything.

It's wild what money can do.

What's even crazier, something that I feel may be the least believable thing I write in this book— something I wouldn't believe if I didn't see and hear it myself, was that this man, a short, white, beer-bellied guy with slicked-back hair, dressed like someone, well, who works at a strip club, used the N-word like a normal person would use "guy" or "man" or "dude."

Hard R and everything. Granted, he was probably in his sixties or seventies, meaning he came of age in a time when that word didn't have the same connotation it does today. Not saying it was an appropriate word back then, I'm just saying people from his generation didn't get fired for using it. Plus, in his defense, he was using it to describe people of all races in the bar, which was a very diverse crowd: racially, that is. Otherwise, everyone had on the same color collar.

But even more shocking than him using *that* word was how the people within earshot received it.

The first time he said it loud enough for others to hear was around the pool table. Even though it was in reference to a white man, being the functional member of society that I am, it made me perk up and prepare myself for any possible consequences. It didn't help that the group of people he was talking to was of mixed race. But just as those he cucked looked the other way, anyone within earshot ignored it and moved the conversation along.

But then he used it in reference to a black man in the same circle of people. To be fair, it wasn't any more malicious than when he used it referring to the white person a few minutes prior. He tapped me on the shoulder, pointed to the black guy he was talking to and said, "This nigger owes me two grand, and thinks he can win it back playing me in pool." I looked at the guy he was pointing at, and I'll never forget the expression on his face.

It wasn't a look of hurt, or pain, but one of helplessness and regret. It was a look that made me think it didn't matter what Jerry called him; his frustration came from knowing that he had to eat whatever shit sandwich Jerry throws his way because of the financial situation he got himself into. And that was probably the saddest thing I saw all night.

Now that Jerry was occupied at the pool table, my value as a companion lessened. He pulled out a $50 bill and asked me to go grab him cigarettes at the Wawa down the street. A better man might have thought himself above being an errand boy, but I couldn't have been happier to get the hell out of that bar. I figured the less time I spend with a guy that everyone wants to punch, the better.

When I got to Wawa, I grabbed a much-needed coffee that would keep me going until his flight. That's when the Boston creme donuts started calling my name. It's not often that they make them that big and that round and that beautiful, and though I try not to eat too many empty calories that late at night, I found myself staring at the donut window the way Ned Flanders was staring at those strippers many moons ago. I just couldn't pass it up.

When I used Jerry's $50 bill to pay, I thought of the wad of cash that it came from. It made me think he wouldn't even notice the extra $3 I spent on a coffee and donut. As I drove back to the bar, I justified what would essentially be stealing by declaring it a convenience fee for getting his cigarettes for him. Plus, it's not like he would notice.

But then I thought about all the men—these grown ass men —most of them in uniforms, exhausted from a long day of work, who Jerry had by the short and curlies because of that one thing... money. And I know the day might come when I sell my soul and sacrifice what's important to me out of necessity, but a coffee and donut ain't it. So I pulled out three single dollar bills from my wallet and put them into the pile of change I had to give back to Jerry.

I sat in my car for a good bit, killing time before heading back into the bar. When I did, I handed Jerry the cigarettes and the forty-some dollars in change.

"Keep the change. I appreciate you going."

I wish I could say I took this moment to reflect on the value of honesty... to attribute his generosity as the universe rewarding me, and take this instance as another reminder as to why you should always tell the truth. In reality, all I could think about was how this dude just gave me $40 for a ten-minute Wawa run. *This really might be the most I ever earn in a night,* I thought.

We were at the bar long enough for him to buy two more rounds for the entire place, each time peeling off bills from his wad of cash like he was giving out penny candy at a parade.

As if it was a mandatory work meeting, seven men and women in their blue Fed-Ex uniforms roll through the door. "Geez, it's after 1 already?" Jerry said upon seeing them, not even looking at his watch. He told me he was going to step outside to have a cigarette, and then we'd head downtown to his office. I couldn't have been happier to get out of that bar.

"Delaware Ave?" I asked when he got into my car after his cigarette. I didn't know whether I should be proud or ashamed that I knew the name of the street his strip club was on.

Ok, who am I kidding, I pride myself in knowing my city like the back of my hand, and I thought this sort of carnal local knowledge gave me some credibility.

"Nah, we aren't heading to the club right now. Maybe later, I don't know if we will have time. Got to stop by my spot downtown first."

"Downtown?" Despite being a top-ten US city, the entirety of downtown Philadelphia can be covered by car at this time of night, or should I say morning, in less than ten minutes, and from Delco, no matter where downtown we were heading, there's really only one way to get there. So I wasn't asking where downtown he was taking me, I was asking *where* downtown he was taking me. Even though I spent the last two hours at the bar with him, and even though I felt an inexplicable sense of responsibility to side with him if his provocation led to a fight (maybe not fight for him, but at least break it up so he doesn't get beat up too badly), and even though he treated me to a much-needed coffee and a delicious donut, I still had no idea who this guy was and what I could be getting into. There is a fine line between paranoia and caution, and when you are driving around strangers to strange places in the middle of the night, it pays to err toward the latter at the risk of the former.

"I have another spot there. You'll see."

"What kind of spot?"

"Jesus Christ, you'll see." He could tell I was hesitant, and oddly enough, his impatience with my suspicion made me feel better. There's something about someone who isn't trying to make me feel comfortable that tends to make me trust them more... it's like they have nothing to hide.

Within fifteen minutes we are downtown and he directs me to a pay-to-park lot I've passed by hundreds of times. The lot was well lit, and there was no missing the signs demanding those who park there when the attendant isn't on duty to put money in the slot corresponding to their parking space, otherwise risk getting towed.

"Do I have to worry about paying?" I wasn't sure how long we were going to be.

"No." He said it so confidently, I felt stupid for asking. That feeling didn't last long, though, because the moment I stepped out of my car a white* guy seemingly appeared out of nowhere and asked for payment.

"That's $20 to park there," the white guy said.

"Ignore him," Jerry said. He was emptying his pockets onto the trunk of my car for reasons he did not explain.

"That's a $400 towing fee if you don't," the white guy pressed on. I looked back to Jerry, who didn't even bother to look up from his pockets' contents that were strewn across my trunk, then back to the white guy. You have to understand, Philly is a blue-collar town full of homeless people, drug addicts, and scammers, and sometimes, you don't know which category of person you are dealing with. This white guy didn't necessarily look homeless, but he didn't look like someone you could trust either. And I know one of the oldest tricks in the book is acting like a parking lot attendant and asking for cash from someone who doesn't know any better.

"That'll be $20," he said again.

"Jerry?"

"Just ignore him, you're fine."

"You don't want a ticket, do you?" the white guy said. He knew I had no idea what kind of lot I parked in.

"Jesus Christ," Jerry exclaimed. I thought he was finally going to sort out this parking situation. I was wrong. "I forgot my fucking

---

*I recognize it may seem odd to some people I would describe this person as a white guy, being that the skin color of a guy in a city parking is usually inconsequential. Plus, it is a pet peeve of mine when someone includes race in a story when it is otherwise irrelevant, which it usually is. This is the long way of saying I am including his skin color, my dear reader, because it would turn out to be relevant to the story.

key." He gathered up his stuff and put it back in his pockets. "Let's go," he said, and started moving across the parking lot.

"I'm not going to get towed, am I?" I asked. I had to put a little pep in my step to keep up with Jerry, meanwhile, the white guy jumped into gear to follow me.

"You're gonna regret not giving me that money, man." Before I could even process the subliminal threat that was in that statement, Jerry stopped in his tracks, turned, and looked the white guy in the eye for the first time since he showed up.

"John, get the FUCK out of here! I swear to God if I see you even breathe on his car," he pointed to a security camera hanging off the building next to the lot, "I'll cut your dick off and shove it so far up your ass…"

"Alright, alright, alright," John said, laughing as though the entertainment he got from frazzling me and stirring Jerry up was worth more than the $20. He turned and walked away, and I could hear him amusing himself until he was out of earshot.

The backside of the parking lot was essentially an alley, but in an old and cramped Northeast city like Philly, it was still technically a street with a name and buildings and addresses. We came up to a set of row homes, and Jerry knocked on a door.

"I feel like a fucking pervert whenever I have to knock on this door," he said.

What a great insight to give me before we head into a strange row house at 1:30 in the morning. He had taken two steps back and set himself square to the door. A slot slid open, but I couldn't see through it.

"Can I help you?" It was a female voice with a thick Asian accent.

"I forgot my fucking key."

"Who is that?"

"It's my driver. He's alright."

The wooden door opens, revealing a stocky middle-aged woman so short that her chest barely cleared the screen of the storm door. Jerry opened the storm door and held it, motioning me to head inside. I stepped through, and immediately regretted my decision. *What the fuck am I thinking walking into a place that I don't even know what the fuck it is, with a guy I don't know behind me.*

I stepped inside onto a dark green carpet that went straight back, unraveling down a dim and red lighted hallway that ended with an ugly yellow string curtain, thinly veiling the living room behind it. To my left, almost as if it was forgotten during the seedy makeover, was a well-lit, small, and messy kitchen. I could hear Jerry locking the multiple deadbolts on the door behind me, and I didn't like the idea of following the short Asian lady as she made her way to the yellow curtain, sandwiching myself between her and Jerry in that creepy hallway, so I peeled into the empty kitchen and allowed Jerry to pass. I didn't know what the hell was going on, but I wanted to make sure I was ready for the absolute worst. I even sized up the kitchen window in case I needed an emergency exit. As I mentally prepped myself for the possibility of an emergency escape that could only entail a superman dive over the pile of dishes stacked up in the sink, through the glass window, and out onto the street, Jerry finally finished securing the door. He turned and saw me standing in the kitchen entrance, doing a very bad job of hiding my uneasiness about the situation .

"What are you, hungry?"

"I just don't know where I'm going." He could tell I was uneasy, shook his head, and continued down the hallway. I followed him through the yellow string curtain into what looked like a living room, with a large, wraparound leather couch. There was a beat-up, square coffee table with some dirty magazines and even dirtier ashtrays on it, and an old stereo system that was playing music through, I kid you not... an iPod. There was nobody else in the room. Jerry told me to take a seat.

"John was breaking his balls when he parked," Jerry said the Asian lady.

"What's he doing working this late?"

"No, White John."

"White John is working for you now?"

"No!"

"Where's Black John?"

"It's Wednesday. I'm thinking about paying him."

"White John?"

"No, Black John."

"That'd be good."

"I owe him money too, could you pay him the next time he's in?"

While I had to bite my tongue to keep from laughing every time I heard "White John" and "Black John" in broken English, this "Who's on First" routine made me think Jerry owned the parking lot. *No wonder he wasn't concerned about parking there.*

They continued to talk for only a few minutes before there was a knock. The Asian lady headed to the door, and came back with a tall white guy and a shorter Asian, both looking like they were in their early twenties. They looked excited to the point of dorky and followed the woman through the yellow curtain and up the staircase that came off of the living room.

"There's bottles of water in the fridge," Jerry said, pointing to a small, clear box in the corner of the room. "Can I get you anything, else?" I declined, and he headed up the stairs as well. I had been trying to piece together the kind of place I was in since I walked through the door, and as I played on my phone, waiting, I thought those two guys that came through all but solidified it. But in case I needed any more verification, what I saw come down the steps fifteen minutes later removed all doubt.

"This way baby," I heard a confident and soothing female voice say, followed by the clonk of heels coming down the steps. Through the staircase beams, I first saw the red shoes. Then, with another step, the thick calves. Two more steps revealed the very large, cellulite-covered thighs, then with another step, the even larger, and much more jiggly stomach. This was followed by the most ginormous, floppy pair of tits I have ever seen. She hit the landing and turned toward me, bringing into focus perhaps the most memorable woman I have ever seen in my life. She had on black lingerie (a bikini-style top and g-string bottom), and not including the very see-through black cover up, due to her size, the amount of her body that was actually covered by clothing was comparable to the amount of water covered by a small boat in the ocean. The bra was so visibly strained that it gave me an urge to give it a little tug, just to see if it would snap or not. It was so tight that it was holding up her breasts to a normal position on her chest (I only knew they were floppy because of the outpouring of breast flesh from every side of the bra).

A girl with the body of a bulldozer dressing as of it's a Ferrari is always a memorable sight, but what really struck me about this woman was that she was the blackest Asian I have ever seen. Black Asian is one of the rarer combinations as is, and I feel like most of the time one look supersedes the other. Not this time. If she had an accent as thick as the madam's I would not have thought twice. At the same time, if she was dropping the N-bomb as freely as Jerry was earlier, I wouldn't have batted an eye. She had a face that would otherwise be characterized as very Asian but with skin as dark as you have ever seen, and an afro pulled back into a bun. She spoke with that familiar Philly attitude that had me thinking she had lived in this city most of her life.

"You can sit here until your friend is finished," she said to her client.

"I think I'll just go," the Asian guy said, and she walked him to the door. She came back to the living room and sat down not too close to me but on the same side of the wraparound couch. She pulled out a small joint from a coin purse.

"You smoke?" she asked, holding up the joint to me. She had a confidence about her that I couldn't help but admire.

"I'm ok for now, thank you."

She grabbed a lighter from the coffee table as I tried to process the situation I was in. Before I could really come to grips with it, I heard that same sound of clonking coming down the steps, though it was nowhere near as loud as it was with the XXL black Asian. This time around, the staircase reveal involved skinny legs, followed by a matching waist, on an average-looking white girl. She was followed by the tall white kid. She brought him straight to the door, and I wondered if the white guy went with the white girl and the Asian guy went with the half-Asian girl by chance, or design. I don't usually attribute too much to race, but this black Asian combination really had my wheels turning.

When the white girl came back to the living room, I thought to myself she might be wearing the exact same outfit as the big girl... not just in style but in size as well, as her outfit actually fit her. I wish I could tell you about some cool hooker talk; some behind-the-scenes trading of stories regarding their recent endeavor or nightmare experience, the kind of thing you would see in a movie. Instead, they just sat there in silence, the big girl smoking and the white girl looking through her phone, like me. As I sat there on the couch, the cliched question of what could have possibly led these women to this point in their lives crept into my head. The white girl looked like a hundred girls I went to school with that got too into drugs and the rest was history. The black Asian? Who knows? I don't think even Tarantino could come up with a believable backstory for a character so improbable.

I caught myself imagining their pasts full of sorrow and troubles that led them to this couch before it dawned on me that I was sitting on that same exact couch. Sure, the roles were different... I didn't just jerk off a stranger in an upstairs bedroom for a couple of bucks. But then again, were they? Was I not playing companion to Jerry all night long for a few dollars? Was I not servicing the needs of my client, whether it was being an errand boy or laughing at his jokes that weren't actually funny? Was I not dancing to that familiar jig of the driver to his passenger, of the employee to his boss, of the hooker to her John?

Point is, who the fuck am I to judge? If anything, they were probably making a lot more money than me. We sat there together, in silence, for another fifteen minutes before there was another knock on the door. Without hesitation, the two girls got up and headed upstairs. They passed the older Asian lady coming down the steps and making her way to the door. Jerry followed and sat on the couch. We watched in silence as a single, middle-aged man, looking desperate and defeated, came through the yellow curtain and headed up the steps without needing to be told where to go.

Before the madam followed him up the steps, Jerry asked if she needed anything else. She declined, and they said goodbye. He motioned me to the door.

"Let's get to the airport."

I tried my best to conceal my sigh of relief. It felt like every second of this night was flirting with potential disaster, and as interesting as it was, I was ready to get paid and get home while I was still in one piece. He motioned for me to exit the living room ahead of him, which I didn't love, but it wasn't anywhere I hadn't been before, and I wanted to get the hell out of there. I parted the ugly yellow curtain as if it was the Red Sea to my freedom and started walking down the red-lit hallway. I was but a few steps away from the door when Jerry stopped in his tracks. "I forgot something." He turned around and headed back upstairs. "Just meet me outside."

To say I was uncomfortable with the situation would be the understatement of the century. At this point, I doubt Jerry would be setting me up for something malicious... but at the same time, everything that just happened seemed like it could very well be setting me up for something malicious. Sure, Jerry hadn't done anything to me personally that would cause me to distrust him, but in the past four hours I have seen him involved in a domestic dispute, brag about banging other dude's wives, and hard R the n-bomb in public. Not to mention, he owes a black John money and there's a white John that he doesn't get along with. What I'm saying is, I know enough about this guy to know that there is no telling what could be on the other side of that door waiting for him, or me, or the both of us, and I'll be damned if I walk out of a brothel into an alley alone at two o'clock in the morning to find out. So I peeled into the kitchen and waited for him to come back.

Waiting in that kitchen for what felt like forever, I couldn't help but notice how the kitchen was very lived in. There were dishes in the sink, a large trash can that needed to be emptied, and reusable shopping bags hanging by the cabinets that made me wonder if their grocery store charged extra for plastic bags, or if these hookers were environmentally conscious. Regardless, this kitchen got my wheels turning. Who is responsible for the grocery shopping in a place like this, and what is on the grocery list? Is it considered a business expense? When do they eat? And perhaps most perplexing, who the fuck does the dishes in a whorehouse?

Jerry comes back and sees me standing in the kitchen.

"Let's go," he said.

"You can go first." I played it cool, but firm.

"Jesus Christ. Still?" Even after all this time, Jerry could tell I still didn't trust the situation, but I didn't care. I wasn't going to be the first one out of that door.

Of course, nothing happened when we stepped outside, and within moments we were back into my car. On the way to the airport, a ways away from the parking lot where I first met him, we passed by White John wandering the streets.

"Hey look. It's White John." I said, laughing to myself at the coincidence.

Jerry didn't even look up from his phone. "Fuckin' asshole."

Seeing White John again sparked a replay of the night in my head as we road to the airport in silence. Jerry getting hit by his girlfriend felt like a week ago, and after everything we went though, the man sitting next to me was more than just a Uber client. He was more like an uncle. Not necessarily an uncle you know and love, but more like your ex-girlfriend's uncle you met a couple times at a family party and you liked hanging around him because he had some wild-ass stories.

At the start of our night, if you recall, he had told me he was flying private, so when we got to the airport, I assumed he wanted to be dropped at terminal A, which is where charter flights fly from. However, he asked me to drop him at Terminal F. He told me it was his friend's jet they were taking, so that's why he needed to be at the other end of the airport. I don't know if he was full of shit about the private jet or what. I also don't know if he actually owned the club he was implying he owned. My guess is a club that size has multiple owners, so maybe he owns a share of it and possibly serves as manager as well. What I do know is he showed me an establishment in Center City Philadelphia I would have otherwise never known existed, with a cash cow of a parking lot to go with it. If that wasn't enough evidence to give validity to his claims, that wad of cash of his that I saw earlier let me know he wasn't completely full of shit.

When we pulled up to the terminal, I popped the trunk and opened my car door to get out and grab his suitcase.

"Wait," he said, as he took that wad of cash back out and started peeling $50 bills from it. He ended up paying me what worked out to be about $45 an hour.

"I wasn't lying to you, right? This is the most you ever earned in a night?" He wanted to make sure he held that title.

I had the cash in my hand at this point, so there was no more need to stroke his ego. "It's up there, but it's not the most."

"You fucking kidding me?"

No, I'm not kidding you. I play the customer service song and dance all night long, laughing at your jokes that aren't that funny, being impressed by your stories that I don't find all that impressive... but once the money is in hand, my friend, that jig stops.

What I actually said was: "I appreciate it, don't get me wrong."

"Well, what the fuck do you want?"

More money you fucking idiot. The good story was a nice little ancillary benefit, sure, but you think I did this for anything other than the almighty dollar?

What I actually said was: "It's fine, I think it's totally fair." Which, in reality, I think it was. I just wasn't about to let this guy think he held the title of my most generous client when he most certainly didn't.

"Jesus Christ." He peeled off another $60 before getting out.

"I appreciate it, I really do."

"Is it the most, now?"

"Look, I'm sorry. I don't know what to tell you. Let me grab your bag."

"You stay in the car," he said with an angry insistence that I knew there was no arguing with. He slammed the trunk and walked to the gate without a goodbye, and his departure made me wonder the whole ride home: Did he get his own bag to compensate for not giving me the most money I ever earned? He let me get the bag at the start of the ride, and he was about to let me get it before he paid me. I wondered if stopping that song and dance of customer service, of standing up for what I actually believed rather than saying something to make the customer happy like a good little Uber slave would, made him respect me a little more.

I can't say for sure if that was the case or if I was just reading into things. Either way, I know this: that was the wildest fucking ride of my life.

2
Uber Daycare

It didn't take long after I signed up for Uber that I had to drive a student to school. It was uncomfortable, being alone with a minor, but being that Uber didn't have any policies in place against it at the time, I would have felt even more uncomfortable kicking her out. Plus, the fact that this rider happened to be black and female made me think it wise to take her without protest and avoid the risk of seeing my picture next to the headline RACIST UBER DRIVER KICKS OUT GIRL TRYING TO GET TO SCHOOL. What I found most ironic about that ride, however, was that on the corner, just a hop, skip, and jump away from the girl's house, were her classmates waiting at the bus stop.

If you have never driven for Uber, I'd bet dollars to donuts that you think about taking a cab to school differently depending on what side of the aisle you're on. I can hear liberals assuming it to be those evil one-percenters, too good for a public school bus and pointing to it as an example of income equality and the need to redistribute the wealth. On the other hand, I can still hear my very Republican uncle, after I told him how often I drive kids to school, saying, "That's exactly why everyone is so god damn broke these days, living above their means and not teaching their kids the value of a dollar." He doesn't have a Southern accent, but when he gets on those rants, that's how I hear it.

Turns out, both sides have some truth to them. I've taken kids to school from government project housing, and from houses that have two front doors. That's right, this house was so damn big that it had two front-facing entrances. I didn't know which one to pull up to, so I kind of split the two. It didn't matter; they ended up coming out of the garage. The convenience and comfort that Uber offered was enough to transcend social class and financial responsibility, and I accepted that giving rides to unaccompanied minors as just another overlooked reality of this gig.

That is until one day, I was in South Philadelphia, near the river that separates Pennsylvania and New Jersey, when I got a request on the other side of the water in Camden. The running joke with New Jersey is that it's such a dump, they don't charge you to come in, but they charge you when you leave. I was a solid twenty minutes away, so I didn't want to commit to crossing the bridge only to have the rider get impatient and call off the trip; then I'd be stuck with the $5 toll to get home. I called my rider to let her know I'm on my way, and she assured me she wouldn't cancel because the ride is for her daughter who needs to get to school.

"Cool, I'll be there soon," I hung up, thinking nothing of it.

Twenty minutes later, I pulled up to a long line of row homes. A mom and three elementary school kids with backpacks were walking out of their front door. I was confused at first, as the woman on the phone only mentioned a daughter. I started dreading the trip ahead. I had given quite a few round trip rides to elementary schools, where the parents will ride along with their little ones (so they weren't alone in the Uber), drop the kids off at school, and then I would take the parent back home or to work. I hated it, because it would usually entail getting stuck in the drop-off line, which, for those who have never experienced it, is the most inefficient form of traffic flow in modern society. I get it, child safety is first. But when you are stuck in that line clearing two dollars an hour and a couple of snot-nosed kids who you don't know are crying in the back seat about going to school, you start thinking about how the world has enough kids as is and get comfortable with the idea of a little less safety precautions and a little more of getting me the fuck out of here.

So I was relieved when the mom and the three kids piled into the car ahead of me. In the adjacent door they came out of, a young girl waved at me through her storm door, pointing at her phone as a way of asking if I was her Uber. I remember thinking that she certainly looked younger but was surprised that she was still high school age. I gave her a thumbs up to indicate I was indeed her Uber. This young woman opened the door and from behind her legs ran a child so small that with every stride she took her Disney schoolbag would hit her calves.

This tiny human sprinted across the lawn, directly to my back door, and grabbed hold of the door handle with both hands. Using all of her body weight, she pulled it open. She got in like it was just another typical morning, but then struggled to reach and pull the door shut, as her size made it nearly impossible. I was shocked that this girl was riding by herself and stepped out of my car thinking the mom might want to talk to me. When the mom saw me get out, however, she quickly waved at me and shut her front door. *I guess this is what we are doing, then,* I thought, as the girl continued to struggle with the door. I walked around to the passenger side of the car, said "Watch your hands and feet," and shut the door.

Looking back, I handled this very poorly. First of all, in the fine print of Uber's terms of use, turns out there were a few lines about people using the service having to be over a certain age. I can't tell you what it said then, but I am sure it was phrased in a way to cover Uber's ass in case anything happened, but buried to make most drivers miss it. More recently, they've been a little more transparent about drivers not taking minors, but when the company was still expanding, they couldn't let something like child safety get in their way.

My second major mistake was, apparently, babies aren't the only people in the world that require car seats. How the fuck was my childless ass supposed to know that kids as old as twelve still need booster seats?

In case you haven't pieced it together yet, as uncomfortable as I was, my dumb ass went ahead with the ride. Immediately after we left, I hear a shuffling in the back seat, and I see in the rearview this girl struggling to put the seatbelt on.

I was surprised when I started getting comments on my YouTube channel demanding I make sure my passengers put on their seatbelts. It didn't even cross my mind that my videos display the more-common-than-not choice people make to not wear one. There's something about riding in a car-for-hire that makes people think they don't need seatbelts, as if a car crash in a ride you paid for doesn't hurt as much as one you didn't. I often want to remind people that my license is the same as anyone else's; it's not like I went through some sort of special rideshare school to qualify me as a safe driving expert. I'm just a financially desperate soul being exploited by Uber for my cheap labor and the fact that I own a car. That said, I learned early on that it's a waste of energy to ask every single person who gets into my Uber to put on a seatbelt. At worst, it's asking for a fight. But seeing this girl struggle was quite the conundrum.

On one hand, it reminded me of the importance of seatbelts, and made me think, yeah, of course this child should be belted in. On the other hand, I operate on a strict no-touching-passengers policy, and that rule could never be more important than when the passenger is a little girl. As I debated the dilemma in my head, I finally heard a *click*— a source of temporary relief. But when I looked into the rearview, I saw the most mangled and twisted seatbelt arrangement you can imagine, with the top strap twisted and tucked directly on the girl's neck.

I couldn't let it stay like that, so I pulled over to the side of the road.

"We're just going to fix that seatbelt for you," I said, before turned and reaching into the back seat. Her face looked exactly like you would expect a girl's face to look when a bearded stranger is turning to her and telling her what to do. I pulled the top strap out and told her to put her arms up and over it, pulling it down under her armpits. It didn't look like the safest thing in the world, but it at least wasn't choking her anymore.

As we got back on our way, it was obvious that she was just as uncomfortable as I was, and the former teacher in me tried to break the ice with small talk.

"So what grade are you in?"

"First."

Good lord.

"What's your favorite subject."

"Recess."

"Other than recess."

"I don't know." She didn't laugh at my "other than recess" tone, making me think I came off a little strong. So I decided to shut the fuck up. Probably for the best, as I had no idea what to talk about with a six-year-old.

The awkwardness was interrupted by a call coming through the Uber app. It was her mother. This posed a problem, as I was already playing traffic-ticket roulette. Not only was I operating a car service that was illegal in New Jersey at the time, and not only was there a young girl who I didn't know in my car, riding without a car seat, but nothing will get a New Jersey cop's attention faster than talking on a cell phone while driving.

If I answer this phone, I thought, *I'm basically begging to get pulled over. But I can't ignore this lady's call when I have her daughter in the car, right?*

I am so glad I made the choice I did.

"Hello," I said, eyes peeled for police.

"I actually put the wrong address in. You are going the wrong way," the mom said, nonchalantly.

"Excuse me?" My heart started pounding. *I don't know how this plays out, but this feels like I'm getting set up for something bad.*

She gave me another address and I prayed that the new destination was actually a school. I didn't know what I would do if it wasn't. I started practicing the speech I would give if I had to explain myself to Law Enforcement or Child Services. "Look, Officer, in retrospect I realize I should've never picked up this kid in the first place, but I swear, I'm not a kidnapper. I don't even like kids!" As I pictured a scenario in which I get pulled over, I caught myself thinking that being a white man with a young black girl would be better than the inverse. I don't subscribe to the idea of white privilege often, but I think you'd be hard pressed to find a solid argument against it here.

Fortunately, after ten more minutes of an awkward silence, as I ran through every worst-case scenario, we pulled up to a school. But I was not yet in the clear. You have to understand something about Camden, New Jersey. It's not what you would call a "nice place." The city was so bad that just two years prior it made national news for abolishing it's entire police force. That's right—the people who were supposed to protect Camden were considered so corrupt that the city decided they were hurting more than helping and let everyone go. At the time, almost 40 percent of its 77,000 residents lived below the poverty line, and the city was home to over 3,000 abandoned buildings, 175 open-air drug markets, and a crime rate high enough to rank it among the most dangerous cities in America. With all that in mind, there was no chance in hell I was leaving the scene until I made sure this girl got into school safely.

The school was in the middle of a city block, and there was only space to pull over across the street from the entrance. Though not part of my usual services, I made an exception and got out of my car to open the girl's door. We can pretend it's because I'm a nice guy, but in reality, I didn't have any other option. She wouldn't have been able to get out otherwise.

I gave her the go ahead to cross the street and was laser focused on her every step, as there was no way I was going through that excruciating ride only to have this kid end up getting hit by a car. She clears the roadway (thank God) and was headed for the school's entrance. Like a lot of city schools, for safety, there's a camera on the door and you have to get buzzed in. Standing on her tippiest of tippy-toes, this little girl reaches up and presses the button.

The door doesn't open.

She does it again. Still nothing. This child was so short that she wasn't coming into view of the camera, and whoever was watching it couldn't see her, so they wouldn't unlock the door.

I'm watching this unfold, not knowing what the hell to do. On one hand, I am definitely not leaving her there, but on the other, I felt a little odd walking up to this school on behalf of a child that I don't know. Like, "Hey, I don't know this six-year-old girl, but I brought here in my car, could you let her in?" I feel like the natural question that scenario creates is, "Sir… what are you doing with this child and can I see some identification?" Next thing I know I'm being told to wait in the Principal's Office and I overhear an adult telling the kid to "show me on the doll where he touched you."

And that's when my self-awareness kicked in. I am a man in my bum-like Uber attire of baggy sweats and well-worn sneakers, with a very unkempt beard to boot, staring intently at a little girl outside of a school. I was not going to leave this girl before I knew that she was safe inside, but I felt the longer I watched, the creepier it would seem. I had to throw all caution to the wind and crossed the street with the intent to buzz this girl in myself, fully aware of the *Dateline: Catch a Predator* vibes I'd give off. Just as I got to the sidewalk, I noticed a mom and two kids heading for the door. I stopped in my tracks, did a one-eighty back to my car, but looking over my shoulder to make sure this lady held the door for my three-foot-tall Uber client.

On my ride back to Philly, I wondered if that woman would tell anyone how she saw a homeless-looking white guy hanging out in front of her kid's school, making a beeline to a young girl before she showed up. I wondered how often that kid takes an Uber to school, and I wondered if her mom was concealing her panic when she realized she had entered the wrong address, or if she was actually as calm as she sounded when she called me with the correct address. After all, your six-year-old daughter in a car with a strange man driving in the wrong direction is a typical start to the day, right?

3
My First Real Scare

I learned the hard way how helpless and alone I am when a ride goes awry.

People are always shocked to find out how little information I get as a driver before I pick someone up. When a request comes in, all I see is a first name and the address of the pickup location. I don't know how much I'll be getting paid, have no idea how many people will be getting in my car, and don't even have a reliable way of confirming that the right person is getting in my car. To top it off, I don't know where the rider is going until I start the trip.*

On one hand, it makes sense for Uber to do that, because otherwise drivers would only accept the trips that would make them a lot of money and only drive to places they want to go. On the other hand, it's complete bullshit for Uber to do that, because Uber doesn't classify drivers as employees—we are independent contractors. If I was really an independent contractor, I would get to choose what job I take before I take it, set my own prices, and I wouldn't get penalized when I don't accept a request. But Uber has Silicon Valley funding, which means they can afford lawyers and lobbyists who make it easy for politicians and judges to ignore labor laws meant to protect the forgettable peasants who drive for Uber. As a result, drivers have very little control over their income, but the even bigger issue has to do

---

*Recently, due to Uber's ongoing court battles to make sure their drivers remain classified as independent contractors, some of these things have changed in certain markets. In Philly, I can now see how much I will earn from a trip and where the rider is going. When I am driving in New Jersey, though, I see neither of those things. Regardless, for all of the stories in the book (including this one), those features were not yet available. All I knew when I accepted a request was the address I needed to pick the rider up at and the first name of the account holder (which isn't always the person getting in the car).

with safety. I realized how vulnerable I was as an Uber driver my very first night working.

It was a Friday night and I had grabbed pizza with my friend Jimmy. Despite his best efforts to get me to go out with him, I was hurting for cash and thought I'd finally give this Uber thing I signed up for a shot. Before I knew it, I was fifteen rides deep and a couple hundred dollars richer. What's more, I had fun doing it. Sitting in my car, listening to music, meeting people and seeing a glimpse of the lives they lead: this gig was sweet. It was now past 3 a.m., and I found myself an hour and half away from home. Like any contractor, time is money, and there was no way in hell I was wasting all that time and gas to drive home, so I figured I'd stay on the app until I got closer. Being that it was the middle of the night and in the middle of nowhere, I was surprised at how quickly a new request came through.

Damn. Do people ever not need rides? It felt like I found an endless source of income.

I followed the GPS through unfamiliar backroads that finally brought me up a dirt path and into the gravel parking lot of a large wooden structure. The outside lights were all off; only a single upstairs room had a light on. I honestly couldn't tell if it was a bar or barn, and I wouldn't be surprised if was once the latter converted to the former.

You have to understand, I don't do well in rural areas. I've always said, I'd prefer the worst neighborhood in a city to some backwoods Deliverance shit. At least in the city, people can hear me scream.

My uneasiness with the situation only escalated when a young man with curly hair and a drifter look to him left the bar and approached my car with a walk so staggered I knew from twenty yards away that he was beyond hammered. We get on our way, and he explained to me that after the average patrons get the boot at 2 a.m., the owners of that bar let a few people drink after hours, causally adding, "but unfortunately tonight was one of the nights the ghost came out, so we had to leave."

People don't say something like that so nonchalantly without wanting to talk about it, so I played along.

"A ghost?" I said with a sarcastic and exaggerated curiosity that a sober person would take offense to, but he took seriously.

"Yeah. There's a ghost that lives upstairs in the attic. If we get too loud he comes out." He spoke the way people do when they are hoping to impress the listener, not just with the craziness of the story they are telling, but in how typical that kind of crazy is for them. A "no big deal, I hang with ghosts" kind of thing. He proceeded to give me a sort of haunted history tour of the area as we drove through it, hoping his horror stories would leave me shocked and awed. Instead, the information went in one ear and out the other. I never understood the fear of ghosts. Even if they do exist, I've never heard of them doing anything other than benign things like opening doors or closing windows. Until I hear a story of a ghost grabbing a gun and jacking someone for their keys, phone, and wallet, I figure it's a waste of energy worrying about them.

Regardless, with customer service in mind, I played along as we drove through the dark and windy roads in God's country. He is in the back seat babbling on and on about this and that being haunted until we finally make a turn into something that almost resembles a neighborhood; really, it's just a bunch of houses sprinkled about along a dark, straight road that stops with a barricaded dead end. On the other side of the barricade is a dense, dark forest. The destination pin on my GPS fell in the middle of those woods.

I continued down the street until there was only one house left before we hit the barricade. I asked him if that was his.

He said, "No."

I was confused. I wasn't about to drive through a forest.

"Well… where do you want me to drop you off?"

He leaned forward, and with a new, lower tone, spoke into my ear: "One time a driver had to call the cops on me."

"Nice, so where do you want to get dropped off?" I snapped back as quickly as possible. My tone was unchanged, and my body was still. I didn't even lean away from him when he got close, as I didn't want to give him a whiff of fear. There was a chance he picked up on it, though, since my heart was pounding so hard he might have heard it. I was scared shitless. A rider, with their destination in the middle of a forest, whispering into my ear about how drivers have had to call the police on him: Uber never gave me a protocol for this sort of thing.

That's when he got even creepier.

"I'll tell you why when you turn your lights off."

I jumped out of my car like my seat was on fire, swung open his back door and put my hands up to let him know I was ready to go.

He throws both his hands up as well, but open, to show he isn't looking for a fight. "No, no, no, it's not like that," he screamed.

"I don't care what it's like. Get the fuck out of my car."

"I just want you to turn the lights off because they are shining into that person's house."

"Sorry dude, lights are staying on."

You have to remember, Uber was still pretty new at that point, and this was my very first night of driving. Perhaps I was naive, or perhaps Uber just did a really good job of marketing to a shmuck like me, but the idea of an Uber ride going south was so far out of the realm of possibility in my mind that when it did get a little weird, I totally panicked.

Once I realized he wasn't looking for a fight (read: once he realized he picked the wrong Uber driver to fuck with), I calmed down a bit, but he still wouldn't get out of my car. He kept trying to justify his actions. This was the first instance of something I would come to see so often in my Uber, occasionally even from myself. When there is any sort of confrontation or disagreement, even after the situation is resolved, some people have this weird need to justify their actions and gain acceptance from the person they disagreed with, even though these situations are all involving strangers. Even after I told him we could drop it and he could go on his way, he babbled on and on, trying desperately to gain my approval. The whole time he talked, I kept thinking, *why does he care so much about what I think of him?*

I wasn't about to turn my back to him, or get back into my car while he was still within striking distance, so I stood there as he talked incessantly. He explained that the reason the driver called the cops on him was because he was so drunk he had put the wrong destination address into the Uber app, and he couldn't remember his actual address.

Seeing his drinking habits tonight, the story made sense. But given the ride we just had, I wouldn't be surprised if he came off a little creepy to the other driver as well. This was my first lesson in perhaps one of the most recurrent and egregious sins of the average person I encounter while driving Uber: the complete and utter lack of self-awareness. This guy was so clueless as to how awful this situation was, he calmly thanked me for the ride, reached into his pocket and pulled out a couple dollars to give me as a tip, and walked away.

Alcohol is one helluva drug.

As I pulled away, I realized that his creepy actions were the result of extreme innocence, rather than ill-intent. I felt a little bad, not necessarily because I handled it inappropriately—at the end of the day, innocent or not, that dude needs to learn how to act in a way that doesn't make strangers he's sitting behind so damn uncomfortable. But I felt a little bad because as I watched him in my rearview, I saw him walk past that last house, up to the dead end, through the barricade, and into the woods.

That was enough excitement for my first night of driving, so I signed out of the app and drove the hour home. I chewed on his exit for most of the way, and it finally dawned on me: Was he trying to tell me that this was an instance of him putting in the wrong address? If that was the case, I really hope he knew where he was going, and that it wasn't too far from those woods he walked into. I didn't like to think that I left a drunk and confused kid to fend for himself on a cold winter night in the middle of nowhere, so I came up with a more comfortable explanation so I can sleep at night: *The rider in my car was actually the ghost he was referring to the whole time, hiding in plain sight.* And it was good I fed his appetite for fear by pretending to be scared by his stories, otherwise he might've jacked me for my keys, phone, and wallet.

In all seriousness, though, if this kid happens to read this story, I'm sorry I left you there. But you gotta understand: *you freaked me the fuck out, bro!*

4
The Craziest Single Night of Uber

Part 1

The craziest single night I ever had driving Uber consisted of three rides. The first was local, the second brought me from Philly to rural New Jersey, and the third ride, in Jersey, is where our story begins.

In order to understand this story, you need to understand that despite its small size, New Jersey runs the gamut of the community spectrum. The big city vibes of New York and Philadelphia bleed into the state, and from those urban centers stem a good chunk of suburban sprawl. Meanwhile, the entire coastline is sprinkled with beach towns that serve as popular vacation destinations every summer. What most people don't realize, though, is that in the middle of it all is a random patchwork of farmlands,* small mountains, and neighborhoods located off multilane lane roadways littered with strip malls, fast food joints, and stoplights every fifty yards. It is such an overlooked area that the question of "does Central Jersey even exist?" is a common debate at dinner tables stretching from Delco to Long Island.

One night, I was summoned by the Uber gods to the mysterious realm of Central Jersey, to perhaps the weirdest neighborhood I have ever seen in my entire life.

I was on a road that was so wide it could've been a highway, yet had a speed limit of 35, when the GPS directed me onto a dark, empty side street. I drove for about a quarter mile. Then with no other neighborhoods in sight, across from a cornfield, the most random neighborhood I'd ever see appeared out of nowhere: dozens of old row homes in a small plot of land, as if someone extracted a handful of city blocks from a rough part of Philly and dropped them in an

---

*Hence the Garden State. Fun fact, the state ranks second in the country in production of culinary herbs and blueberries, and boasts more horses than Kentucky.

empty field. It was 1:30 a.m. on a Saturday in the summer, and the whole neighborhood was out. I didn't know if this was typical, or if I caught the tail end of a block party, but there were kids playing on front lawns, teenagers hanging on the corner, and adults sitting on their porches drinking. I could see it was a racially diverse neighborhood and I wondered if a community consisting of row houses on farmland qualifies as urban, or rural, or both. On the way to find my passengers I passed by an old black man, sitting alone in front of his house in a lawn chair, with a trucker hat on and a can in his hand. He was sitting next to an old box stereo BLARING country music so loud it echoed throughout the entire neighborhood.

Where the hell am I?!

I was sitting at the pickup location for a few minutes, soaking in the experience and enjoying the aforementioned country music playing a few blocks away, before my passenger finally came out. It was a young white dude wearing a doo rag and a beater. The first thing he says to me is, "My niggas will be here in just a minute."

Now there are few things in this world that make me more uncomfortable than when a white dude I don't know uses the N-word. And I don't mean like I think he's racist, or that I get personally offended, so don't think I'm posturing to appear accepting or woke or any of that nonsense. I mean that when a white dude uses that word as a term of endearment it can only mean two things: Either he has absolutely no idea about the way society works, or he does, but doesn't care. Either way, it's a major red flag.

After a minute or so his N-word's come out, a white guy and girl looking like extras in *Breaking Bad*. For the record, I've never seen *Breaking Bad*, but I have seen meth addicts. And they fit the bill.

The girl sits in the front and the two dudes get in the back. Everyone seemed to be acting funny, and I assumed that they were either high, socially awkward, or both. It would be about a half-hour ride, and there wasn't much chatter during it, until about halfway through when the girl asked if we could stop at a CVS. She told me it was a bit out of the way, but she could direct me.

I figured she wanted something drug related, but that's not my business: driving is. And nothing cuts into my hourly rate more than when a passenger want to stop and shop as I sit and wait for them. And I know what you're thinking: "Don't you get paid to wait?" Yeah, I get paid about ten cents a minute. You know what you can get for ten cents a minute in 2022? Loads and loads of credit card debt.

I told her I don't make stops, as it really cuts into my earnings. This is when normal people offer me cash to make it worth my time. She took a different route.

"I really need a tampon. It's my time."

A lesser man might have caved due to shock value, but unfortunately for her, I used to teach high school math. And nothing sets off my BS meter more than when a girl inserts something like that so comfortably into the conversation. As an adult male teacher that wanted to keep his job, I'd have to bite my tongue from confronting a teenage girl with, "Look, smart ass, I know there is no way your time of the month just happens to coincide with every quiz and test we have."

But the beautiful thing about Uber is that the only boss I have to answer to is me. And what I really wanted to say to her obvious bullshit was, "Lady, you don't have to lie to me. I don't care if you inject into yourself a tampon or a needle. The only thing I care about is making my rent this month."

Instead, I took the high road and said, "I'm sorry, I really can't." That's one thing I've learned while working for myself: Now that I have the freedom to say the things I couldn't when I had a job, I find it much easier to refrain. It's funny how much more patience a man has when he doesn't feel controlled.

"Please, I really need to stop." She was not letting this go.

"How about if we pass by one, and you promise to be quick, I'll stop." I wasn't about to go out of my way to lose money, but if we were driving right past one, I'd feel like an asshole if I didn't stop. As I started to wonder whether I'm a nice guy, or just a sucker, I noticed the girl look back at Du Rag Beater Boy in seeming disappointment.

That was odd.

We don't pass a pharmacy, but as we get closer to the destination, the one dude asked if I could drop him off separately. "If you turn right at the next light, I'm just a minute up the road, I'll tell you where to stop."

I felt bad about the pharmacy situation (I'm definitely a sucker) and him jumping out of the car a minute up the road is no big deal, so I agreed without hesitation.

I turned and drove a minute out of the way. And then two. And then five. Remember, this is central Jersey: all signs of civilization are slowly fading away.

I finally asked, "How much further am I heading?"

Almost together, the two guys responded, "Oh, I'm right up that road there."

"Make the left after the train tracks."

That was another red flag. If I hadn't asked, would they have said anything?

I make the left onto a long, empty road. I pass a lone streetlight before seeing up ahead nothing but darkness and trees. Not a house in sight.

It was then I noticed Du Rag Beater Boy in my rearview. He was sitting up like a dog waiting for a bone, with a stare so intense it could've burned a hole through me.

My Spidey senses went through the fucking roof. *This is it. It's about to go down.*

Call me sexist, but the ninety-five-pound girl sitting in my passenger seat may as well have not even existed at that point. My only focus was, *How the fuck am I going to handle the two cracked out dudes sitting behind me?* My first thought was about the knife I keep accessible in a hidden location. I always thought I was being responsible and safe by keeping one handy for times like this, but now that I was actually in a situation where I could use it, I realized, *What the hell am I gonna do with a knife?* I've never been in a knife fight before. I don't have the first fucking clue on how to use it, especially in a close combat situation with two guys sitting behind me while I'm belted in. If I pulled it out, the odds-on favorite result was me getting stabbed with my own knife.

I had to think on my feet. I cocked my steering wheel just so, and threw my car in reverse. The dudes in the back weren't wearing seat belts, so my plan was, the second this thing escalated: brace myself, punch the gas, and launch this Honda Civic right into that light pole. I hoped to God that would be enough to at least stun them and give myself time to make an exit. I lifted my left foot onto the brake and slid my right foot onto the gas pedal. I was ready to rock.

I say to the guys, "Look, I can either drive you to the original destination, or you can get out here... but I'm not going down that road." What I was really saying was, *Are we going to do this the easy way, or are we going to do this the hard way?* Yippie kai yay motherfuckers!

I could feel the contemplation permeate from the back seat. And as Du Rag Beater Boy and his N-words considered whether attempting to rob me would be worth it, I kid you not, on the road I just turned off of, a cop car, sirens blaring and lights on, flies down the street so fast it looked as though he caught air from the train tracks. He passed behind us and zoomed down that perpendicular road.

This only made me more nervous because I now knew if I have to call 911, the closest cop is busy doing something else. But fortunately, criminals are idiots, and they didn't recognize that a cop speeding away from you is actually the best time to commit a crime. Instead, they were visibly shaken up.

"We'll just get out here," Du Rag Beater Boy said, defeat in his voice.

And that's when I knew I wasn't being paranoid. Initially, it was just the one guy that said he wanted to get dropped off there, and now all three of them were getting out in the middle of nowhere, miles away from the original destination.

The next day, out of curiosity, I google mapped the location where they got out, and it was nothing but woods for miles and miles. Kind of crazy to think about what might have happened if I didn't listen to my gut.

It was a little after 2 a.m. when they got out of my car, and I felt like I had just dodged a bullet (or more realistically, a self-inflicted stab wound). I decided to call it a night and head home. Minutes after crossing the bridge back into Philly, my first rider of the night called me on my cellphone. And that is where Part 1 of this story ends and Part 2 will begin.

Part 2

Before I went on the excursion with Du Rag Beater Boy and Co., the first ride of my night was this guy who reminded me of half the dudes I grew up with in Delco. His arms were covered in tattoos, and he was wearing cargo shorts, a tank top, and a flat brim snapback. He had a badass beard that stretched down to his collarbone and carried a thirty-rack of Bud heavy as he headed to his friend's house to watch a UFC event. It turned out we had bet on some of the same fighters, and that lead to a great conversation. It was one of those rides that leave a driver thinking, *Why can't they all be this easy?*

Before it ended, he asked for my number and said he would hit me up later if he needed a ride home—not an atypical occurrence for a five-star driver like myself. I told him I never know where the night is going to take me, but if I was around when he called, I'd be happy to take him. After I dropped him off, as you may recall, I got a ride that brought me into Jersey, followed by the one where I narrowly escaped death by meth heads, before calling it a night and heading home. I had just crossed the bridge back into Pennsylvania when Badass Beard Tattoo Guy gives me a call.

"We hit our bets baby!" was the first thing he said to me before asking if I was around Delco, hoping I could pick him up. I was in a pretty bad mood from what had happened earlier, but I knew the guy was cool and assumed he would be heading back to his house, which was not far from my place. I'd be stupid to pass up what I thought would be an easy fare.

He gets in the car with the same energy he had on the phone and tries to sell me on going to the casino with him. I told him I'd be happy to take him there, but it was almost 3 a.m. at this point and I didn't have the bandwidth to be in that kind of environment. He tried to sell me on it a little longer, but I wasn't budging, so he told me to take him home.

As we're about to pull up to his house he says, "Hey, uh… like no offense or anything but… are you gay?"

"And why would that be offensive?" I asked, as if I was offended. In reality, I just wanted to make him sweat a little bit as punishment for asking an irrelevant question.

"Oh no, sorry, I mean like, see, well, my boy said he got an Uber driver named Eddie. He was super cool, and all, and he was gay… and I was just wondering if—"

"Sorry man, must be another Ed."

"Oh yeah, no, I'm sorry. Must be another Ed for sure. But, uh, hey, um… you want to come inside and crush the rest of this case with me? My girlfriend's out of town so it's just me."

I declined, but he persisted, which only forced me to reject his offer to hang out several more times. Eventually, he realized I would not be swayed. He got out and I drove away.

On my way home, I replayed the peculiar end of that ride in my head. I like to think I'm fun to be around, but I've never had a stranger sell me so hard on spending time with them, especially after so many rejections. I started to wonder if that was more than a friendly invite to be a drinking buddy. The thing is, if there's one thing I am not good at, it's flirting. I can't tell you how many times people think I'm flirting when I'm just being friendly and how many times friends have told me I'm giving off homosexual vibes because I'm being nice to a guy. So I started doing the math: he was happy to see me, but so are most Uber riders, since I'm their way home. He laughed at all my jokes, but hey, I like to think I'm a funny guy. He was very engaged in our conversation, but I like to consider myself a professional conversationalist. Plus, a lot of Uber rides fit these characteristics—not to mention, as do most conversations with my Grandmother. And it should go without saying Granny certainly isn't flirting with me. So I was still unsure of how to gauge Badass Beard Tattoo Guy's intentions.

But then I thought about how he invited me into his home at three in the morning.

To drink with him.

Alone.

Was he hitting on me?

The more I thought about it, the more I was sure that he wasn't asking to just hang out. He was asking to *hang* out. But then I had to reel my thoughts back in: *Come on, Ed. Don't be the guy that thinks every gay guy wants to get with him. You're better than that. I mean, you don't even know that he was gay. He did ask if you were gay, which is a pretty gay thing to do. No straight guy would ever ask that question.*

As I was pondering the sexuality of a man I thought I'd never see again, my phone rings. It was him.

"Hey, uh, sorry to bother you, but I think I left my keys in your car. I can't find them and I'm locked out."

Is this guy pulling the old "leave behind" move? There's no way.

I told him I'd look, so I turned off the road I was on and into what happened to be a cul-de-sac. I don't typically involve the specifics of the type of roadway I am traveling on unless it's relevant to the story, and in this instance, it is. I need you to understand I am essentially heading into a dead end, with no way out other than the way I came in. So as I'm going down the bottleneck of the cul-de-sac, there's a car parked halfway on the sidewalk, still running, with the driver's door wide open and a bare leg hanging out. When I pull up next to it, I see a glamorous young woman, dressed as if she came from an upscale night club, motionless in the front seat. I couldn't even tell if she was breathing. I rolled my window down and yelled "Yo!" to try to wake her. Nothing.

My yelling gradually grew louder and louder, nearly maxing out my volume and still getting nothing. I undid my seatbelt, opened my door, and debated getting out. I didn't want to get too close to her, but I felt like I had to do something. I don't know if it was a delayed reaction from my yelling, or the ding from my seatbelt being undone, but she finally woke up. She looks directly at me, says "FUCK OFF," slams her car door, and goes back to sleep in the driver's seat.

While it was certainly not how I expected it would go, it at least made the decision easy for me to keep it moving. *Not my monkey, not my circus.* I pull further into the cul-de-sac and start digging through my car looking for this guy's keys. I haven't even been stopped for an entire minute before I see a police car rolling down the bottleneck. I got out of my car because I assumed he was coming to see what the hell I was doing and I didn't want to be crouched in my back seat reaching around the floorboard when a stranger with a gun is trying to decide if I'm a criminal or not. So I am standing there waiting, watching this officer drive right past the running car parked halfway on the sidewalk with a person passed out in the front seat. He stops a few yards in front of me. Then, at a little after three o'clock in the morning, in a well-lit and otherwise empty cul-de-sac, as he is looking at me looking at him... this cop turns his lights on and gives a short blast of his siren.

Well don't we have a regular Sherlock Holmes here.

Typically, I let police officers take the lead in the situation because after all, that's what they are trained to do. Plus, I always figured that control is why most of them signed up for the gig in the first place. But before he even said anything, I wanted to nip this situation in the bud. If he thought it was prudent and necessary to blast his siren there, I really didn't want to see any more decision-making capabilities this armed police officer might have.

"Hey, I'm an Uber driver and my last passenger just lost his keys, I'm just looking for them."

"Are you okay?" The police officer asked, which is cop talk for "keep talking so I can figure out if you're drunk, high, or just actually an Uber driver who got the shit end of the stick, stuck in a cul-de-sac at 3 a.m. looking for some guy's keys."

Can't a man earn an honest buck without being harassed?

"I'm good, but you might want to check on that car up there." *The one that's running and hanging off the sidewalk that you drove right past, you dumbass.*

As if on cue, the girl got out of the car, and I see her try to close her door as quietly as possible before she started moving toward her house across the street. My guess is Sherlock woke her up when he turned his siren on. The cop sees her in his mirror, punches a U-turn, and as if the cop car's movement was the starting gun in a track meet, she takes off across her front lawn in a barefooted all-out sprint, heels in hand, getting to her front door just as the cop is pulling up. Inside, she turns back to the cop, and screams, "Leave me the fuck alone!" before slamming the door.

The officer is stopped in between her house and her car. He stares at her drunken park job, shakes his head, and decides to drive away. Apparently it is not his monkey either.

What the fuck is happening tonight?

I call back Maybe Gay Guy and I tell him I'm sorry, but I couldn't find his keys.

He says, "My girlfriend won't be home until Monday, otherwise I wouldn't be so worried."

I didn't believe the girlfriend bit, but I wasn't going to leave this guy hanging. I circled back to his place and he jumped in my front seat. He asked if I could drive him to a friend's house, but first had to call his friend and make sure it was okay.

Since I'm sitting right next to him, I was able to hear the entire conversation.

"Hey man, I locked myself out. Is it cool if I come over?"

"Where's Christie?"

"Christie's out of town."

Oh snap! Maybe he really does have a girlfriend. See, this is why you can't assume things about people.

"Are you sure it's cool? Your parents aren't home, right?"

And look at that, he's even being considerate. I started to get a little ashamed of myself. Was this gig turning me into someone who assumes everybody has ulterior motives, or is lying, or is up to something?

As he's putting his phone down into the cup holder console area, I noticed that whoever the friend he was talking to was saved in his phone as "Mom."

Mom? That didn't sound like his—wait a second...

I knew it! I fucking knew it! He wanted a piece of this five-star-rated Uber driver ass!

After I dropped him off, I tried to piece together the implications of his male sidepiece saved in his phone as "Mom." Anybody capable of the smallest bit of deception knows the fake contact is Cheating 101, but to go with "Mom?" Bold move. I wondered if his girlfriend thought it was endearing how much he talked with his "Mom," totally oblivious to the situation.

She had to be oblivious, right? Remember, my first impression of Maybe Gay Guy was Badass Beard Tattoo Guy. With cargo shorts! What kind of homosexual wears cargo shorts? I thought they were supposed to know fashion. I guess the Delco (read: white trash) in him trumps the gay.

I know there's a million possibilities here (he could be bi, she could be cool with it, etc.) but the hidden contact, the cryptic conversation on the phone, asking me if I was gay: I was fairly certain that Badass Beard Tattoo Guy was in the closet and his poor girlfriend had no fucking idea. I wondered how long that could go on for, and I wondered what kind of pressures are in his life that he feels the need to live like that in this day and age, not only lying to himself but lying to someone else as well. Most of all, I wondered how the hell he was so comfortable calling his sneaky link in front of me after just hitting on me. I started feeling a certain way—like, he had a backup plan this whole time?! Did he ever really like me, or was I just what was available in the moment?

I did think about his girlfriend, and what a weird position she is in. If and when it comes out that he is gay (hopefully, for her sake, it's not because she caught him cheating), he isn't going to be looked at the way I would be if I got caught cheating. Badass Beard Tattoo Guy is viewed as having a personal struggle, living as a closeted gay man, and when he is caught fucking some dude behind his girlfriend's back he will be considered brave and strong for standing up to whatever pressures that kept him from being his true self. There will be no mention of what a fucking asshole he was, not just for cheating on Christie, but for using their entire relationship as a prop to conceal his cover.

And I'm not saying this to disparage Badass Beard Tattoo Guy, I'm saying this out of jealousy. He's got homosexual privilege: a "get out of jail free" card that can be used whenever he gets caught cheating. On behalf of all the straight men in relationships who can't get something strange without social and personal repercussions— that's total bullshit!

As I was driving home, still trying to make sense of everything that transpired, in a very safe, pretty wealthy part of Delaware County, I saw what I thought was a typical traffic stop. As I got closer, I realized it was anything but. There were four men lying on the pavement next to their very used car, arms and legs spread, and two cops standing over them—both with their guns drawn and barking orders. I know I don't know the whole story, but to me, they looked like students from the nearby college, pulled over for driving a beat-up car in a nice neighborhood late at night. And maybe I thought that because I've been harassed by police in that same area, for that same reason, multiple times before.

Of course, all four men on the ground had to be black, and both of the police officers had to be white.

Maaan, I hated what I was about to admit to myself. *That's the least surprising thing I've seen all night.*

5
Sex in the Uber

There are few things that will overtake the cab of a car like the scent of a postcoital vagina. The first time I experienced this, it felt like I got smacked in the face with a dead fish. It's something that really surprised me about driving Uber: when someone gets in my car, the way they smell is very apparent. I don't know if it's due to the way air circulates in a vehicle, or perhaps it's a result of air wafting toward me when the car door is opened and closed. No matter the reason, it is immediately obvious if my passenger recently showered, or hasn't showered in awhile, or if they smoke, or a hundred other things that can be detected by the power of the human nose. But above all else, believe me when I say there is nothing as pungent as the smell of a stanky pussy that's just been put to work.

That smell has entered my Uber several times, and I think it's worth noting that each time, the pickup location was at a remote beach entrance, and each time the man and the woman did not Uber to the same destination. While it is no surprise that girls who fuck guys they just met on the beach do not cuddle with them afterward, the small sample size observed in my Uber implies that there may be a correlation worth exploring between the likelihood of a girl fucking a guy they just met at the beach and the stankiness of their pussy. I don't know if it has to do with sweating their asses off in a jam-packed shore bar before their escapade, or if it has something to do with the way the salt air and sand mixes with their lady parts; I'm just relaying data here.

While it's not uncommon to come across that fishy smell after a romp on the beach, or hear that sloppy slap of French kissing coming from my back seat, or come across dash cam footage of riders discreetly putting their hands onto and into the no-no squares of their partners, the never-ending sexcapade that *Taxicab Confessionals* portrayed on HBO has not been my experience as an Uber driver. I have a few theories as to why, be it due to the lack of a partition that an Uber has vs. a traditional taxi, or perhaps because people today are more aware that they are always being recorded, and that recording has the possibility of going viral overnight. Gone are the days where the consequences of flashing your tits on a late-night HBO special lasts as long as the segment. The titties of today get tagged and properly attributed to their owner, living on the internet forever. So instead of my Uber being a locale for love-making, I am quite literally the transition home. Sometimes it is before the act, taking couples with the kind of sexual tension you can feel to a place where they can finally be alone. Other times, after the act takes place, aiding the late-night escape of someone who got what they came for and didn't want to stay a second longer, or the morning after, my rider still in last night's clothes, calling upon my services to commence the modern walk of shame. So when I get the common question about sex in my Uber, I tell this story instead.

It was the busiest bar night of the year: the night before Thanksgiving. With the entire country off the next day, and every college kid back home, it means there is money to be made driving Uber, so instead of going to an overcrowded bar and having that godawful conversation of "What are you up to these days" with someone I won't see again until next Thanksgiving, I opted to drive.

Before going out, I was relaxing at home, watching television, when I saw a commercial promoting the *Titanic* movie marathon. In the commercial, they showed the iconic shot of Rose's hand sliding down the steamy car window as she and Jack made love in the back seat. This stood out to me because as a third grader who had begged to see *Titanic* in theatres, that was one of the two scenes that my wonderful mother made me leave the theatre for. Whether my mom was being overprotective or not is up for debate, but I will admit that even as an adult, I was a little surprised seeing that hand on the foggy glass, not only on daytime television, but in the commercial at that. When I pointed it out to my mom, she shook her head and said something about deteriorating values and the moral decay of society that I didn't need to listen to in order to know what she was saying. Looking back, I think that commercial was just the universe's way of reminding me of the injustice I suffered as an eight year old that just wanted to see a pair of boobies, and letting me know that today would be the day the scales of justice were balanced.

I starting Ubering in the late afternoon, and it was as busy as I expected. Before I knew it, it was after midnight when I get a request in a cul-de-sac of an upper-class suburban neighborhood. This is the kind of neighborhood that doesn't have sidewalks or streetlights, so it was pretty dark. There was only one car parked in the cul-de-sac, and the owner had left the headlights on. The car was empty... or so I thought.

As I'm sitting there waiting for my rider, I thought I saw the car shake a little bit. When I gave it a closer look, I noticed that the car did not match the neighborhood, as it seemed as old as some of the houses in it. The windows were fogged up, just like they were in that scene from *Titanic*, and now that I was paying closer attention to it, I was all but positive that I saw what I thought was an empty car shake yet again. It took me a moment, as it was about fifteen yards away from me in the dark cul-de-sac, but I finally made out the shadowy silhouettes of two figures inside the vehicle. One was clearly in the back seat, and the other looked contorted over the middle console, stretching from the front seat to the back seat. Being that I was seeing this with fresh eyes and not in the context of a story titled "Sex in the Uber" equipped with various references and foreshadowing of car sex, I didn't immediately process what was going on, and as embarrassing as it is to admit, as the car began to shake more and more violently, my first thought was:

Are they fighting?

You have to understand, save an accidental glance when I walked into the wrong room during Senior Week, I've never actually seen people have sex. It is not like what they show in movies. In the movies, it's an activity I see and think, damn, I wish I was doing that. In real life, in that back seat, it looked like a wrestling match between two people who are both having seizures.

When my initial confusion wore off, I deduced by the curvature of the silhouettes that I was looking at an aggressive display of doggy style. I had a gut reaction that I'm not sure if I should call normal, or insane, since it's not often I get to confer with people who have found themselves in a similar situation. I think a small part of the reason I would interpret the situation the way that I did had to do with the surprising amount of physical exertion involved with the act, as the dude was going so incredibly hard it made me wonder if I had been doing sex all wrong this whole time. But I think the majority of it had to do with the toxicity the media was shoving down my throat at every turn.

You have to understand, this was November 2017, right around the time the Harvey Weinstein story broke. From influencers to politicians, from the activists on college campuses to corporations playing activist, the media was playing and replaying the idea that there are predatory men in our midst, and there is a war against women; and if you aren't actively fighting for women, then you are fighting against them.

So my first thought when I realized I was witnessing a good old-fashioned fucking was not that this situation most likely involved two willing participants having a little adolescent fun in a back seat because it's the most privacy they can find at this stage of their life— my first thought was about the war being waged on women. *Was this part of the war effort?* If so, I sure as hell better do something about it.

But then the angel on my right shoulder—my women's right's shoulder—said, *Come on, Ed. You've read* The Feminine Mystique. *She's a grown woman!* (Read: probably drunk and underage). *She can make her own choices. She doesn't need you to save her!*

So as I'm contemplating whether or not I'm morally obligated to intrude on this woman's sexual expression, or stand idly by as a #Metoo unfolds right in front of me, the most unexpected thing happens. Another dude comes walking out of the house that the car was parked in front of, and he was heading directly to that car.

When I saw this, my heart started pounding. As socially progressive as I claim to be, there was something that felt so wrong about the situation if this dude tried to join in. On one hand, I would imagine the majority of threesomes are not formal, planned events and probably begin with the kind of impulsivity and randomness unfolding here. And if I'm supposed to respect the independence of the modern woman like a good feminist would want me to, I should expect this woman to be totally comfortable and capable with accepting or rejecting the advances of the random dude trying to get into the car.

On the other hand, if she wasn't into the idea, the pressure of two dudes pushing for it may be too much for her to stand up against in the moment, especially if alcohol was involved (which, given the situation, was most likely the case).

So, like most things, I was forced to come up with my own idea of when a line is being crossed. And for me, my thought was that earlier in the night, when the sober version of that girl was getting ready to go out, doing her hair and putting on her makeup, she wasn't thinking to herself, "I sure do hope tonight is the night I get railed by two dudes in the back of a '97 Toyota Camry." And to be clear, she could have very well wanted that, and no judgment on her if she did. Shit, I don't know the first thing about the female sexual desire. I'm just saying, it felt wrong to watch a guy insert himself into that situation, because if she didn't want it to happen, it would not have been her decision to make. So at the risk of being a cock block for three consenting adults (read: drunk minors), I wasn't going to let this new guy get into that car.

With every step New Dude took toward the couple (still busy getting busy), the closer I found myself to a confrontation with two young men, both of whom were bigger than me, and at least one of them much more physically gifted—evidenced by his domineering performance in that back seat. I don't know the typical way dudes react when a bystander interrupts their potential threesome, but I wasn't ruling out a physical fight, and the prospect of coming to blows with two guys, one being completely naked, was almost enough for me to let this woman fend for herself. I mean, the #Metoo movement made it seem like this kind of thing happens every second of every day. So what's one more, right? Is it really necessary to risk my own personal safety for a woman I don't know? Would she do the same for me?

But the closer New Dude got to the car, the more I could feel that something was not right about this situation. I don't know if I could live with myself if I didn't at least try to intervene, even if it came with an ass kicking. I put my window down, unlocked my door, and unbuckled my seat belt, ready to spring into action if need be. I didn't know what I would do if this went south. I briefly considered the knife that I still kept with me, even though (as you might recall from my Craziest Night of Uber), I already decided that when it comes to my ability to use knives, odds are there's a better chance of my own weapon being used against me. And if I got stabbed by my own knife by a naked man, I'd probably tell the paramedics to let me bleed out. There's no coming back from that.

I mentally prepped myself for the possibility of a good old-fashioned beat down as I prayed to God that New Dude would not climb into that back seat. Unfortunately, those prayers went unanswered. He could not have been more casual in his stride to the car, opening that backdoor like he had every right in the world to get into that back seat. As the door swung open, the inside lights illuminated the car's interior, revealing two youthful and connected bodies. Before I even have the chance to get out of my car, New Dude screamed, "Oh shit! This ain't my Uber!" The couple disconnected themselves and scrambled for any random articles of clothing they could get their hands on for cover.

"Yo!" I yelled, my head and hand hanging out of the window. "Um… you looking for Eddie?" New Dude apologized to the couple and gingerly closes the car door before walking over to me. The inside lights go out in the Camry, but you could still make out the shadowy struggle of two people trying to put clothes on in the back seat of a car. My passenger got in the front, and without acknowledging what he just saw, informed me that a few of his buddies were leaving the party with him and that they should be out in a few minutes.

We sat in that cul-de-sac for his friends, in direct view of the two silhouettes sitting shoulder to shoulder, half naked in that back seat, waiting for us to leave before making their next move. I could only imagine what the inside of that car must have smelled like.

6
Weirdest Thing I Ever Saw

"Get me the fuck out of here. My P.O. was being a pain in my fuckin' ass!" he said, skipping any sort of greeting, or even a confirmation that I was his Uber.

When a request came through with a pickup location that read "Delaware County Adult Probation Office," I knew there was potential for an interesting ride, but I had no idea that it would produce one of the most unexpected moments in my Uber-driving career.

He sat down in the back seat, and I could feel how stressed he was. He continued on about his probation officer. "That fuckin' bitch. I thought she was gonna make me pee today."

"Did she?" I was quietly proud of myself for rolling with such an intense greeting.

"Nope."

"It's like my grandmother always said, it's always a good day when you're P.O. doesn't make you pee." I must have deadpanned my delivery a little too hard, though, because what I thought was solid gold comedy went right over his head.

"I was ready for it though," he said. Much to my surprise, unbuckled his belt and started undoing his pants.

Having a stranger undo their pants while sitting behind me in a car that I'm driving is a cause for concern in any context, especially considering the only thing I know about this stranger is that he has a criminal history. But the way this guy came into my car, bypassing the pleasantries that "normal" people do with strangers (but would never do with people they are actually comfortable with), gave me a feeling a familiarity and trust. Sure, maybe not to the point of letting him get naked in my back seat without wondering what the hell is happening, but I could feel there wasn't any ill intent. There's always been something about people who don't hide from their social abnormalities, who own things like trips to the probation office and their fear of having to pee that make me trust them more than I would had they acted "normal." After all, I know deep down we all have flaws; the difference with this guy is he wasn't pretending he didn't.

"Where you from?" he asked, now digging into his pants.

"Springfield."

"Oh shit. You know Bobby Smalls?"

"Hell yeah. I grew up playing football with him."

"That's my cousin.

"Saw 'em in the paper recently too." I laughed, assuming he knew the story.

"Dumbass." He did.

It was the weirdest feeling of nostalgia when I saw Bobby's mugshot on the front page of the county paper. I read the whole story before even buying the paper, and afterward, felt an odd sense of pride that I knew the guy. As it was reported, Bobby had to get something from the county courthouse for some reason, and he went despite having a warrant out for his arrest. While he was there, he was recognized since—well, he is at the county courthouse and there is a warrant for his arrest. When a cop asked him to take his hands out of his pockets, Bobby knew what was happening and decided to run. The problem was, he ran into the basement of the courthouse, which naturally had no way out. A cop mocked him in the report, saying that "usually wanted persons don't make it that easy," but maybe because I always liked the guy I couldn't help but respect the never-say-quit mentality it takes to even attempt an escape.

"How's he doing?" I asked. "I don't think I've seen him since high school."

"Man, fuck that nigga,"* he said, still digging in his underwear. "Owes me money. Imma beat his ass when I catch 'em."

---

* My editor told me I need to specify the race of the rider, and the person he is referring to, since it is such a racially charged word. I told him the fact that I don't specify the race of the rider, or the person he is referring to, is enough information for the reader to figure it out, because if it was any other race other than the race that's allowed to say it, it would have warranted a reaction. That lead to a bit of an argument over if I did include this person's race, given the fact that I didn't bat an eye when he said it, it may seem like I am going out of my way to say that I think its okay for certain people to use that word so freely, when in reality, I think that is one of the most detrimental aspects of American culture. But that's certainly not a battle I'm going to pick in my Uber with a guy that society says is allowed to use it, and being that I'm a white guy, I know people would say it's not my place to feel that way at all, so I thought it best to not include that opinion in this book.

"Well if I run into him, I'll be sure to let him know." Another attempt at dry humor that went completely unnoticed. But it was understandable this time, as he now had both of his hands down his pants. I don't know what he was digging for, but it was a full-body activity at this point, writhing around and contorting as necessary to achieve whatever goal he was working toward.

Worst case scenario, I thought, *he's got a weapon on him.* With that in mind, any other concern (specifically, anything that had to do with his private parts and what he might do with them if he whipped it out) was a distant second on my list of worries. Regardless, I still didn't get any sort of threatening vibes from this guy and thought it was most likely he hid some weed in his pants for a post P.O. smoke. Sure, he didn't seem like someone who was stupid enough to bring drugs to a probation meeting, but if I've learned one thing from driving Uber it's that you can't count anything out.

As I debated whether or not I even wanted to know what was happening back there, he finally yanked something out of his pants. "Like I said, I was ready for it."

I look in my rearview and see him smiling with pride, holding a small, soft, tubular-looking thing. If you assumed I was talking about his dick—small, soft, and tubular could describe many a penis—you must not remember, this guy can use the N-word. I doubt there's any chance that a very average* white boy like me would ever describe this guy's dick as small. Whatever he was holding was something I had never seen before.

"What the hell is that?"

Still beaming, he shoved it forward, holding it over my middle console for me to examine. I looked back and forth between the road ahead of me and this thing beside me, trying to figure out what it was I was looking at. There was a malleable, clear, plastic tube, with small, pillow-looking things hugging it and multiple rubber bands keeping it all together. Inside the tube was a yellow liquid.

"Is that...?"

"*Yessssir!*" My passenger was holding a hospital-grade plastic bag of piss in my back seat. "And it's clean as a whistle. I give my boy $20 to piss in this thing, and then it fits right up under my dick."

Now I have encountered puking from riders who got too drunk to keep it down, bloodstains from people who got too drunk to keep their balance, and even instances of passengers who wet themselves—and my back seat—because they got too drunk to

---

*Okay, fine… below average. But at least I'm a reliable narrator.

control their bladder (and once on account of being six[*]). But a contained bodily fluid being proudly displayed in my Uber was new territory. As I looked at this ingenious contraption, I couldn't figure out what the tiny pillows were.

"Hand warmers," he explained, "in case they check the temperature. I got to be careful how I put it in my pants though, because if the hand warmers touch my nuts, it burns like a motherfucker." Occupational hazard, I suppose.

I've always been amazed at the ingenuity necessity creates. When I dropped him off in a very seedy part of town, I wondered what would have happened if this guy was dealt a couple different cards in his life. Rather than a guy jammed up for small-time drug charges outsmarting his probation officer every month, he could've been a legitimate entrepreneur or engineer. I mean, the same year I gave this ride, a water bottle company by the name of CamelBak, made famous for their water packs designed for hiking, sold for over $400 million. And their flagship product, which is essentially a plastic bag in a backpack with a straw, seems like child's play to this kid's one-of-a-kind, climate-controlled urine receptacle, which he made on little to no budget, mind you. Dude should be working for NASA, or taking a cut of a $400 million acquisition, not spending his weekday at the county courthouse.

If there was any thought left in me that the war on drugs was the biggest waste of time, money, and energy on earth, that thought right then and there, and was immediately replaced with the idea that it was about time I Lysol my back seat.

---

[*] Her age made it easy to be sympathetic to the situation, but unfortunately, kindness and compassion didn't get the smell of urine out of my car.

7
The Wildest Question Ever Asked

Two beautiful young women were waiting for me on an empty sidewalk on the backside of a Jersey Shore bar. One was standing, eyes darting back and forth between her phone and every car that passed, while the other was sitting on the curb, head in her hands. I knew immediately what was happening here: this is the universal positioning of the responsible friend calling an Uber to take the drunk friend home.

When I got there, the sitting girl stood up, took two steps forward before stumbling backward, catching her balance in a perfect parallel squat, arms out front to aid her balancing act. She smiled with pride in herself for not falling. She held that squat, and smile, for what felt like forever, stiff as a board, fighting with all of her might to maintain her balance. Slowly but surely, however, gravity took over. I watched in awe as she maintained her posture despite the slow backward tilt that started. Millimeter by millimeter, that tilt picked up speed, until finally graduating to a full-blown, unabated fall, and boy oh boy did she go down hard, right square on her pooper, yet never breaking from her squat stance, even after she hit the ground. I don't know how they judge gymnastics, but I'm giving that girl a ten out of ten for style on the sheer fact that she was fully committed to the pose despite the cement opposition.

The thud of her tailbone hitting the concrete sidewalk bothered me more than her. She was on her back, knees still at a ninety-degree angle, laughing hysterically. She lay there until the other girl, Alyssa, got her up and over to my car. Before I let them in, I asked Squat Girl if she was feeling sick at all. She assured me she wasn't, and I told her if she does start to feel a little queasy, it's not a big deal, as long as she lets me know so I can pull over. Squat Girl collapses into the back seat, and Alyssa sat in the front, and we got on our way.

There is a song by Hozier called "Someone New," and if there was a soundtrack to my career as an Uber driver, that would most certainly be on it. It goes, *"I fall in love just a little oh little bit, every day, with someone new."* It makes me think of how there is occasionally a connection I make with riders; a clear chemistry between us that makes me think we would be very good friends in a different life. To be clear, this connection doesn't necessarily have a sexual component, and even if it did, I tend to err on the side of caution with my approach to women in general, but especially in my Uber, as the thought of being characterized as a creepy Uber driver would be almost enough to off myself if there was validity to the claim.

So at first, despite the obvious connection I felt with Alyssa— she was friendly, engaging, and most importantly, laughed at all my jokes—I thought she was acting like this because she felt bad about the potential throw-up hazard she brought into my car. Plus, I'm the type of guy where the most obvious of advances go over my head.* Even when she asked for my number, I wasn't sure that she was into me, as I'd never assume that a good-looking woman who just left a bar, filled with literally hundreds of men doing their best modern-day mating call, would resort to picking up an Uber driver—even if that Uber driver was as charming as me. So I thought she wanted my number to hit me up for a ride later that weekend, as it is not an uncommon occurrence for riders to want to circumvent the Uber app and contact me directly for my five-star service.

"I'm sorry, I actually won't be driving tomorrow, I'm heading back to Philly."

"Even better, I just moved there for school. We could grab drinks there next week."

Holy shit. She was flirting with me. Now I'm a firm believer in the idea that any country club that would let me join is a country club I don't want to belong to. In other words, any girl that is going to leave the bar alone and end up trying to pick up her Uber driver probably has a few screws loose. But Alyssa was fucking hot, so I tossed that normally sound reasoning out the window.

Now that I knew I wasn't reading into things, I was even more comfortable with the conversation, and I could tell she felt the same. As we got closer to her house, she said she didn't want the ride to end and invited me to party at their place when we got back. Believe it or not, though this was the first time implications of a sexual nature hung in the balance, being invited in by a rider was not uncommon. And I

---

*You may remember that from my experience with Maybe Gay Guy from chapter 4.

made the mistake of taking riders up on that invite too many times to know that it was never the right move.

If you consider the point of view from the rider inviting me in, it's a movie-esque idea, reminiscent of something that would happen in *The Hangover*, and to a drunk mind it sounds funny to randomly show up to a place with the Uber driver. The problem is, while the idea is funny, in practice it goes like this: my rider introduces me to the rest of the party with a big smile on his face that says "Look at me… I'm so wild and crazy and unpredictable I just showed up with my Uber driver. Isn't that hilarious?" Meanwhile, the rest of the party is looking at me and thinking, *Who the fuck is this guy and why is he here?* To top it off, I can't drink because I'm driving, so I'm just a weird sober guy being introduced to people who don't want to meet him.

So when it came to partying with passengers, I learned the hard way that the idea of it would always be a thousand times better than the reality. And that was with regard to entirely platonic situations. If I had any chance of ever hooking up with Alyssa, I don't think heading into an unknown house with two girls I just met, one of whom is blacked out, was a good starting point. I'd much rather end this night on a high note and shoot my shot when the stars are more properly aligned.

As if Squat Girl in the back seat was just as turned off by Alyssa inviting me in as I was, she came out of her drunken coma and made the familiar sound that would make any Uber driver's heart skip a beat. When I heard the gag, I didn't pull over as much as I just stopped with my car titled toward the side of the road.

"Get her out!" I yelled at Alyssa, who sprung into action as quickly as I could have hoped. Perhaps it was a testament to our chemistry, but I'm sure the fact the ride was on her account had something to do with it. Alyssa rips open the back door and yanks her barely-conscious friend halfway out of the car. Squat Girl is now hanging horizontally out the back door, her head facing the pavement and her body parallel to the ground. Alyssa contorts her body against my car to clear herself of the prospective splash zone, grabs hold of either side of Squat Girl's head, and aims it away from my car as if it was a twisted version of a point-and-shoot water gun carnival game. The only difference is that instead of water, she was shooting chunks of some sort of red, fruity drink, and instead of winning a stuffed animal, she was hoping to avoid a $300 cleanup fee.

Her aim was *almost* perfect—she didn't account for the splatter that hit the pavement and splashed up onto my car door. I don't know how they judge throw-up prevention tactics, but I'd give a nine out of ten based on the result: a minimal amount of juice that landed on the forgettable area of the underside of my car door. As disgusting as it was, it was hard to be upset about it considering that the brunt of the splatter landed all over Squat Girl's face and in her hair.

After the bulk of it came out, Alyssa tied her friend's hair back before letting her head go. She told Squat Girl not to sit back up until she was sure it was all out. Alyssa got back into the front seat, apologizing. I wasn't happy, but given the way we were getting along beforehand, I couldn't really be mad either. Accidents happen, after all. As we waited in an awkward silence for Squat Girl to give us the all-clear, while she was still hanging out of the open back door, I moved the car up a few feet so her face would no longer be hovering over the pile of puke she just made. Plus, I wanted to get away from the overbearing stench that was invading my car. It smelled like an animal had died in a tub full of fruit and alcohol.

Eventually, she nodded when asked if she could keep it together for thirty more seconds until we reached their house. Alyssa and I rode in silence for that short distance that felt like forever, holding our breath listening for any sound of discomfort that might come from the back. Fortunately, Squat Girl held strong.

We both knew that any feelings of continuing the night were crushed, so I didn't have to come up with an excuse about why I didn't want to hang out. She reminded me to text her before opening the back door and trying to help her friend get out of the car.

Unfortunately, Squat Girl had lost all motor function, and being that Alyssa might have weighed a hundred pounds soaking wet, she was having a hard time wrangling the dead weight of her friend out of the back seat. Alyssa somehow manages to get her friend out of the car and to her feet, before Squat Girl falls into a clumsy half-spin away from Alyssa and bounces onto the trunk. It looked bad, and sounded worse. Unlike her first fall, I couldn't give her any style points for this one. She laid there still, slumped over my car. She wasn't asleep, but was blacked out to the point that she might as well have been.

Alyssa began making futile attempts to get her to stand—every time she was hoisted up, Squat Girl would fall back onto my car. So I got out and asked how I could help. I told Alyssa that I didn't really want to carry her, but I didn't know any other way to get her inside. Alyssa tried assisting her off the trunk of the car one more time. She managed to get Squat Girl out of the street and onto the sidewalk before she stumbled headfirst onto the front lawn.

"Umm—" I considered how to politely inform her that she is too weak and her friend is too drunk. "I'm not sure this will work."

"I think you're right."

I stood there in silence, since I already offered to carry her once and didn't want to push the issue if it wasn't welcome. Plus, I didn't know who was inside that house, and the idea of carrying a blacked-out girl inside of it was not very appealing. If she wasn't going to let me carry her, I didn't know how we were going to solve this problem, and it was in this moment of decision that she asked me the wildest question I've ever been asked, a question I never in a million years would have expected her to ask.

"I think her brother is inside, let me go get him... could you just wait here and make sure she's okay?"

"Sure."

"You're not gonna like, rape her, are you?"

What the fuck did she just say?!

And I don't know what was crazier: the question itself, or the manner in which she asked it, as casual as a cashier asking if I want fries with my burger.

How the fuck am I supposed to answer that question? I imagine if she thinks I might rape her friend, she probably also thinks that I would lie, too, right? I can't imagine most would-be rapists are honest about their intentions. So with a question like that, the answer is not really about what you say, but how you say it. But what is the appropriate level of denial? If I gave an over-the-top, emphatic NO, (which, by the way, *is* how I feel about rape), could that be looked at as too dramatic? Like I was trying to get her off my tail? And if I play it too cool, like responding with a simple "nah," would that be taken as too ambivalent? As if I'm only saying no because I'm not in the mood. Something like, "You know, normally I would, but I've had such a long day and I'm just not up for a rape right now."

I thought about deflecting with humor, saying, "I was planning on it, why? Do you not want me to?" But I didn't need an actuary to tell me that the risk/reward of that joke landing was not ROI positive. So I responded with, "Are you fucking kidding me, right now?" Choosing to go the route of not even entertaining a question that has an answer so obvious it doesn't need to be said. I don't know if that was the answer she was looking for, but she said "okay" and headed inside to get help.

So there I was, leaning against my car at three in the morning, in front of multimillion-dollar beach house, with a girl I don't know a few yards away from me who's passed out on a front lawn with pieces of throw up in her hair and the shine of puke residue on her chin, ruminating on the fact that I was just asked if I was going to force myself onto said passed-out girl—*with pieces of throw up in her hair and the shine of puke residue on her chin*. It's bad enough she would consider me capable of that horrendous act at all, but capable of doing it to *her*?! Gross. She might as well have asked if I was a necrophiliac.

As I waited for Alyssa to come back, with that preposterous question and all its implications still in mind, I couldn't help but wonder about the kind of world some women live in. The same guy she gave her number to, insisted on going out with, and invited inside: she also wondered if she left that guy alone for two minutes he might be inclined to rape her half-dead, puke-covered friend in public?

I *knew* I was right about women who hit on Uber drivers having a screw loose.

And while thinking she might prevent a rape by asking that question is certifiably stupid, I'm not saying she is crazy for not trusting me, no matter how well we were getting along. She had quite literally met me via the internet less than thirty minutes before all this happened. All I'm saying is that it was an interesting lens into the world the way some women view it—like every potential mate is also a potential date-rape. No wonder so many of them are fucking nuts.

After a few minutes, Squat Girl moaned and rolled, lifting her head to see where she was. She looked at me, and though I am positive she had absolutely no idea who I was, she smiled... and then dropped her head back to the ground. She closed her eyes but kept the smile on her face. I shook my head and laughed to myself, as this was the complete opposite end of the spectrum Alyssa was on. Squat Girl was operating in this world with a security unmatched, drinking herself to oblivion half an hour from her home knowing full well she would be relying on the kindness of others to get her back in one piece. Then again, maybe she's drinking to that point in the first place because she wants to escape the same reality Alyssa lives in. Who knows.

The brother came out, thanked me, and carried his sister inside. Alyssa gave me a hug and told me she hopes to see me again, and I went on my way.

Despite the wild end to our ride, she texted me the next day. We went back and forth for a week or two, half-heartedly trying to meet up before I let it fizzle out. As hot as she was, I just couldn't get over how casually she asked that question. I guess I'll never know if I left an opportunity on the table, or if I was finally wise enough to hear my big head telling my little head that it wasn't worth it. But what I do know is this: that was the craziest fucking thing I've ever been asked.

8
The Rider Who Spit at Me

I always loved driving Uber on Halloween. In general, any holiday is great for driving Uber from a money-making standpoint; plus, because most people are off work and celebrating, the riders usually have good vibes. All Hallows Eve is especially enjoyable, though, due to the fun of seeing adults play dress-up, and most importantly—the, uh, wholesome and conservative costumes today's modern woman chooses to wear.

I drove to a nearby college town knowing that was where the highest earning potential would be, and to reiterate my earlier point, the sights of a college campus on Halloween were a nice ancillary benefit. The night was going great. I was making more money than usual while taking in the extremely creative costumes college girls wear, ranging from slutty nurses, to slutty schoolgirls, to slutty [insert literally any profession]. There was even one girl I saw wearing a short black robe, and she had cut out the chest area to let those puppies breathe. I wasn't sure what she was going for until I saw the gavel in her hand— obviously she was slutty Supreme Court Justice. Of course, she could have just been a slutty judge, not necessarily one for the highest Court in the land—but just because her ass cheeks were exposed to the world every time the wind blew doesn't mean she couldn't have the highest aspirations.

All night long, I saw every variation of slutty costumes, but perhaps my favorite was found among a group of girls I drove home right before the bars closed. When I asked them what they were dressed as, one girl, who was practically in lingerie, responded, "Nothing really. I just wore the sluttiest outfit I could find."

Ah, so a slutty slut. Well played.

I dropped them off right as the surge pricing hit its peak, which meant my next request was going to be a payday. Within moments, I get a ping to pick up an "Alex" at a bar. On my way there,

I kept thinking about how much I appreciated that last girl's assessment of her own costume, and thought about every other outfit I saw while driving. It dawned on me that on a night where you can dress up to be anything you want to be, the overwhelming majority of women choose to be sluts.

I wanted to dive into the implications of that, as I thought it might help in man's never-ending quest to understand the fairer sex, but before I could, I pulled up to the pickup spot. There was a group of six standing on the corner, and everyone is dressed for Halloween, except for one guy. That guy turned out to be Alex.

He comes up to my car, confirms I'm his Uber, and motions to his friends to get in. He sits in my front seat with a beer bottle in hand. Before I could even address the bottle, I saw all five of his friends trying to squeeze into the back.

"Whoa, hold up," I said, looking at the five drunk adults in costumes smushed together in the back of my tiny Honda Civic. "I can only take four."

"No, no, no, we're good, just go." Alex said.

I wanted to say "no, no no, you're not, get the fuck out of my car," as there are few things that piss me off more than someone getting into *my* car and telling *me* how to conduct *my* business.

But, like I said, the surge pricing on this particular ride was insane, and if I canceled the trip, I might not get another one. There is nothing that makes a service worker more patient than the potential for a huge payday. So I kept it respectful, using my go-to excuse of "there's just so many cops out tonight, I'm sorry but I just can't take more than four."

Alex went from zero to a hundred real quick. "This is fucking bullshit. You know what I paid for this? You're taking us. Let's go."

Again, this kind of behavior would normally warrant a cancellation. But the amount of shit I am willing to put up with directly correlates to how much money putting up with it gets me.

"I'm sorry," I said, cringing at myself for apologizing to this asshole, but that's the game we play in the service world. "I can only take four."

Despite my calm and kind demeanor, Alex could tell I wasn't going to budge on this. "Fuck you then," he said, and ordered his friends to get out.

"Thanks."

He slammed my car door hard enough to spike my blood pressure, but I was still willing to let this go until he slammed the beer bottle onto the trunk of my car and kicked my rear panel as he was walking away. I put the car in park and got out.

As I walked to the back my car to see if it was damaged, Alex started mocking me, saying, "Oh, that piece of shit is fine."

"You better hope it is," I said.

At this, Alex stopped, turned, and charged at me, looking like he wanted a fight. He was coming from about ten yards away, so I had time to gather myself. I didn't charge back—I knew that would only escalate things—but I did take a step forward to show I wasn't going anywhere. I balled my fists and raised them to my chest. I was ready.

I size up just about every passenger from every ride, just to have a bearing on my course of action if things were to go south. I knew from the jump Alex was not a big man, and other than his beard, there was nothing about him that was the least bit intimidating.

"What the fuck are you gonna do about it?" Alex said, still coming toward me. Time had slowed down and I was processing a million things in a millisecond. If this guy was going to get in my face, especially with five friends behind him, there was no way I was going to wait for him to hit me before I felt justified in swinging. My fists were clenched, locked, and loaded with every ounce of disrespect and disregard I've received, not just from Alex, but from every other entitled, rude, and ignorant person I've come across Ubering, and I was ready to unleash that bottled-up fury directly onto Alex's jaw. He's getting closer, and closer, and closer, and my fist is ready, and the moment before he's within striking distance, as I'm homed in on my target—his beard caught my eye.

That's a weird beard. Wait… is that…fake? I looked at the rest of Alex's face, with its soft features and smooth skin. Then I took into account his short stature and wide hips, and noticed long hair creeping out of his beanie, which matched the rest of his 90s skater-type outfit. And it dawned on me: Alex did dress up for Halloween… as a boy.

I unclenched my fist and let my hands hang the moment before it would have been time to swing. She got right in my face and says, "What the fuck are you gonna do? Hit a girl?"

Then, in a very ungraceful motion, she turned her head to the side and flung it forward for momentum as she tried to spit on me.

For the sake of the story, it would be cool if I could say I dodged her saliva matrix-style, but this idiot timed the spit wrong and ending up getting most of it on herself.

Her friends had been half-heartedly involved in this whole event, from the moment Alex started giving me attitude in the car, with a sort of *here we go again* kind of attitude. After the failed loogie launch, one of them finally yelled out, "Alexandra, leave it alone. Let's fucking go!"

She walked away, as I wrestled with my emotions of shock and anger. I hated being treated like that, but I couldn't believe how close I was to knocking this bitch's block off. I mean, if I swung, there's a 95 percent chance she hits the ground, and lord knows the ramifications that would come with that. Meanwhile my only defense would be victim blaming: *How the hell was I supposed to know? It's her fault for not dressing like a total whore like every other girl!*

I understand this circumstance was the result of Alex's extremely convincing Halloween costume, but it made me wonder: for every other day of the year, what is the etiquette for fighting with the transgendered community? We've all seemed to agree that equality for the sexes stops when things get physical, as there is almost no justification for hitting a woman, even if she is hitting you. But how does that pertain to someone who *used to be a woman* but is now a man? Or what if they started as a man, but now identify as a woman? And how do surgical procedures play into this? Like if a chick has a dick, can I throw a fist? And if a dude with a cooch gives me a smack, is there no excuse for me to hit back? These are legitimate questions that need to be addressed as long as we are going to entertain this gender-blender insanity.

But to add to the disrespect and turmoil, I was incredibly pissed that I missed out on the busiest part of the night. The surge pricing was now gone, and if I canceled this very long, very profitable trip, I'd only get $5 for the cancellation fee, as opposed to the nearly $200 fare I'd get for the insane surge that was attached to that trip. So not only did this bitch treat me like a piece of garbage, almost tricking me into committing assault and battery with a side of social suicide, but she quite literally impeded me from putting food on my table. And that I could not abide.

Since I already started the trip, I knew that if she canceled, I would get most, if not all, of the fare. The problem was, she wasn't canceling it for that very reason. So I went ahead and completed the trip anyway, driving all the way to that bitch's house without her or any of her friends in my car, getting the full fare, and calls and texts from Alex, begging me to cancel so she could call another Uber and avoid getting charged.

I'm not saying it's right what I did, but if I'm being honest, I don't feel the slightest bit of remorse for it either. They say if you come for the king, you best not miss. It would seem the same applies for spitting on your Uber driver, *bitch.*

9
Frank the Felon

"For Frank?" I asked, as this very large, athletic black man gets into my car. He was walking down a barren road that parallels the highway. Had I been new to driving, I would've been a little wary of the situation. And no, not because he's black, you asshole, but because the pickup location wasn't even an actual address; it was a dropped pin on the Uber map. There wasn't a single manmade structure anywhere in sight, and it made absolutely no sense as to why someone would be on this road. But at this point, I had been driving long enough to know that the ways people lead their lives will never cease to amaze me, and being that it was daylight, and I was well outside of the city limits, I wasn't worried about how this ride would go. But that changed within moments of him getting in my car.

"Yup, that's me," he said, in a voice that matched his description.

"What's up, man?"

There was silence, which I would've thought nothing of, as some people don't think replying to a conversational greeting is necessary, especially when it's coming from their Uber driver. God forbid you give the servant class the chance for human interaction.

I realized this silence was intentional, however, when I caught his eyes burning a hole through me in my rearview. When I met them in the mirror, he broke it.

"What do you mean by "man?" He sounded serious, and pissed. I was so confused. "I identify as a woman, and I'd appreciate if from here on out, you address me as Francine."

Oh, shit.

When I tell you I was speechless, it's not so much that I was surprised—I mean sure, I would've never expected that statement from a guy who looked like he could be catching touchdown passes for the Philadelphia Eagles every Sunday—but I was more concerned with what the hell I was supposed to say to this hulk of a man, er, woman, sitting behind me, that I just pissed off. If I said the wrong thing and things got violent, not only would this be a fight I am sure I would lose, but there would be dash cam footage showing that I got beat up by a girl.

"*Ahhh*—" I started.

With a very accentuated and purposeful feminine flare to his voice, he said, "Can't you tell? I am Francine and I am fabulous."

He was too kind to wait for my response this time and started busting out laughing.

"I'm just fucking with you, dog." After a breath of relief, I joined in the laughter.

"I was going to say, I've meant some interesting characters; but someone that looks like you—that says they are *that*—well, that would be an all-time curveball."

That naturally led him to ask about some of the other crazy characters I've encountered while Ubering. After telling him one or two of my classics,* he asked, "Have you ever had any felons?"

Well I do now, I thought. After all, only a felon would ask that question, in that way. So I knew the guy behind me had a good story, and I wanted to hear it. I needed to answer his question in a way that let him know he was in a safe space to tell it.

"The long answer is that sometimes I wonder how many people in my car have a record. I studied criminology in school, and being that the land of the free and the home of the brave boasts the most prisoners per capita in the entire world, it doesn't escape me that there's a lot of people in my car that have a record that I'll never know about.

"I hear that."

"But the short answer is yeah, I've had quite a few people share their *criminal history*, for lack of a better term. I hate that term. It makes it sound like being a criminal is in their DNA; like when a doctor asks if you have a family history of high blood pressure or some shit."

"That's real talk coming from a white boy."

---

* In case you are wondering, I usually open with "just this weekend," and relay whatever recent insanity Uber brought to me, as there never seems to be a shortage of those kind of experiences with this gig, and then, if they seem interested in more, I follow up with an abridged version of the girl who came out of her blackout in the Uber (chapter 12). I think that story paints a pretty good picture, in a short amount of time, of how insane this job can be.

"Hey now—" it was my turn to get serious. "Who the fuck said I identify as white?"

My joke landed so well that I flirted with the idea of tagging it with "I'm blacker than you, my nigga," but the risk of upsetting the knockoff Lebron James sitting behind me was not worth the reward, and I reminded myself this is an Uber, not an open mic. And he still wasn't sharing his story, so I wanted to make the invitation to tell it even more obvious.

"For real though, something that always struck me about when I have felons in my car is that I'm never nervous. Granted, I've never heard someone admit to murder, but even that, I know it's something like 95 percent of murders are committed between people who know each other, and my thinking is, if someone is going to tell me about the murder they committed, or any other crime for that matter, there's an element of honesty that makes me trust them more than it makes me nervous. Like why would they volunteer that information to me if they were up to no good? But anyway, my point is, these people tell me stories about going to jail for drugs or a DUI or a bar fight. Things that seem more like one-off mistakes or victimless crimes. I'm starting to ramble here, I know, but it's something I think about a lot." I paused for a second, hoping he'd take the opportunity to start the story I knew he had.

Still nothing.

So I continued: "It always amazes me when I'll have a felon in my car or, hell, people committing a crime—so to speak—by being intoxicated in public, drinking underage, or high: all things that a police officer could quite literally cite them for. And yet I feel totally safe with these "criminals" that are total strangers to me. Like when I pass by a cop car with a felon in my Uber, I think, *This friendly guy in my back seat is who you are supposed to be protecting me from?* Meanwhile, whether I have a passenger in my car or not, I get nervous every time I see a cop on the road because I've learned the hard way how bad they can jam me up with the bullshit traffic tickets they love to hand out, all under the guise of it being for my own good. It's almost like I can rely on criminals more than I can rely on cops: at least with a criminal I know what I'm getting." I paused again, thinking I couldn't create a safer space for a felon tell-all. Plus, I needed to take a few breaths, as this topic can get me a little heated and I didn't want my Irish temper overtaking the otherwise fun ride.

"Maybe you really aren't white," he finally said.

"I don't know, I'm a millennial from Delco. We all wanted to be black at some point in our lives."

"Well you can add another to list of criminals in your car."

"I kind of figured."

"How so? Asking about felons?"

"Nah. Cause you're black."

I finally worked up the guts for a risky joke. It landed thank God.

"I was selling weed. Fucking weed. Got me for twelve years. I wasn't even a big time or anything like that. I was selling dime bags to people in the neighborhood just so I could smoke for free, maybe make a couple extra bucks. My son was four years old when I went away; I came back, and he was sixteen. Grown ass man. I missed his whole life. How the fuck am I supposed to play Dad now?"

Before I drove for Uber, I was in social work. It's never fun to hear a personal story like that, but unfortunately, it's not unique. These kinds of stories are what those "hard on crime" zealots don't account for. Ironically, those same people are typically champions of the nuclear family, and how the demise of the family is the demise of society, and how kids need fathers. To be clear, I have no issues with that; the importance of family 100 percent spot on. What drives me crazy, though, is wondering how the hell those people can take the father out of the neighborhood over victimless crimes like selling weed to competent adults, and then turn around and say the problem with the neighborhood is that there aren't fathers around? I get that some people, typically older people, have been brainwashed to think that marijuana is a dangerous drug, but just because *they* think marijuana is bad, should a man be put away for twelve years?

But this somewhat common situation and my unoriginal rant to go with it is not why I wanted to share this story. What Frank said next is something I still think about to this day.

"You know what's fucked up though? I'm not outta prison for two months, and Philly decriminalizes weed. Would you believe it, the same motherfucker who was prosecutor for my trial stood at a fucking podium in front of TV cameras and reporters, and said, 'It's about time this city stopped the unfair prosecution of people, especially people of color, for using this harmless, and even helpful, plant.'"

He got visibly upset revisiting this memory, making me think when God built this generic Lebron James, he included a heaping scoop of Irish temper as well.

"This motherfucker stood in a courtroom, and in front of my family, called me a predator—said I preyed on my own neighbors. Man, I was selling weed to grandmas that couldn't go to a doctor for arthritis. Callin' me a fuckin' predator, saying I need to be put away like an animal. Then twelve years later he turns around and plays politics for the camera, acting like he wasn't the motherfucker putting people in prison for the exact thing he was talking about. And they ate that shit up in the press. No one called him out."

Damn.

"I never thought about it like that."

Our conversation continued, and it eventually turned back to the lighthearted jokes that it began with. Before he got out, I said, "I wish the best for you Francis," and fabulously flicked my wrist for punctuation. He lost it.

After I dropped him off, I couldn't help but think about how it must feel to be a few years early for monumental changes. How it must feel to know you spent twelve years in prison for something that gets you a slap on the wrist today. How it must have felt for those who graduated a year before schools were integrated, or those who turned eighteen on the last day of the draft, or those who boarded the last train to Auschwitz.

I would assume that most people do not hold any animosity toward those who benefit from the improvements that they missed out on. It's not like those who benefitted were the ones that caused the problem. I do wonder, though, about the rage that comes from considering these injustices. Of course it's not only reserved for victims, as I too am no fan of the Holocaust, sending people to war against their will, or putting people in prison for marijuana. But what is the result of this rage directed at politicians, at shadows of the past; at faceless prosecutors willing to play either side of the coin for personal gain at any given moment, with no regard for the actual human lives hanging in the balance? Consider Frank's situation: not only was he affected, but also his wife and his young son—the majority of his childhood robbed of a two-parent household. Not to mention, the ripple effects it had throughout the community.

My encounter with Frank forces me to look differently at every politician—especially those that have been in office for a while —and makes me wonder when I see them righting the wrongs of the past: How much responsibility in creating those wrongs did they have in the first place? It's almost like they started a fire, then want to be thanked for using a taxpayer-funded firehose for putting it out.

Yet despite my rage, there I am at the ballot box every election like a good citizen, pretending I'm making a difference, pretending that endorsing the lesser of two evils isn't still endorsing an evil.

I wonder, does that make me a hypocrite? But then again, what is my recourse? After all, I'm just a fucking Uber driver.

10
A Drug Run to Kensington

West Chester University is a medium-sized state school that crams fifteen thousand college kids into a small town that doesn't even cover two square miles. Located forty-five minutes outside of Philadelphia, it's filled with bars and student housing and consistently ranks in the nation's top-five party schools, and for an Uber driver, that translates to an opportunity to make some money. Plus, being around youthful and hopeful partygoers that have not yet been made bitter by adulthood is a nice ancillary benefit, and I will never complain about the fact that it seems most women can earn their bachelor's degree without learning what kind of clothes you are supposed to wear in the winter. They must save that lesson for grad school, or the modern college female is immune to cold weather. Regardless, since a Thursday to a college kid is the same as a Friday to an adult, every Thursday night I'd made it a point to take my Uber services to campus.

On this particular Thirsty Thursday, it was exceptionally busy, and I was giving ride after ride, every single one for young men and women dressed for a bar or house party, going to a bar or house party, or coming home from a bar or house party. So you can imagine my surprise when, on the other side of midnight, a young man strolls across his front lawn to my car, wearing a loose sweatshirt, baggy sweatpants, and well-worn slip-ons. Dressed like that, I assumed he was catching a quick ride to some other on-campus housing, perhaps to continue the party with friends, or maybe a post-bar booty call—that is, if it was a sure thing. After all, he'd be showing up in sweatpants and slides. Given his disheveled appearance, I didn't count out the possibility he was either going to or leaving a late night study group; cramming for a test or finishing up a project. But when I started the trip, I was very surprised to see that his destination was over an hour away, dispelling every idea I had of what he might be getting into. I was even more surprised to see that this tall, skinny young man was heading to Kensington.

Unlike West Chester, which is the kind of place I'd feel comfortable falling asleep on a park bench when taking a break from the long, drunk walk home in the middle of the night,* I don't know too many people who feel comfortable driving through Kensington even during the day. The insanity of that part of Philadelphia can be summed up by a round-trip ride I gave one summer day, where a young mom was picking up something from her in-laws. When we arrived at her in-laws, before getting out, she looked at the ground and said "ah, fuck" before reassuring me she would be quick, begging me not to leave her there.

When she got back in, she said she was mad at herself because she knows better than to wear flip-flops in Kensington. The of risk getting pricked by one of the thousands of needles discarded on the ground in that neighborhood is too great for open footwear.

I recognize that every documentary or exposé on drug use claims the area they are covering to be the heroin capital of the world, or have the most overdoses per capita, or whatever other way they can twist the numbers to make it seem like the city they are in is the worst in America. I can't sit here and claim that Kensington is factually the worse place in America, but I can say that I'd rather be fucking anywhere else. I'll roll the dice on whatever skid row you can find in sunny California, or whatever desolation and poverty you can find in Appalachia . Kensington is a monster of its own kind, the sort of place that if you've seen it, no explanation is necessary, and if you have not, no explanation will suffice—but I'll try my best. For all intents and purposes, it is an open-air drug market that serves as the final destination for the teens and young adults from the surrounding areas who could no longer stave off their addiction with the prescription pills stolen from medicine cabinets, and graduated to something more serious. At any time of day, you can find hundreds, if not thousands, of people openly dealing, using, and leaning that familiar zombie lean on Kensington Avenue or around McPherson Square, better known as "Needle Park." In the middle of Needle Park is a building that looks like a small Jefferson Monument that most outsiders assume is vacant due to the simple notion that no one in their right mind would walk through that sea of users in order to get to it. In actually, it's a public library. A fucking *public library*. A not-so-fun fact about that library is that every librarian who works there is

---

*May or may not be speaking from experience.

equipped with multiple doses of NARCAN—the agent used to reverse an opioid overdose—and trained to use it, as it is not uncommon for a child to find a junkie close to death, lying in between bookcases or in the library bathroom.

And these are all events that can be witnessed during broad daylight. So when this very suburban, very green college kid told me that he was heading down there to pick something up for his work, and was hoping I could drive him back, it didn't add up. But this was going to be a nice little fare to bring me right back to where I wanted to be, so I didn't hesitate.

That said, I wanted to have some idea of what the hell I was getting into, and gently probed about his work and what he was picking up. He spun some story about keys he needed for the next day that he had to get from his boss, and the more he talked, the less it lined up. I didn't believe for one second he was Ubering all the way to Kensington and back for a set of car keys, and I assumed it was the classic tale of a drug addict lying about doing drugs. Why he was going all the way to Kensington for it, I didn't know. But I didn't feel threatened by this kid, so at the end of the day, what he does, and where he buys it from, is his business. Eventually we settled into the long drive in silence, which was good, because the only thing that scared me more than going into Kensington in the middle of the night was the thought of making small talk for a two-hour round trip.

The exact destination address was a rundown row home, that may have been empty, on a desolate block that had more buildings vacant than not. I didn't love it, but was also expecting as much, so I was not in panic mode yet. He promises he won't be long, but then again, if I had a dollar for every time a rider told me they won't be long at a stop, I wouldn't have to drive Uber. So I wanted assurance he would be quick.

"Just call me if anything changes, I don't want to sit here for too long." That was my nice way of saying, if you aren't quick, I'm leaving.

"Alright," he said, looking at his phone. "Actually, my phone's about to die—" he kind of hesitated, realizing the implications a dead phone would bring. "I promise you, I'll be right back."

"Well, in that case, five minutes max, and I'm out."

He gets out, and instead of going into the house we stopped in front of, he disappears around the corner. Again, I expected as much; I didn't think he would be dumb enough to have his Uber pull up to exactly where gets his fix. That wouldn't be good for anyone. So I sit and I wait in my Honda Civic, with no tints and stock everything, surveying the area because I know I don't look like I belong. Anyone who saw me would think I'm a potential customer, which means I have cash on hand, or I am lost, which means I'm a sucker prime for the picking.

There was a car on the corner, running, but without its lights on. There were two guys in the car, and the driver-side window was halfway down. I could see the dude staring right at me while he smoked. By the look of his car, my bet was that it was an unmarked police vehicle, and the cops inside assumed I'm just another suburban kid looking for a fix. That's not a problem because even if I was using, cops in Kensington rarely arrest people for selling drugs, let alone for using them. I did consider the possibility that whoever was in that car was tasked as lookout for whatever dealer operation was going on in that area, and the longer I sat, the more suspicious I looked. Of course, there was a chance these guys were adversaries of whatever dealer operation was going on there, and the longer I sat, the higher chance I'd wind up in some sort of crossfire. These were certainly not possibilities that I wanted to see come to fruition, so as to not be a sitting duck, I decided to do a once around the block, hoping my passenger was ready to go when I got back.

When I pulled around the corner where my passenger had disappeared to, I saw a crowd of at least twenty people around a stoop, waiting to get their fix. I looked to see if my passenger was among those standing there, but a quick glance did not yield any results. *Maybe this kid is actually meeting up with his boss.* I didn't think it would be smart to stop and stare in hopes of finding him though, so I kept it moving.

After circling the entire block, I was back to the original drop-off location and the undercover cop/drug dealer/murderous rival was still in the same spot, still eyeing me up. I positioned my car so that I was not directly facing him anymore, and also so that I'd be ready to get the hell out of that neighborhood when my rider came back. My eyes were going back and forth, from the shady running car in my rearview mirror, to the sideview mirror that showed the corner I hoped my passenger would be walking around soon.

I'm not sure if we hit the five-minute mark or not, but I started to get a bad vibe from the whole situation, and was not about to become a drug-related statistic because I didn't meet an arbitrary deadline with an Uber rider. I decided to give him one last chance and gave him a phone call.

Straight to voicemail.

Fuck.

I tried twice more, hoping it was just a matter of bad service. Both straight to voicemail. His fucking phone died.

For the sake of drama, let's pretend I put the car in drive with the intent to pull away before I had a change of heart—but if you think that I put my car in park at any point during this waiting game then I got a bridge in Brooklyn to sell you. The point is, just as I was about to leave this kid to fend for himself, it dawned on me that with a dead phone, he would have no way of calling another Uber. And you couldn't catch a cab in Kensington even before Uber ran most of them out of business, so he had no shot of finding one in the post-rideshare world, especially at this time of night.

I tried to convince myself that he wasn't my problem, but as weird as it sounds, the fact that he was my passenger, and so young and dumb looking, gave me this sense of responsibility toward him. It wasn't just the leaving him stranded part—if something did happen to him, I'd feel bad because the only reason I had for leaving at the moment was my own fear.

There are few things in this world that motivate me more than not being a pussy, so I stuck it out, and as if the universe was rewarding my choice, I finally see him come back around the corner.

Thank God. Now let's get the hell out of here.

Does he walk to my car? Of course not.

This son of a bitch ducks into the alley on the backside of the rowhome that all those people were gathered in front of. Since I moved my car, I had a clear line of sight down the alley, and he was too focused on the task at hand to notice. He had some sort of metal object—I don't know if it was a pocketknife or a spoon or what—but he had used it to scoop something out of the bag he was holding. He put the bag into his pocket, pulled out a lighter, and held a flame under that metal object and whatever was on it.

I thought this kid was about to get high in the alley right in front of me and there was no way I was going to wait for him to zoot himself to zombieland, only to then have to drag him out of that alley to get into my car. So I start doing that hushed yell out the window— you know that weird thing where you're trying to be loud quietly: *Yo... Yo... Yo! Brandon. Yo!*

Preoccupied, he doesn't register my calls... but someone else did. A head poked out from the corner that he had just reappeared from; the same corner where I discovered the crowd of twenty junkies in congregation. I didn't know who this head belonged to, be it a user or dealer, but I did not care to find out. That was my tipping point. I jumped out of my car, took one step toward the alley Brandon was "hiding" in, and used my outside voice for the first time. "Yo, Brandon! Three seconds and I'm fucking leaving!"

He knew I meant it, because he was out of that alley and in my car in no time, and we got the hell out of there.

He tried to say something about how his boss couldn't find the keys, but quickly realized I wasn't interested in his bullshit. I was too angry with the situation that he put me in to even feign a response. On the silent ride home, I was surprised that he didn't pass out, as I assumed he would have had he gotten high, and I was trying to piece together what exactly he was doing in that alley.

I considered the idea that maybe he was using a different kind of drug, an upper that wouldn't turn him into the kind of lifeless body that can be seen leaning all over Kensington at all hours of the day, but his demeanor didn't change at all from the ride down there. He seemed just as sober as when I picked him up. Plus, I still couldn't understand, no matter what kind of drug he was using, why he would go all the way to Kensington to get it. He lived at a college that is a nationally ranked party school. Anyone with a pulse would be able to find drugs at West Chester University.

If I thought he would tell me the truth, I would have asked him what he was burning in that alleyway and why. Outside of alcohol and the occasional joint, I don't do drugs, so the methods of drug use are out of my realm of expertise; though I will say, if he was trying to get high, I think he would have gone about it a little differently than burning something on the edge of a utensil. What was his next move? Inhale the smoke? Lick off the melted residue? That said, I do know that burning a product is a way to test its purity, but whether you can do that by eyesight and in a dark alley, I don't know. Regardless, it got me thinking: maybe I was wrong to assume he was trying to get high in that alley. Maybe he really was down there for "work." It wouldn't make sense for him to go all the way to Kensington to get drugs for himself—but it would make sense if he was going to get drugs for everyone else. What if this kid was the campus kingpin, and I was the guy taking him to the wholesaler? Perhaps when he lit up in the alley he was just giving his purchase a quick taste test. Maybe what happened in that alley was not some kid trying to use drugs: that was an entrepreneur doing quality control.

What I thought was an out-of-his-element addict who needed my help was more likely the campus dealer that had more street smarts than I did. As I was wondering how many ounces, or pounds, of an illegal substance I was currently transporting, it dawned on me that this asshole could have been telling me the truth the whole time about the keys he had to pick up from his boss.

As in, the kilos he had to purchase from the dealer that he answers to.

That slick motherfucker.

After this realization, I moved into the right lane and made sure to drive exactly the speed limit, not a mile an hour more, the entire ride home. I was not risking getting pulled over and having the dude in the back seat throw his drugs under my seat, so that if they are discovered he can swear "those aren't mine, officer, they must belong to the driver." I played out that worst-case scenario in my head until Brandon cut through the silence.

"Excuse me," he said. I looked at him in my rearview, not knowing if I should be even more frustrated by my new perspective of him, or impressed.

"My phone died… do you have a charger?"

11
Avalon's Finest

I've made it a point on my YouTube channel to wage a war against traffic enforcement as it is undeniably the basis of the degradation of modern American society. I admit, considering that in the past few years we have seen unforgettable footage of police brutality, a range of "mostly peaceful protests" to violent riots across the entire country regarding law enforcement, and a mass exodus of police officers from the profession as citizens call for them to be defunded, I too would find the idea that it all starts with a traffic ticket absolutely absurd: that is, had I not been enlightened by this story I am about to tell you.

It was the weekend of the Polar Bear Plunge in the Jersey Shore town of Sea Isle City, a winter event held under the guise of raising money for charity. In reality, though, this is a marketing ploy by the town's business community to get customers into town during the otherwise dead offseason. I understand how cynical that may sound, though it should be noted that it is a data-driven cynicism. Every year while Ubering during the Plunge, out of genuine curiosity, I ask my passengers what charity is benefiting from the event. Not once, in the hundreds of rides I've given, has anyone been able to answer that question. The most common response was summed up by one particular rider who so eloquently said, "I have no idea. I'm just here to get fucked up."

Being the forward-thinking entrepreneur that I am, I would drive down the shore for this event, following the crowd of partygoers and cashing in on the influx of people in an area that had a shortage of drivers. It was the perfect recipe for those astronomical surge prices that can make a driver's week, and it was worth the three-hour round trip as long as everything went according to plan.

Unfortunately, on this particular Polar Bear Plunge, things would not go according to plan.

Compared to previous years, I was not getting the number of ride requests I had in past years, and there was not a single surge the entire afternoon or early evening. The bars were just as full, so I assumed it had to do with the rise in popularity of the gig working economy. There were more Uber and Lyft cars than ever before. In simple terms, even though the Plunge was popping, because there were more rideshare cars available, the less I get rides, *and* the less the rides cost, so the less I get paid. Despite this, it was steady enough, and as long as I positioned myself by the bars at 2 a.m., that time of the night when hundreds of people call an Uber at the same time and jack the prices up out of this world, then I'd make my nut and the long drive home at three in the morning would be worth it.

So with half an hour to go until the Sea Isle bars close, I found myself in Avalon, the neighboring shore point. Avalon bills itself as "cooler by a mile," as it sits in the Atlantic Ocean a mile further than the other islands, but "cooler by a tax bracket or two" would work just as well, as most people know it as the wealthiest shore point in South Jersey. The only thing more astonishing than the size of most of these houses is the fact that almost all of them are second homes, used sparingly. So you can imagine my surprise when, at 1:30 in the morning, I get a pickup request at one of these mansions.

Typically, at this time of night, I never get anyone leaving their house, and on the rare chance I do, it's a young guy or girl opting out of the "stand" portion of a "one night stand." So when a couple in their fifties came walking out the front door and into my car, I was beyond baffled as to what their situation could be. To make it even more confusing, they reeked of alcohol and were heading to a bar in Sea Isle.

"I'll try my best to get you there before they close, but no guarantees." That was my customer service way of saying, *I'm not risking a speeding ticket for you.*

"Oh, we aren't going into the bar," the guy said. "We just have to pick up my car." He explained how they had driven over to Sea Isle in the morning, spent all day drinking, and took an Uber home around dinner time, making the wise choice to leave their car at the bar. They were Ubering back to grab their car, which, by the smell of things, was *not* the wise choice.

"There's no judgment coming from me," *[which translates to "There is definitely judgment coming from me]* "but the cops are out in full force tonight."

"I told you we should have just waited until morning," the woman said.

"Honey, I'm fine. I stopped drinking when we left the bar."

"Kevin, you just finished a six pack."

"Yeah. Over four hours."

"Ok. But you were still drinking," she laughed. She was more excited that she was winning this argument than worried about getting in a car with him behind the wheel.

"It was beer though," he said.

"Sir..." she said with an inflection that let me know a question was coming my way.

Dammit. She is about to bring me into this.

"Could you help settle something for us?"

"What's that?" *Of course I would love to weigh in on a debate between a married couple, one of which I agree with and the other whose name is on the account.*

"Does beer count as drinking?"

"Oh, that's a tough one." *Of course it fucking does. But if I side with you, lady, not only will it bruise your husband's ego, but it's going to kill any chance of a tip.* "What kind of beer was it?"

"Bud Light," the guy said.

"Oh, now if it was something heavy, I'd say for sure. But Bud Light? That's basically water."

"I knew I liked this guy," he said. She laughed.

"I will say though, I don't know if it reads on a breathalyzer like water. And I just saw a cop posted at the base of the bridge. So be mindful of that." There is only one bridge that connects Sea Isle to Avalon, and sitting there in hopes of catching drunk drivers after the bars close would be like catching fish in a barrel.

"That's why I brought my copilot with me. She'll keep me alert."

Having driven Uber for a while now, I've seen enough visibly intoxicated drivers to know that driving drunk is a lot more common than the mothers against it make it out to be. I'm not saying it's a good thing, I'm just saying I wasn't about to take a moral stand and refuse to take this man where he wants to go. That would produce nothing but an argument, which would then ruin my timing of getting to the bars right as they were letting out, and all for what? For him to call another Uber to take him to his car. Sure, I'd bet dollars to donuts he was over the legal limit, but that threshold is crossed after two drinks. It's not like he had a hard time walking or talking or anything like that. Shoot, for all I knew it was the woman who was producing most of that scent of alcohol.

As I defended my decision to take this man to his car in the imaginary debate I was having with my own conscience, we approached the bridge.

"Check it out," I said, pointing to the base of the bridge. "The cop is still there."

"Alright. Maybe we'll take the parkway."

Great. Now instead of fifteen-minute drive home on a 25 mph single road they'll be booze cruising down a multi-lane highway. Nice one, Ed.

I passed the cop and made it onto the bridge when I saw him pull out of his spot.

"Actually, it might be you're lucky day. He just pulled out."

He seemed like he was in a hurry and moved so quickly he was behind me before I was even halfway across the very short bridge. He was riding my bumper so close on the one-lane bridge I'm surprised our cars didn't touch.

The fuck am I supposed to do, asshole? I'm not about to speed on a narrow bridge with you behind me. Give me a fuckin' break.

When we get to the end of the bridge, I wasn't surprised to see his lights immediately turn on. I was surprised, however, when I moved to the side of the road to let him pass that he pulled up behind me.

"Is he pulling you over?" The woman was just as confused as I was.

I racked my brain with what this could possibly be about, but more importantly, how we can get this over with quickly. I didn't have any time to spare if I was going to get to the bars for that closing time surge, so before my car even came to a complete stop I had opened my glove compartment and was reaching into it, looking for my license and registration. I was quickly reminded that I've been putting off cleaning out my car, as what I found was a glovebox full of the most useless junk in the most disorganized fashion, only adding frustration to the pressure of finding these documents quickly. As I desperately dug through the mess, due to my quick, sudden movements, my seatbelt locked. Now my distressed attempt to locate the paperwork was literally being held back by a seat belt that wouldn't budge, and the harder I fought the restraint, the tighter the grip the belt had on me.

My internal clock was ticking. I knew this cop was going to ask for paperwork, and I wanted to have it in hand before he got to the car, hoping to speed up the frustrating and familiar song and dance of a traffic stop; the song and dance that mainstream media has told me, as a white man, I shouldn't be so accustomed to but unfortunately know all too well. Then maybe, just maybe, I could get to the bars in time for closing.

I calmly reminded myself that haste makes waste, took a breath, freed myself by unbuckling my seat belt, and gathered up my paperwork. I was able to locate the documents just as I heard the officer's door close, setting them on the dash and putting my hands on the steering wheel. I mentally prepped myself for the yes-sir and no-sir bootlicking that I've learned is the best route to take during a traffic stop.

The officer was a chubby, clumsy kid who looked so young that if you told me he was still in high school, I would have believed you. After walking past the Lyft and Uber stickers in my back window, and two passengers sitting in my back seat (with no one in the front), the first thing out of Avalon's Finest's mouth was, "So what has you out on the road so late?"

Who the fuck forged your transcript? Take a wild guess, Sherlock.

"I'm just out here working, sir. Can I ask why you pulled me over?"

"I clocked you going 30 back there."

My blood boiled. *30 mph? In what, a 25? This guy has to be kidding me.*

"Sir, I apologize, I thought I was under. I actually saw you when I came on to the island and knew you were there. I had no idea I was over. What was it, 25?"

"Try 15."

"*Fifteen?*" I can run faster than 15 miles an hour. "I'm sorry sir, did they just change it or something? I've driven on this road many times and I could've sworn the limit was 35."

"It was, but there was a temporary speed reduction for the number of cyclists we expected this weekend."

It is 1:50 in the fucking morning. And you've pulled me over in the name of cyclist safety? I caught myself from voicing my frustration. "Sir, I've been working all day. I apologize, but I really had no idea. A ticket would really jam me up."

"Do you have your license and registration?" I handed him the paperwork. He took it without saying anything and went back to his car.

"I apologize for the hold up here. I had no idea they dropped it to 15," I said to my riders.

"Yeah, sometimes they do that to get out-of-towners on a weekend like this," the guy in my back seat said. "They got to make their money somehow."

I really hoped I wouldn't be part of that somehow.

As we were waiting, a Jitney pulls up on the other side of the road. Ten visibly intoxicated people pour out. They are singing, screaming, and stumbling, as one guy beelines to a bush that is barely off the sidewalk, emptying his bladder in clear view. I looked in my rearview to see the officer pounding away on his keyboard and shook my head at the situation. There is literally a small bus's worth of drunks carrying on the in the street, publicly intoxicated, disturbing the peace at now 1:55 a.m., with one of them proudly and publicly urinating for all to see. Meanwhile, in my back seat, though not committing a crime in the moment, are two individuals who smell like they wouldn't pass a breathalyzer test until Wednesday, on the way to drive a motor vehicle. Despite all of that debauchery, the great state of New Jersey has invested its power and resources into investigating me, the dumb schmuck who opted out of partying all day in hopes of earning an honest buck.

Ain't that America.

I don't know what this cop was doing back there, but he was taking his sweet-ass time. It was almost 2 a.m., and I was still at least ten minutes and a drop off away from getting to the bars for closing time. He finally gets out of his squad car and comes back to me.

I braced myself for the moment of truth.

"I'm not going to give you a speeding ticket."

"Oh, thank you so much sir. I really appreciate it."

"But when I walked up to your car, I noticed your seatbelt was off, so I'm going to give you a ticket for that."

Are. You. Fucking. Kidding me. I couldn't keep up with the good citizen charade.

"Are you serious? I had it on, I took it off to get the license and registration."

"It wasn't on when I came up to the car, what can I say."

"Don't you remember I had the paperwork ready. The car wasn't even moving, is this even legal?"

"I can't know for sure when you took it off."

"You *can* know because I'm telling you." Though upset, I was keeping it respectful. But my patience was running thin.

"The ticket is already written."

"Dude, if I didn't have it on while driving, this car would beep like crazy. I got passengers in the car—"

"He had it on the whole time," the woman chimed in.

"This doesn't concern you ma'am." The cop quickly shut her down.

"Did you put your seatbelt on when you sat in your car to write this bullshit ticket?"

"Watch your fucking tone."

There are few things more infuriating than being told by an overweight, inexperienced, low IQ asshole on a power trip to watch my tone.

"If you want, I can give you that speeding ticket. Since, you were double the limit, you could lose your license. Would you prefer that?" Turns out, being blackmailed by an overweight, inexperienced, low IQ asshole on a power trip is one of those things. "In fact, I think I deserve a thank you for cutting you a break."

I scowled at him in a way that let him know what I really think of him, but I knew if I said anything else I would do nothing but dig myself into a deeper hole. I looked away from him at the road ahead. My knuckles turned white as I gripped the steering wheel.

"Are you going to say 'thank you' or do I need to write this ticket?"

This motherfucker was serious about that?

I have no qualms about my position in life. I don't feel a certain way when I spend a Saturday night working, driving around people who have the means to pop down to their second home that have closets bigger than my apartment and drink the day away. And while it's beyond frustrating, I understand the unchecked authority of even the lowliest cop on the street is enough to ruin lives, but that's the way the world works and there's nothing I can do to change it, especially in my present situation.

But every man has his line. And I was ready to spend the night in jail before I thanked this cocksucker for anything.

I turned back toward him and met his eyes with a look that said as much.

"Just let him go, this is taking too long," the woman called out.

I've never felt like such a bitch in my entire life. It was like I was the horse pulling the carriage of my impatient, wealthy masters sitting behind me, as the threat of another ticket hovered over me, and my ability to make this month's rent hanging in the balance. Meanwhile, the officer is standing there, immediately to my left, and I'm stuck there, sitting with my face at his midsection. It was in this moment I realized our positioning is a damn near perfect metaphor for what happens at every traffic stop. But even if his point of view, looking down on me as I looked up at him, gave him the angle that fulfilled his tyrannical, sadistic desires, I wasn't breaking eye contact. If

I was going to get hit with his load of shit, I was going to take this load like a champ.

Maybe he respected that more than the yes-sir and the no-sir dick sucking our interaction began with. Maybe the woman saying something snapped him out of cop mode and back into humanity. Maybe he just didn't want to deal with the paperwork and was bluffing the whole time. I don't know. But for whatever reason, he didn't write any other tickets. He handed me the seatbelt violation and said "have a great night." Before walking back to his car, with a smug smile, he added, "remember to buckle up."

I wish I could say I was shocked by the way this cop treated me. Unfortunately, the kind of people that would be surprised by this cop's actions are the kind of people who haven't had to deal with police much, and that ain't me. For whatever reason, I seem to attract traffic cops like crumbs attract ants. Instead, now that the episode with Avalon's Finest was over, my mind went back to the clock. It was past 2 a.m.

FUCK!

"I'm sorry that took so long, I don't know what that guys problem was," I said to my passengers, crossing my fingers that there would still be surge pricing after I dropped them off.

"He was terrible!" the woman said. And then she said something that I still think about today: "You know, you hear those stories on the news about cops be racist and violent and killing innocent people, and I never believed them. I always thought they were sensationalized for TV. But after that... I don't know. It makes me wonder."

Before I had time to fully process that statement, we arrived at their destination.

"That beauty right there," the man said, pointing to a classic baby-blue Corvette in excellent condition. He handed me two single dollar bills, patted me on the shoulder, and said, "Hang in there, kid."

Two dollars? Two fucking dollars?!

I finally understood why in some parts of the world tipping is seen as an insult. I pick this guy up from a fucking mansion, drive him to a fucking car that is worth more than my life, where he's going to risk getting a $10,000 DUI because he doesn't want to be inconvenienced the next morning, and when he sees me losing my shit over a $46 traffic ticket that wasn't my fault, he gives me two dollars?! I'd rather him give me a bottle of scotch and a handgun so I can blow my fucking brains out.

I know, it was probably all the money he had in his pocket. But the juxtaposition of two dirty, crumpled dollar bills against the backdrop of the wealth and power that was being shoved down my throat was too much to ignore. As I watched him open the door of that beautiful automobile, I couldn't help but think I was doing something wrong. I don't know how people make it that far in life, but I was learning the hard way it sure as hell isn't by driving Uber.

C'est la fuckin' vie, I said to myself as he got into his car, shaking my head at the road in front of me as I pulled away, praying I'd make it to the bars while the prices were still high.

They were not.

The worst part about missing that window of the post-bar surge is that, similar to how bars and restaurants generate most of their revenue during specific days of the week, the majority of my earnings rely on particular hours of the day or night—the most lucrative being when the bars let out. I've had rides at that time that double my earnings for the entire week. And thanks to Avalon's Finest and his crafty detective work, I missed it. So not only did that ticket erase three hours of my pay, it made me miss my highest earning potential. As a result, in order to meet the goal I set so I could make my rent, I had to stay out two hours later, chasing more rides for much less money.

Over the course of playing catch up, I passed by the speed trap and had my eye out for the temporary speed limit sign that I missed before. It was off to the side of the wide road, partially blocked by a tree, and smaller than the size of a regular speed limit sign. *No wonder I fucking missed it.*

By the time four o'clock came around, I started the trek home. I was too tired to make it all the way and was forced to get a room at the Hotel Honda Civic at a rest stop in Jersey. I don't like sleeping in the back seat after a full day and night of strangers sitting in it, so I reclined in my driver seat, folded my sweatshirt into a makeshift pillow and tried my best to get some shuteye. I was too tired to drive, but I was too frustrated to sleep, either. I lay there, trying my best to recharge, until the sun came up and I got back on my way.

Driving home, I wondered if this cop realized the consequences of his actions. Sure, it forced me to work an extra two hours, which lead to me sleeping in my car just so I could make rent that month. But as frustrating as that is, that's the life of an entrepreneur.

Sure, it reinforced my belief that police aren't there to help you and are more likely going to hurt you. But I've dealt with so many assholes hiding behind a badge that it's more memorable when I meet a cop that actually acts like the public servant he's supposed to be.

But what this cop did to the woman in my back seat was the most consequential. He made her question her belief in the goodness of police. We are talking about a wealthy, white, older woman. If there was one demographic left that unequivocally supports police, it's that one. And he fucking turned one of his biggest supports against him.

And that's the first part of why traffic tickets are the demise of American society: the only time the majority of law-abiding citizens deal with police is during traffic stops for violations that are committed every day by every driver and enforced at random. And not only are these law-abiding citizens forced to have an interaction that by its very nature is unpleasant, they have to do so with an armed officer that is most likely an asshole. You are talking about people who sign up for a job that entails harassing their neighbors over laws that they didn't create and might not even agree with. If you think I'm being dramatic, I'll take it back when you show me an officer who writes himself a speeding ticket, or calls the cops on his own kids for drinking underage.

What nobody admits, though, is that you want cops to be assholes. If your house is broken into by masked men with weapons, you don't want to have a "nice guy" show up to save you. You want a fucking brute that is going to kick ass first and take names later. The few times I actually needed police help, as it turns out, they actually helped. Isn't that a wild concept? When the police don't go out of their way to harass citizens and wait until the public request their services, the public actually appreciates them. Who woulda thought?

Ever wonder why there are quite literally nationwide riots over policing at least once every decade, yet you never hear a single peep about firefighters, even though the firefighter and the policeman are basically the same person? They both have the ego needed to volunteer for a job that literally entails risking their own lives to save the lives of strangers in the kind of high-stakes situations most normal people can't even fathom, let alone operate in. And they both have that "fuck with one, fuck with all of us" mentality that most adults left in high school, except for those in gangs and prison. The reason everyone loves firefighters, though, is because the only time we see them is when we actually need them. They aren't randomly knocking on doors, invading people's living rooms, and fining them $80 because they have one too many cords plugged into a power strip.

Meanwhile, the government, in all its wisdom, thought it wise to ask police officers—the same people who are supposed to protect us from murderers and thieves and villains—to enforce victimless traffic violations like not wearing a seatbelt. So what happens? Law-abiding citizens, who never encounter police otherwise (like the old, rich, white woman in my back seat), see the kind of dirty tactics and rough demeanor that job entails during these traffic stops, and they lose faith in the idea of the upstanding, hero police officer they want to believe in.

But that's just the half of it. Months later, during the summer, I was back down the shore, and the winds of Uber took me into Avalon. As fate would have it, when I arrived at my riders' destination, there were several Avalon cop cars stopped in the middle of the street, lights flashing. It looked like Christmas in July. As my passengers got out, a few more squad cars and several bike cops joined the scene. They were congregating, confused, and looking around every which way. One of the cops came up to my car and asked me if I had recently seen a guy wearing a red shirt.

Maybe I did. Maybe I didn't. Maybe you can go fuck yourself, is what I wanted to say. I know it wasn't the same cop who pulled me over months before, but it was the same department that fucked me over. Why would I ever want to help them? So they can jam up this red shirt guy who I never met and I don't have a problem with? For all I know, it's over some bullshit just like it was with me.

I know better than to give a cop attitude for no reason, so I simply said "no" and went on my way, wondering what could have happened in a wealthy resort town to draw so much attention. Perhaps an underage kid was drunk and bruised an officer's ego; history has shown me that's all it could take.

And that's when it dawned on me — the cyclical nature of shitty police officers and community relations. The Avalon Police Department fucks me over, so now I have no inclination to help them when they ask. Imagine that at scale: an entire community mistreated by their police, even over seemingly trivial things like a $46 traffic ticket, results in an entire community not trusting their police, let alone be willing to help them. In turn, that only makes the cop's job all but impossible. Could you imagine trying to protect a community that doesn't like having you around? I know when the cult of Blue Lives Matter turns a blind eye to bad cops, they do so with the mantra that "it's only a few bad apples." The problem is, they ignore the rest of the saying: "a few bad apples spoil the whole bunch."

I thought this was where this story would end, stashed into my brain as a bad memory and the most damning examples I've experienced personally of why traffic tickets are the downfall of the criminal justice system. But this story would get a nice little bow wrapped around it years later, when I found myself once again in Avalon, picking up a middle-aged passenger from his beautiful beachfront property.

"So you're the guy who put me out of business?" he said, with a smile on his face when he opened the door. He had a friendly demeanor and spoke in a way that made me think this was his go-to story whenever he took an Uber. He explained to me that among his many ventures, he bought a cab company in the area sometime around 2010. And what he said made everything make sense.

For those of you familiar with the Uber Files—the classified documents a former Uber exec leaked because he felt guilty about what he did during his time working at Uber—you understand why Uber was illegal and the lengths city governments went to do away with them. For those of you who aren't familiar, in short, the cab industry held a monopoly for so many years because they had to buy very expensive medallions in order to operate legally within a city. The money from those medallions, along with the tax revenue generated by those businesses, went to the city. In return, these cab companies knew that as long as they had these medallions of limited supply, they would have the market cornered. It honestly wasn't too much different from the mob extorting businesses for protection, other than the fact that because it's the government, it's legal, and the fact that they aren't as willing to enforce their extortion with baseball bats and crowbars.

Well, when Uber came along, they said their drivers were independent contractors and didn't require a medallion. Of course, this meant much less overhead than traditional cab companies, but even more importantly, allowed Uber to avoid paying local and state taxes by claiming that the driver—not Uber—was the business entity operating in the area and as a third-party service they weren't subject to most tax regulations. That meant city governments lost revenue: they were collecting less in taxes (it's not like uber drivers paid taxes to every single city, town, or borough they picked someone up in), and the price of medallions plummeted. In New York City, they fell from around $1.3 million each to about $160,000. Here in Philly, they dropped from a high of $545,000 to a measly $10,000. And this was happening all across the country. As you can imagine, this didn't make the city governments very happy.

My passenger alluded to the idea that he was involved in city and state politics, and told me that there was a directive to the police departments target Uber and Lyft drivers in hopes of keeping the cab industry alive.

When he said that, it all made sense: put up a temporary speed limit that's not obvious to anyone from out of town, wait for an Uber driver with out-of-state plates, and give him a ticket to make him not want to come back. I wondered if that cop who pulled me over at the plunge was smart enough to realize that doing it when the bars let out directly helped any cabbies that were looking for fares at that time. Regardless, it made me think he was playing dumb when he asked me why I was out on the road so late, and it brought me comfort to know that a guy the government gave a gun and the authority to use it wasn't as stupid as he seemed. Don't get it twisted: he is still an overweight, inexperienced, low IQ asshole on a power trip. But at least he knew what he was doing.

So a quick recap: in hopes of keeping the local taxpaying, medallion-buying cab industry alive, the city and state governments use local police departments to target Uber drivers, giving me a bullshit ticket that forces me to sleep in my car and undermines a rich white woman's faith in the police. A few months later, when the local police department asks for my help, I tell them to fuck off (at least in my head), and now the local police department has a harder time doing actual police work because the community they are trying to protect won't help them. Meanwhile, Uber finally comes to an agreement to pay an absurd amount of money to the state of New Jersey in back taxes, and all of a sudden, the targeting of Uber drivers stops, and most cab companies go out of business.

So the working man is harassed, and the cop's job becomes next to impossible, only for the cab companies to go under when Big Tech pays off the government. And the Uber Files proved this happened in so many cities and countries across the globe, all in the name of revenue for the state.

All of sudden, using a charity event as an excuse to drink reality away makes a lot more sense, doesn't it?

12
The Scariest Moment in my Uber

Stereotypes get a bad rap. They are nothing but the gamble we make on the information at hand, be it consciously or subconsciously, every second of every day. They're like the unreliable compass that we need in order to navigate this crazy world of ours. And one of the most prevalent stereotypes that we all bet on is the notion that poverty is associated with danger and crime; wealth with safety, security, and class. That's why when I pulled up to a mansion on the Main Line—the wealthiest part of the Philly metropolitan area—I would have never in a million years bet that a beautiful young female in a ball gown would give me the scariest moment of my Uber career.

I knew this would be memorable trip the moment I saw this house party had valet parking. I knew I was white trash the moment I processed a formal event at an estate as "a house party," so let me rephrase. A founder or CEO was hosting the company holiday party at their personal residence: a sprawling estate so big it took me longer to drive the length of the driveway than to circle my three-building apartment complex. I passed scores of luxury vehicles, from sedans to coupes to classics, meticulously aligned on the grass, only to have my untinted, 2012 Honda Civic pull into the three-car-wide porte cochere —the covered part of the driveway where vehicles can stop so their wealthy passengers don't have to deal with the elements. Getting rained on is for poor people.

I stopped in the porte cochere between two tinted-out sedans. Their drivers were wearing suits and waiting in the car. I noticed two workers in tuxedos at a valet stand by the door. Seeing them, working on a Friday night during the holiday season as the rest of the world partied, catering to the same upper echelon of society that I would be chauffeuring soon, I felt a certain kinship to them. But whether it was my used car that stuck out like a sore thumb among the hundreds of luxury vehicles in sight, or my backward hat and hoody that didn't quite match the formal attire of everyone else, these valet workers didn't seem to want anything to do with me.

It wasn't just that they didn't say anything to me, but I knew that look very well. It was a look that said, *What the fuck is this guy doing here?*

"What's up guys?" I greeted them as if they were my people. After all, they were. The service worker in a tux is a still a fucking service worker. "I'm an Uber, picking up a Monica."

Neither of them responded, and kind of looked away, as if to disassociate themselves from me. I'm guessing it wasn't only because my car was at least $50,000 less than the next cheapest vehicle in sight, but being that it was 2016, I was most likely the first and maybe only Uber to be called to this party that was otherwise chauffeured. They were probably unsure of how to handle this situation and feared getting in trouble with their boss. *Fuck these guys*, I thought. Sure, they look better than me, and are probably making a lot more money than me, but at least I'm not looking over my shoulder, worried about Mastah.

Monica comes out in a beautiful red ball gown that accentuated her figure in a way that turned the heads of the valets as if it was instinct. There's nothing that turns the elitist into an everyman as quickly as good old-fashioned tits and ass.

She got in the front. In my experience, the people who sit in the front of an Uber are the kind of people who are hoping to engage in a friendly conversation. Beautiful, wealthy, professional, friendly, and female—this ride had all the signs of being a cakewalk. But in a book about the unexpected experiences of Uber, I don't think I need to give a spoiler alert when I tell you this ride would be anything but.

She stayed awake long enough for me to confirm the destination, a forty-minute ride to Center City Philadelphia, before she rolled the window down and laid her head on my door, seemingly out cold. I did not see that coming.

Oh well, I thought. *A passed-out passenger is still an easy passenger*, and I started to drive.

In perhaps the most amazing display of directional consciousness, moments before any turn I had to make, she popped her head up, eyes barely open, and told me where to go. Like everyone else born after 1985, I find it amusing when people feel the need to provide me with directions, but that amusement turns to confusion in the Uber, as my riders quite literally used a GPS-based app to summon me in the first place. I always wanted to ask them how they think I found them when they weren't in my car to direct me. Alcohol does the funny things to the mind I guess.

The wildest thing about Monica's directions were that, despite the fact her eyes were closed the entire time, she wasn't wrong once. I guess once we hit the highway, she thought her responsibilities as navigator were through and passed out completely. I settled in for what I assumed would be smooth sailing for the remainder of the long ride, and wondered if this woman was acting like this out of exhaustion, or intoxication, or maybe a little bit of both.

We rode in silence for about twenty minutes until upon my ears fell the scariest thing I ever heard in my Uber.

"Who are you?" the woman in the seat next to me said.

Is she on the phone? I didn't see one in her hand.

"Where am I?" she asked, with panic setting in.

Is she talking to me?

Finally, in a voice of pure terror, she screams, "Where are you taking me?!"

Oh, fuck.

As if this was an emergency situation she had trained for, in one smooth, swift motion, this chick undoes her seatbelt, grabs the door handle, and while we are going seventy miles an hour on the highway, yanks the door handle so hard I'm surprised it didn't break. When it didn't work the first time, she tried again, this time putting her shoulder into the door, hoping to bust it open. *Thank God* my old Honda was new enough to come with automatic locks that lock when the car is in motion. Otherwise, this would have been a story of how my Uber rider accidentally offed herself on the Schuylkill Expressway.*

So literally by the car's design she is locked in, and as a result, she thinks she's trapped. I don't know if what happened next was an actual panic attack, or her fight or flight response started to kick in, but either way, she started breathing quickly and heavily, looking and moving all around as if to figure out another escape. I wish I could tell you I played it cool, but instead, I gave into my own panic that befell me when I thought my Uber rider was going to turn herself into highway hamburger meat. I started screaming at her: "I'm your Uber driver! Look at your phone!"

While I repeated my pleas to check her phone, my Civic decided to chime in with that painful ding that doesn't stop until all riders are buckled. It was like it was queued up to make my current situation more difficult. If Honda only knew the chaos that was

---

*It's a one-and-a-half-syllable word pronounced *skookle*. Welcome to Philly.

happening in my car right now, they'd have built in an option to substitute the seatbelt ding with a notification to not jump out of a moving vehicle.

I kept trying to convince her she is totally safe and heading home, and to keep her hands off the fucking door locks, when I heard something coming from... her crotch?

"What's up? ... Monica? Hello?"

Da fuck?

I noticed a glow coming through the overflow in the crotch area of her ball gown.

"Hello! Monica! Answer me!"

Is her vagina talking?

She pulled out her phone from under the dress. *Her vagina was talking!* She was trying to be discreet about it, because, after all, she still thinks she is trapped by a strange man that wants to kidnap her. On the phone, I see the face of a concerned friend on FaceTime.

Oh, good, I thought. *A person she trusts that can easily clear up the confusion my rider can't seem to understand because she is hammered and convinced she's starring in the next installment of the* Taken *franchise.* But what I didn't account for was the overestimation of discreetness drunk people have —as in, this chick thought she was undetected in her FaceTime for help. So when I told her to tell her friends on the phone that she is in an Uber, she shoved her phone back up her dress like she was caught trying to escape.

"Take the phone out!" I ordered, in a tone that in no way could have made her feel more comfortable.

"Monica!" The vagina was screaming.

She slides it back out, and now there are two concerned people on the FaceTime.

"Tell them you are OK!" I demanded. Definitely not a thing a kidnapper would say, right?

She slides her phone back into her dress and left it there. She stared at the highway ahead in a frozen panic. Her vagina is still talking, and with each sound it made the glow coming from between her legs seems more and more like the answer to all my problems. It was a devil's dilemma, as the beautiful, flowing gown opened at the bottom like the gates of heaven, inviting me in to find the peace I need, the peace that I know exists, if I could just get a hold of that phone and clear up the confusion. Then again, the gumption it would take to reach up a drunk woman's skirt, no matter how long it was nor the reward that came with it, was most certainly not worth the risk.

Instead, I kept telling her to open her Uber app, and she'll see a picture of me. But the next time she took her phone out, she was still on FaceTime. Whoever she called must have been at a party, and that person must have corralled the whole crew out of concern for Monica because this time, there was a whole screen full of worried faces.

"Tell your friends you are OK!" I have since come to realize that someone who is completely innocent but not believed can quickly become frustrated, and that frustration can sound a lot like guilt. In other words, in retrospect, I sounded like a kidnapper trying to bully his victim into saying exactly what a kidnapper would want them to say.

She hung up the phone without a word.

Great.

All I could think about was that the next call might be 911, and Lord knows what kind of implications or accusations a drunk chick in a panic might make.

I know the kind of person I am, but I'm also no dummy. I know how stereotypes work. The prospect of having my word—the word of an Uber driver—versus that of a young, beautiful, wealthy woman was not appealing. It's just me and her in the car, and if this chick had any sort of imagination, what leg would I have to stand on? My fucking Uber rating? If even the valets looked down on me, how do you think I'd play in front of a jury? Sure, I had the truth on my side, but an unverifiable truth in the American justice system is a truth that can help you sleep at night—in your prison cell. As I start mentally prepping my statement to police—*of course my DNA is all over her, it's my car*—I replay the specifics of how I caught her shoulder when she fell into my car, or the times our elbows bumped over the middle console. I'm thinking that's all the proof Benson and Stabler are going to need to put me away for years. So as a final act of desperation, I began shouting out any landmarks she might recognize on her way home.

After a few minutes of this, when I pointed out the Art Museum, something clicked in her drunken brain. She finally calmed down, put her phone away, and we sat in silence for the remainder of the ride. When we pull up to her very expensive Rittenhouse apartment, she gets out of the car, turns square to me, and yells, "You need to learn your directions better." I can see and hear that scene clear as day in my head, mainly because it left me incredibly confused. *Of all things to say in that moment?* Her tone got the sentiment across, for sure, but the words made no fucking sense.

The realization of the risks I take driving with strangers was enough to make me call it quits for the night. I signed off the app and drove straight home, contemplating the situation. What I couldn't get past is how in a situation like this, the doubt would inevitably be cast upon me, a guy out here just trying to earn an honest buck, while society would feel the need to protect and believe the party who drank so irresponsibly she forgot where she was.

I couldn't come to a conclusion as to why that was, other than the assumed innocence of beauty, and the assumed guilt of the brute. But what I did know was this: it's high time I got myself a dash camera.

13
Apparently, I'm Racist

There's a video on my YouTube channel where a guy gets into my car using an account with a female name. It's a rainy night, and the route we take brings me down a sketchy street. The guy lingers in my car longer than I thought he would, and I got a little spooked by the situation. Much to my surprise, the comments came flooding in, accusing me of being racist, saying that I only acted that way because the guy was black.

These comments reminded me how many stupid people there are in the world. Like, what was my masterplan? Let me drive around this exclusively black neighborhood, and when a request with a very ethnic name comes through, I accept it on the off chance that it's the first white person named Tiana to come out of West Philadelphia? Then, when instead of a female, a very large, bearded black man, with a sweatshirt that reads ROB THE RICH, comes to my car, I let him in to sit behind me, because nothing says WHITE POWER like providing providing cab service to black people. That'll show 'em!

And much like idiots on the internet desperate to find instances of racism, it is not an uncommon occurrence to be called a racist by passengers when they aren't getting their way. It might be my white privilege talking—or perhaps, the fact that I know I'm not racist —but almost every accusation that came my way sounded more like a default excuse as to why they weren't getting their way than anything based on evidence. And every time, I wanted to respond to that charge with, "Do you really think I'd be driving in this neighborhood if I had a thing against minorities?" That would be like hating sand and going to the beach.

The most ridiculous episode tied to my alleged racism happened in a neighborhood that could be on a poster for underserved communities. Two non-white women come out, one holding a baby, and five little kids in tow. Every single one of them was small enough to require a car seat.*

"Hi, how are you guys doing? Can I ask when you are heading before I start the trip?" I'm being as polite and open-minded as possible, but I knew what was going on the second I saw them pile out of that house.

"Southwest." We were in North Philly. That meant it was going to be a long trip on multiple highways and byways on a busy Saturday night. It would be one thing if they were only going a couple blocks (then again, with the infant, I probably still wouldn't have done it), but there was absolutely no chance in hell I'm taking two adults, five kids and a baby, and risk a lifetime of guilt when a reckless driver rear-ends me, sending a few little kids through my windshield... just to make $20.

"Um, were you all planning on coming in this car, or is there another Uber on the way?" I knew the answer, but I also had a feeling of how this was going to go and was trying to lead into it as softly as possible.

"Oh, no, we can all fit, it's fine."

"Oh, I'm sorry. I can only take as many as there are seatbelts. And I'm going to have to ask you to get car seats for them."

I knew there would probably be static, but I would have never predicted how quickly it would escalate. The first woman—short and shaped like a bowling ball—went from zero to hundred real quick.

"Are you fucking kidding me? Don't be such an asshole, other drivers take us all the time."

"Well, I'm sorry, I'm not other drivers," I said, as I wondered how often the tactic of calling someone an asshole works for her. "You can certainly cancel and call another Uber if you want."

This is when the second lady chimed in with, "He's just saying this cuz he's white!"

"Excuse me?" *Because I'm white I follow traffic laws? Because I'm white I want people to wear seatbelts? Because I'm white I care about the safety of your kids?* I checked the fine print on my white privilege card and I did not see those qualifications anywhere. Call me crazy, but I'm pretty sure those attributes apply to non-ratchet people of all races.

"You heard me, racist-ass motherfucker."

"Alright. I'm sorry, I won't be able to take you. You'll have to cancel and get another Uber."

---

*I learned from my Uber Daycare experience in chapter 2

"I ain't canceling and getting charged $5," the Bowling Ball snapped back. "You better cancel!"

I expected a response like that, as it's rare for anyone to accept a cancellation fee without protest. What I was not expecting was what would happen next. It is still, to this day, the funniest thing I have ever seen while driving Uber.

See, a lot of drivers would start arguing with her because, at the end of the day, she is wrong. And if I cancel as the driver, not only do I lose money, but my account gets dinged for canceling a ride, and I run the risk of getting kicked off of the Uber platform. But at some point in my Uber career, I learned that there is no value in proving myself to strangers that I'll never see again; the only thing that matters in a disagreement is getting the desired outcome. And all I wanted was my cancellation fee and not to be penalized by Uber. In order for that to happen, I had to wait another minute and forty-two seconds for the Uber timer to run out. That way, Uber could see I was at the pickup point and gave the rider ample time to come out. Then, and only then, would I be able to cancel without penalty and collect my $5.

So I politely responded to her request to cancel with a "sure thing, ma'am," and drove fifteen yards up the road with zero intent on following through with it. There was now a minute and twenty-seven seconds left on the countdown. The only problem was, if I drove too far away from the pickup point, the Uber GPS would see that I'm not in a position to pick up the rider, and the countdown on the cancellation timer would stop. So I had to make sure not to get too far from where I was supposed to pick them up—from where they were all still standing—for only another minute and four seconds now.

As I stared at the countdown, it seemed to move slower with every second. Bowling Ball was behind me, standing in the middle of the street, trying to request another Uber. Naturally, because our ride was never canceled, she couldn't. I watched her in my rearview connect the dots: looking at her phone, then looking at me, then back at her phone, then back at me... then bolting up the street toward my car (well, at least as much as a bowling ball can bolt).

"HAAAY!! Hay you! You better cancel, motherfucker! You better cancel this shit!"

As she moved toward me, I saw her avatar on the Uber map getting closer to my car. I wasn't about to risk this lady damaging my vehicle for a $5 cancellation fee, so I started inching forward, expecting the timer to stop when I got too far from her house.

But it just kept ticking.

It dawned on me that the pickup area, and cancellation timer that went with it, wasn't based on the pickup address—it was the GPS of the rider's phone. In other words, as the woman got closer to my car, it extended the area where I could go without the timer stopping. So as this very large, very rotund, very angry woman barreled after me with kill in her eyes, I kept slowly rolling away from her, watching the countdown to make sure I didn't get so far ahead of her that it stopped. My eyes darted back and forth between the timer and the butterball in my rearview, not because I thought there was any chance of her catching me, but because I had never seen something so round and so angry work so hard, and the slight incline of the street only added to the entertainment. The harder she tried, the more her run looked like a waddle. It looked like I was being chased by a giant penguin on cocaine.

There was only 24 seconds left until I could cancel but she was picking up speed.

By 21 seconds she was looking very winded.

At 18 seconds, she stops and put her hands on her knees. *That didn't last long,* I thought. I slammed the brakes to make sure I stayed within range.

17 seconds: *Shit! It was a fake out! She's on the move again!* I hit the gas.

12 seconds: *Slow it down, Ed. Can't get too far.*

9 seconds: *She's getting a little close for comfort.* Who knew a Bowling Ball could roll uphill? *Need to pick up the pace!*

5 seconds: *She'll never make it.*

To her credit, she lasted longer than I thought she would, and fortunately for everyone, the timer ran out before that woman gave herself a heart attack. I canceled, collected my $5, and sped off.

Needless to say, I didn't pick anyone else up in that neighborhood, because let's be real: I fucking hate minorities.

Relax, I'm obviously kidding. For real though, I don't know how you envisioned these women who called me racist, but if you look back at the story, I only referred to them as non-white. And no, I didn't do that because I'm some snowflake millennial who's trying to sound woke. I did that because the only thing that pertains to this story is the fact that they weren't white, and they thought I was treating them a certain way because I am and they're not. Specifying their skin color would do nothing but reinforce stereotypes. People who act like that are jackasses, no matter their color. The real victims are their children who have to grow up learning about this world through that bullshit lens of race-based victimhood from their jackass parents, and of course, that poor, white (but incredibly handsome and charming) Uber driver that had to deal with their bullshit.

I wanted to point that out because over the course of my Uber career, I was surprised how quickly I started making assumptions about riders based on previous rides. I was even more surprised at how often my assumptions would turn out right. Now, if you are looking for some high-minded explanation as why that's bad, you'll have to ask someone who doesn't live in the real world. The real danger with assumptions is allowing them to morph into expectations. When that happens, you treat people a certain way before giving them a real shot. And you end up missing out on a lot of life that way.

14
That's Assault, Brother

It was just after 10 on a Saturday night in West Chester, Pennsylvania, a small college town with a high median income and a drinking problem. This is the time of night when adults start to head in and college kids start to come out, so when I got a pickup request at Lorenzo's, a pizza shop next to a bar, my guess was that this ride would consist of young adults grabbing food and responsibly calling it a night. I was right on all accounts, except for the part about them being responsible.

My passenger finally comes out carrying a pizza—a beautiful, tall, slim woman in her mid-twenties. She's dressed like she knows what she's doing. There was a guy behind her, athletic and husky, looking like could've played linebacker in college. Without any sort of provocation, the guy delivers a UFC quality shin kick from behind, catching the inside of her leg. By some sort of miracle, she kept her balance, and then froze, her face caught in between shock and pain. She stood there in disbelief as he walked by laughing.

She said something to the effect of "Are you serious?" But there was nothing about it that made me think it was a joke that got out of hand. That's assault, brother. I was just as shocked as she was: not only I had never seen a guy kick a girl so viciously but also because he did it in the middle of a public street, directly in front of my car, literally illuminated by my headlights. It's like he waited until he was in the spotlight to attack a woman.

The girl opened my car door and said "Hello" in that distinct "distressed but trying to keep it cool" voice. She sat in the back seat, but when she tried to close the door, the guy jumped from the sidewalk and grabbed the side of the door, preventing her from closing it.

"You're not coming in!" she said, as she blocked any sort of entrance he could make into the back seat. He cursed at her and then slammed the door.

"Do you know him?" I asked.

"Nope," she laughed.

"You really don't know him?" I couldn't believe it.

"No," she gave another breathy laugh.

"I just saw him kick you."

"Yeah, it's kind of fucked up." She was turned around, looking out of the back window, making sure he was walking away.

"Who the fuck was that?" I asked.

"I don't know, dude," she said, like it was nothing.

I didn't understand how she was so nonchalant about this. She just got kicked by some random dude who then tried to force his way into the car. The internal debate inside me raged. On one hand, I hate getting involved with things that I'm not involved in. On the other hand, if there is a random dude running around West Chester assaulting women he doesn't know, that's a problem I did not want to ignore. But how was I supposed to handle this? Do I suggest filing a police report? Get out and confront the dude? Thing is, I know from experience involving the police is almost always the wrong course of action. At best, it proves to be futile, and at worst, it hurts more than it helps. And as far as confronting the guy, I'm a firm believer in the philosophy, "Don't pull that thang out unless you plan to bang." In other words, this isn't like downvoting a Twitter post. Calling out a drunk dude on a dark street doesn't offer the protection of the other side of a screen, and his reaction will not be mitigated by the social restraint of the classroom or the corporate office. So I'm not getting out of my car without the very real expectation of getting into a fight with this guy. Of course, no one wants to get beat up, but I've been beat up before. It was more that I wasn't sure if I was willing to risk getting beat up for this girl who didn't really even seem to care.

As I sat there, debating my course of action, she broke the silence with a sad truth that caused the thoughts racing through my head to come to a sudden halt.

"That's actually my boyfriend. So just… you can just… go."

"Oh. Alright. Sorry."

I confirmed her destination and she continued to look over her shoulder. There was a lot I was processing—seeing her get kicked, the dude charging into my car, and her lying about it being a stranger. But above all, I was embarrassed for her: caught in her lie, forced to admit that she did indeed know who kicked her, and she knew him intimately.

At this point, I had driven scores of young women fighting back the tears that often accompany a night of drinking, and I am typically able to laugh off the melodrama, which usually involves a guy not showing interest or a girlfriend being catty, knowing that it's really the alcohol crying. But the whimpers I heard coming from the back seat on this night were different.

"You alright?"

"I'm good." She was trying hard to keep it together. "Thank you."

"It's really not good. I know it's not my business but—"

"*Yeahhhh*, I know." She cut me off, as if she had been given a lecture on the topic many times before.

"Sorry."

"You saw that though, right?" she asked.

"Saw it? It happened right in front of me. I literally have it on camera."

"Can you send that to me?"

"Absolutely. Text me your email. I'll send it tomorrow. That was so fucked up."

As I gave her my number, she tried to keep it light by singing out the digits, with nervous laughs in between. And despite being so far from where we left her boyfriend, she was still looking behind us, making sure he wasn't following. I don't know if I ever felt so sorry for a passenger.

There was an awkward silence, before I asked if her leg was okay. Her answer, and what happened later in the ride, is the reason I wanted to share this story.

"My leg is fine. I am strong," she said, with a victim's tone of pride, satisfied with herself and her ability to overcome the adversity that life has thrown at her.

There was another awkward silence before I couldn't keep it in any longer.

"I feel like I'm obligated to tell you, it's not good for somebody to do that to you."

"Yeah, trust me, I know. I know."

Apparently, you don't. I've lived enough life to know that it was probably not the first time something like this had happened to her.

I bit my tongue, and would have resigned the rest of the ride to the silence had it not been for the sounds of crying that continued to come from the back seat. To lighten the mood, I asked what kind of pizza she got, and she welcomed the change of topic.

"Okay, on a scale of one to ten, how much do you like Hawaiian pizza?" she asked, her mood lifted.

"I'd say a five. I don't dislike it, but I would never order it.

"Hawaiian is my favorite kind of pizza," she said passionately.

Ahhh, so that's why he kicked you. Even the comedian in me knew the risk/reward for that joke was not there. As I felt the mood in the car lift, I never appreciated the value of small talk as much as I did in that moment. I always saw it as a sign of conformity, commiserating about the weather, or talking about the local sports team, or thanking God that it's Friday—a simple way of saying hey, we are part of this human experience together. But I never understood how the most meaningless of things, like the way my palate receives the allocation of a tropical fruit on a cooked arrangement of dough, sauce, and cheese —or in other words, if I like pineapple on pizza—could be the saving grace for a woman on the verge of a breakdown after being physically assaulted by someone she trusts.

There was an unintended consequence of cheering this woman up, though, and I was afraid I knew what she was doing the moment she started typing away on her phone. There's a fine line between cynicism and reality, and I absolutely despise the cynic in me, not only for his negative outlook on life, but also for how often he is right. And when I saw her texting and texting and texting every time I looked in the rearview, the part of me that still has faith in the world wanted to believe she was reaching out to a friend or a roommate. But I think anyone who has ever encountered a situation like this knew exactly who she was reaching out to, and though it was never explicitly confirmed, what she said next only reinforced my assumption.

"Should I call him?"

"Who's that?" Deep down, I was pretty sure I knew who she was talking about, but I wanted to give her the benefit of the doubt.

"The guy that fucking kicked me," she snapped at me like I was the one being stupid; as if I wasn't keeping up with the conversation. *So sorry for not assuming you'd chase after a guy that just physically assaulted you.* My knee-jerk reaction to her question was, *No you shouldn't call him you dumb bitch!* But I tried my best to tone it down.

"I don't want to tell you your business, but I would just… avoid him."

"I'm not—" I assumed she was going to say, "I'm not going to see him tonight." But before she could finish her thought—"Well, it went right to voicemail, so…" She was disappointed.

I knew it wasn't my business, but I also knew this woman was a lost cause from the moment she said, "I'm strong." So my curiosity got the best of me, and I couldn't help but ask, "What would you say to him?"

"I'd say what the fuck did you kick me for? Like grow the fuck up?"

"Does he do that a lot?"

The pause she took before answering said it all. And I think she knew this, because instead of lying like she did before, she admitted it wasn't the first time.

"Kind of," she said, with the sound of tears creeping back into her voice.

"That's really not good, Avery."

"I know." She paused. "Can you send that video to me?"

"Absolutely."

"I'm going to show it to his mom on Mother's Day."

If there was any hope I had that this woman was actually going to stand up for herself, it was gone right there. *Why the hell are you still planning on going to Mother's Day with him?* I don't know if this is right or wrong, but I decided that I wasn't going to send her that video unless she contacted me for it the next day when she was sober, and via text. That way there was a record of her reaching out to me. Last thing I need is to look like I'm trying to play Superman and insert myself into a situation like this. At the risk of giving the cynic in me too much of a spotlight, I thought chances are this girl was more likely to tell her boyfriend I was hitting on her while trying to help than show his mom this video.

As we pulled up to her house, I said "I really hope it stops, because... look, I'm a little older than you, and I've seen my share of this kind of thing, and chances are... well, it doesn't get better."

"Yeah, I know," she said in her shakiest voice yet, right as we stopped in front of her place.

"Do you have someone to talk to? Like a friend or something?"

She laughed like that was the dumbest idea ever. "Well, I have you're number now, is that okay?"

Oh, HELL NO, sweetheart. What makes you think I'm interested in getting involved in this drama? Meanwhile, the cynic in me was chalking up another W.

"No, I mean like, somebody you can trust. And if I were you, maybe tonight is not the best night to keep calling him. I'm sure you were both drinking..."

"I'm not drinking, but thank you." I don't know if she was telling the truth about that or not, but I do know that she thought she was putting herself in a better light by saying she wasn't drinking. In reality, that just made her look worse. At least if she was drunk, alcohol could be an excuse for her stupidity.

"Ok, well maybe he was," I said, just trying to reiterate that calling him tonight was not a smart move. "Look, I don't know the situation at all, but I just know that what I saw isn't good."

"Yeah," she sounded like she couldn't have been closer to losing her composure.

I could see in my rearview that she had been fixated on me speaking since the moment we pulled up to her house, so I turned to look at her. For a brief moment, our eyes met.

"Nobody deserves that," I said. This single sentence put her on the verge of a complete meltdown. She fought back tears as she looked away in shame and embarrassment.

"Thank you," she said, and escapes my car before I witnessed the brunt of her tears.

I don't know the science or biology behind it, but there is something to be said about the vulnerability people feel when eyes meet. Windowpanes of the soul kind of thing. But what I find even more amazing is how people tend to have a harder time hearing a kind word in a moment of need than they do a negative one. She didn't lose it until I told her that she deserves better. She dealt with a leg kick better than the idea of self-worth.

As I drove away, I didn't think about that poor girl, or that asshole guy, or how I could've handled the situation differently. It was how she said, "My leg is fine. I am strong" that kept reverberating in my head. Nobody on earth needs to be told that domestic violence is wrong, including the guy who kicked her. But the fact of the matter is, as long as the world turns, there will be men that use their physical advantage against their wives and girlfriends. And my mind kept going toward the baby girl I was expecting in a few weeks, and how I would explain a situation like this to her.

I'd want to tell my daughter that often there is a fine line between strength and stupidity, but in this instance, the distinction was clear. This woman was an idiot. Putting up with physical pain in order to protect a relationship doesn't make you strong, it makes you stupid. Now I don't know this woman's story, or what led up to it, but I do know there was absolutely no excuse for that guy to kick her like that. I also know that just because there is no excuse for something doesn't mean that it won't happen. We live in a broken world, and all you can do is focus on what you can control. And the moment you start making excuses for that kind of behavior is the moment you start contributing to the situation. The great lie is that your strength is keeping you in the situation, when in reality, what's keeping you in the situation is a fear of ending it. Strength is found in confronting that fear. And I don't mean fighting back; I mean getting out of that relationship. And I know, it's easier said than done. That's why it's important to nip that shit in the bud the first time it rears its ugly head because the longer you put up with it, the more normalized it becomes, and the harder it is to walk away.

I'd want to tell my daughter it is never her fault if someone hits her. But if it happens more than once, she has to ask herself how she contributed to the situation. And I don't mean like what she said or did to cause the violence; I mean like why the fuck was she still with this guy after he showed his true colors. Sort of like, "Get kicked once, shame on him. Get kicked twice, still shame on him... but why are you still within striking distance?"

I hope my daughter never has to confront a problem like this, but if she does, I can only hope that I raise her in a way that helps her get the hell away from that situation as fast as possible.

As far as that girl in my car? I hope the fact that she never contacted me for the video doesn't mean what I think it means.

15
A Holy Day of Debauchery

It was as if all of the consequences of alcohol gathered on a single city block. At one end, there was a small but sturdy blonde, with a chest to remember, pinned against a wall in the narrow alleyway. A large man, built like a loaf of bread, was shoving his tongue down her throat. At first, it startled me. The out-of-rhythm kisses, him standing in a sort of split so that his lips and hips were more even with hers, and the awkward, occasional pelvic thrusts; it would have made me wonder if the girl needed help had it not been for the fact that it was broad daylight, and they were less than five yards into an alley off a busy sidewalk. Plus, she seemed to be teasing him with the possibility of an over-the-pants hand job.

At the other end of the block was another couple on the entirely opposite end of the relationship spectrum. It was as if they traveled through the assembly line of intoxication I was staring at and came out the other side bitter and angry. Though they complemented each other well with their equally good looks, matching athletic physiques, and a similar style of dress that said, "I think I'm cooler than you," they did not seem at all compatible. With these two, the roles were reversed, and it was the man with his back against the wall, and the woman standing square in front of him, with a finger pointed in his face, screaming. The guy was holding his hands out, and his shoulders were up to his ears, giving the universal "what do you want me to do?" shrug of a man defeated.

Back at the end of the block this story opened on, on the sidewalk and within arm's reach of the mismatched couple in the alley (still publicly displaying their affection), there were three girls, all wearing headbands with shamrocks on springs. The girl in the middle was bawling her eyes out, and her shamrocks were dancing along with her short, choppy, panic attack sort of breaths, sobbing as she unsuccessfully tried to form words to her friends who kept asking what was the matter and telling her to calm down.

And there, right in the middle of the love-making, and the fighting, and the crying, a young man was sitting on the bottom step of a stoop of a closed business directly in front of me, puking every bit of his insides out onto the sidewalk.

I don't think Da Vinci could have envisioned a more accurate depiction of what happens after the party. To make it even better, because it was Saint Patty's Day, every single one of them had on some shade of green, making it seem like they were part of the same team, fighting the same fight, which, from my sober perspective, seemed to be exactly that.

Boasting one of the highest Irish per capita populations in the United States, Philadelphia celebrates Saint Patrick's Day with a city-wide bar crawl known as the Erin Express, which would take place over multiple weekends leading up to the Holy Day. On this final Saturday of the Erin Express, I started Ubering early knowing there was money to be made, and seeing that scene unfold while it was still daylight let me know I made the right call.

I gave ride after ride to drunk after drunk from dawn 'til dusk, with the intoxication of each rider rising as the sun was setting. Before I knew it, the night was upon us, and I found myself waiting for a pickup at my alma mater, Temple University. The rider came up from behind my car, and when I heard my back door open, I turned to see the first person I saw all day that did not have a single piece of green in their outfit. She looked like an average college girl, and she was laughing hysterically.

"I just fell into hole!"

"What?" I hadn't heard a genuine laugh all day, so I had a hard time deciphering whether or not she was being drunk, or if she was actually happy.

"There was a random hole outside of my house and I didn't even see it!"

She was laughing so hard she was having a problem explaining. But when she did manage to get some words out, her speech wasn't slurred; she made total sense.

By golly, I think she is actually happy.

From what I gathered, someone forgot to cover a manhole at an unfinished construction job (or perhaps a college kid removed it to be stupid) and she stepped into as if she was recreating a scene in *Home Alone*. Fortunately, she fell in a way that left her leg dangling underground but caught herself from otherwise being more seriously hurt. This led into a friendly conversation, as I couldn't help but mention that I went to Temple myself, and she told me she was there now studying nursing, with a minor in gender studies. Who would have thought—an intelligible, enjoyable conversation after sunset on this Holy Day of Debauchery? It was going great until I brought her outfit into question.

"I have to say, I've been driving since noon and you are the first person I've seen that isn't wearing green. Not a fan of St. Patty's Day?

"Oh, no, I was partying earlier. I'm heading into work now."

"Ah, gotcha. Where do you work?" It was the natural follow-up question, but I was particularly curious as to what kind of job she could go to after a day drink.

"I'm a dancer."

"Like, at a theatre?"

"No, at a gentlemen's club." I could hear in her tone that she enjoyed the shock value of that answer, as if she was on the front lines of the sexual revolution they fantasize about in gender studies classrooms.

What she didn't understand about me is that I used to work in psychiatric research, interviewing drug addicts about their day-to-day activities. My Monday through Friday quite literally consisted of asking crack addicts to tell me some of their crackey tales. So when it comes to shocking revelations, she was going to have to do better than talking about a job that any eighteen-year-old with a little bit of rhythm and a vagina can do. What did surprise me, though, was that this woman just refuted the Stripper Myth—the theory that all strippers are lying when they tell you that they are stripping to pay their tuition.

I guess Chris Rock was wrong: colleges do take dollar bills.

I had a million questions I wanted to ask her, as the strip club from a stripper's perspective seemed like an interesting one. Problem is, I started with the wrong question. Remembering that our destination was on Delaware Ave, I assumed I knew where she worked.

"Oh, no way! You work at Show and Tel?"

I could feel the mood in the car change.

"Excuse me?"

"That's pretty cool." I was confused as to why my enthusiasm was off-putting.

"You think I work at Show and Tel?"

"I thought you said —"

"I'm at Risque."

Oh shoot. I forgot about Risque. Risque is the kind of gentleman's club you could bring your wife to. There are Yelp reviews that say as much. My favorite review was a mom who brought her twenty-four-year-old son there for his birthday. He had special needs, and the mom went on and on about how professional and courteous the staff was toward him and their whole family. All that is to say my passenger worked in an upscale, topless-only environment the whole family can enjoy.

Now Risque is a stone's throw—or should I say, a crumpled up dollar-bill toss—away from Show and Tel.* The difference between Risque and Show and Tel is that at Show and Tel, you can take that same crumpled-up dollar, head inside, and there will be a fully nude woman, on her back, spreading her legs, and everything else that can be spread, and inviting you to shoot that dollar bill inside of her. Puts a hole new meaning to aim small, miss small.†

If you recall my traumatic experience the first time I ever went to a strip club in chapter 1, this was where it took place. When a girl dad says his only job is to keep his daughter off the pole, Show and Tel is the worst-case scenario kind of place they envision. So even with her Power to the Pussy feminist ideology, she was offended that I would assume she would work at a place like that. I tried to recover, asking generic questions like "What's the craziest thing that ever happened to you? Do you ever feel unsafe? What's the most money you've made in a night?" I cringed when I realized that these are all the same questions Uber riders ask me.

But the ship had sailed. She was giving me one-word answers that had an undertone of "fuck off, asshole." It was so obvious she was upset with me that I started to feel like the one being disrespected in my own car like that. I dropped the attempt to win her back, and we rode the rest of the way in silence. And though I was working a job most people in academia look down on, I parlayed the silent treatment the stripper in my back seat was giving me into a time of quiet contemplation, confronting the realities of this world that are too uncomfortable for the safe space of the modern college classroom.

I get that she wants to brag about being an exotic dancer, and at the same time, not have people assume she is spreading her pussy

---

*In case you have been wondering, this is not a typo. Whether it was a marketing decision or they just wanted to save money by having one less neon-lit letter to buy, this is how it is actually spelled.

† Also not a typo—I couldn't resist the pun.

lips for dirty dollar bills to be darted at them. But her problem was in thinking people look at the dancer at Risque differently than the one at Show and Tel. Gender studies professors can talk feminist theory until they are blue in the face trying to convince us otherwise, but at the end of the day, nothing will change the fact that a whore is a whore is a whore. Shoot, I don't care if you are a fucking NFL cheerleader: if the main function of your job is providing sex appeal, you're a whore.

And sure, I'm well aware that it's much more socially acceptable to be an NFL cheerleader than a stripper, just like the activities at Risque are more socially acceptable than those at Show and Tel. But whether the cleavage is out on stage at a strip club, or during halftime of a football game, or during a sales pitch in a board room, it's all the same game, sweetheart. If anything, at least the stripper is being honest about it. If I have one problem with that sexual revolution bullshit they plug in academia, it's not that women can express their own sexuality as they see fit. The problem is acting like that expression doesn't have consequence. If you're going to show a little cleavage when you are closing a sale, that's fine… just don't act like gender equality has been set back fifty years if a client starts to hit on you.

When we arrived at her highly esteemed place of employment, I wondered about the appropriate farewell for someone who is about to show her tits for dollar bills. I had a feeling "Don't shake your ass too hard" or "Hope nobody grabs your cooter tonight" wouldn't fly, so I played it safe with "Have a good shift." And while I've always found those who work in tip-dependent industries are extremely generous tippers themselves, I was not at all surprised when she exited my car without even a goodbye, let alone a gratuity.

With the angry stripper gone, the night rolls on, and a little after ten, I get a pickup request at a bar near the river. Four young men get into my car, heading to McGillians. McGillians is a bar known for being the oldest operating bar in Philadelphia, and due to its location in the heart of Center City, it's known by most Uber drivers as a pain in the ass to get to, especially during the Erin Express.

Fuck, I thought when I saw the destination. *I'm going to be stuck in traffic for at least half an hour.*

"Fuck," the guy said in the front seat, almost as if he echoed my own thought. "She's leaving McGillians."

"Where are they going?" A friend in the back seat asked.

"Home."

"Fuck."

"I knew we shouldn't have left."

"If you didn't take so long," he said to his friend, "they'd still be there!"

It was such a familiar situation it's almost cliche. Guys leave a bar in hopes of linking up with a group of girls at another bar. The girls bail. Now the guys are stuck between a rock and a hard place: Do they wait in line to go back into the bar they were just at? Or do they give the new bar a shot, not knowing how it is?

I saw this as my window of opportunity to dissuade them from McGillians. "I drove by McGillians earlier… it was even more crowded than here," I said, praying these guys would bail on the ride and save me the trip to Center City.

There was a general consensus in the group that there were no girls to be had for them back in that bar, and that was enough for them to want a change in scenery. As I start to pull away, the guy in the front seat half-jokingly said, "At this point, we might as well just go to the strip club."

There was not an immediate and vocal rejection of the idea, and it made me think the guys in the back were not entirely opposed to it. I'm not proud of what I did, as I don't like to encourage people to do things that they might regret the next day. But I really did not want to drive to Center City.

"I actually just dropped a stripper off at Risque earlier tonight. She was one of the most beautiful girls I ever saw." You can add lying to the list of things I'm not proud of, right after being a bad influence. The angry stripper was a seven at best.

"Should we?" someone finally asked from the back seat.

"I'm telling you, McGillians is crazy packed right now," I said.

"Let me text that girl one more time," the dude in the front said to the group. I don't know what she said back, or if she said anything at all, but within moments, he said, "Fuck it. Let's go to the strip club."

The dudes in the back erupted with that douchey excitement guys put on when they don't want to admit how they really feel, and I kept my excitement bottled up for the same reason. It was as if I was witnessing yet another part of the Chris Rock stripper bit in real life: "You know those guys that can't function in a normal club? They go to a normal club, ask one girl to dance…

"Excuse me, would you like to dance?"

"No, not right now, maybe later."

"Yo man, let's go to the titty bar man. These bitches is stuck up, man!"

Granted, there was some slight variation to the way it played out, but it was close enough for me to feel like I was seeing that iconic stand-up bit play out in real time.

It would have made for a great story if they had asked to go to the same club that Angry Stripper worked at, but the truth is, they asked to get dropped off at Delilah's. It worked out great for me, not only because it was closer, but also because it weighed less on my conscience. It's not fully nude, they have a dress code to get in, and you can't even bring your own beer. In the realm of Philly strip clubs, Delilah's was closer to a kindergarten center than to a Show and Tel.

My logistical luck would continue as my next ride request was conveniently at Delilah's. Those four guys get out and a new rider gets in without me even taking my foot off the brake. At this pace, I bet I was giving more rides to guys I didn't know than the Angry Stripper. And I bet she was still making more money than me.

I was surprised to see this new rider's destination was a hotel in Delaware, forty-five minutes away, and I was even more surprised that he was noticeably alert the whole ride there. Typically, this is the point of the night when people begin to pass out on the way home, especially on longer rides. I thought perhaps he was jacked up on adrenaline from the strip club, or maybe he was feeling good from the booger sugar that often accompanies a place like that. My assumptions would change when we got to the destination.

It was a decent hotel located off of a highway in a suburban neighborhood, and it was a bit of a head scratcher as to why my passenger was staying there, so far away from where he celebrated St. Patty's Day. When we pull up, there was a very curvy Latino woman in a tight red dress standing next to the lobby doors smoking a cigarette. I remember that dress as clear as day, not only because it was my second sighting of an outfit without any green in it, but also because it was way too cold to be wearing only that. I remember she was Latino because I caught myself judging her less for not wearing green due to her ethnicity. I wondered if that was me being realistic, or if I was being a bit racist. Or maybe it was both.

My passenger thanked me for the ride, and when he got out, walked directly toward the woman in the red dress. She held up a finger at me, as if telling me to wait. I rolled my window down as she motioned my passenger to head into the lobby. I heard her say to him, "Just wait inside, baby. I'll be right back."

She comes to my car and says in a beautiful accent, "There's a bank two minutes down the road. I'll give you $50 dollars if you drive me there and back."

Fifty bucks cash for a ten-minute trip? There was definitely something shady going on here, but that rate works out to be $300 an hour. "Sounds good to me." She opens the door and sits down in the front seat.

While that kind of money will get me to take even the shadiest of rides without hesitation, I was still on high alert. After all, I was driving to an empty parking lot of a closed bank around midnight with a stranger not using the Uber app. As illogical as it sounds, though, I didn't get any bad vibes from this woman, and that made me comfortable. She directed me to the self-service ATM, got out of my car, and pulled out a handful of cash from her chest. She deposited it into the ATM, came back to my car, and we headed back to the hotel. When we got back, I noticed she was on a first name basis with the attendant standing in front of the hotel.

While the several people I told this story to seem to immediately pick up on what was going on here, it wasn't until she exited my vehicle that the thought dawned on me: *Did I just take a hooker to the bank?*

Admittedly, this is speculation, but I'm pretty sure I drove that guy from a strip club forty-five minutes away to a working woman operating out of a hotel, and then took said working woman to safely deposit her previous earnings into her account so she wasn't walking into her next client cash heavy. And if that's the case, I'm definitely racist for thinking she wasn't wearing green because she's Latino. She wasn't wearing green because she's a whore!

After that, I headed toward the nearby college town, getting a few short rides of St. Patty's partiers heading home, until a long one brought me out to the farmlands of Bucks County, a good forty minutes away. It was a college-aged kid, riding solo, and he passed out within moments of getting in the car.

After all the wildcards I had been dealt today, finally, a familiar kind of ride. I was relieved. It didn't escape me, however, that the baseline of normalcy for a late night Uber ride was somebody so hammered they can't function. What has this job done to my view of the world?

When we got to his destination, the typical vocal nudges did not work in waking him up. So I yelled. And then I yelled a little louder. Still nothing. This dude was out.

I have a strict rule of not touching passengers, especially when a passenger is passed out. I have no interest in learning how a sleeping, drunk stranger in my back seat will react when they wake up to their Uber driver touching them. Plus, I wouldn't even know the right way to go about it. Do I shake them violently to make sure they wake up immediately, but at the risk of them coming to thinking they are in the middle of a fight? Next thing I know I'm in hand-to-hand combat with a blackout drunk in my own car. Or do I opt to go with the gentle and soothing touch, so as not to startle them, but risk giving the vibe of a sexual advance, waking this poor guy up with a move reminiscent of the over-the-pants handiwork I saw at the start of my day. Now my rider is left wondering what else happened while he was asleep, or even worse, encourages me to continue.*

Instead, I lifted my foot off the brake and let my car roll just a little bit before jerking to a stop. His head fell forward, but he was still asleep. I did it again... and again... and again, each time going a little faster and stopping a little harder. It got to a point where I was worried I might give him whiplash. After the fifth or sixth time, I double checked to make sure he was still breathing. It was then I realized my stop-and-go routine brought us about forty yards away from his house.

If this guy was too drunk to notice my self-inflicted turbulence, there was no way I would expect him to be able to walk that distance when he did wake up. So I put it my car reverse, and his upper body slumped forward as I started to go backward to the original drop-off point. This time, knowing he had the seat to cushion his head, I picked up a decent amount of speed before I punched the brakes so hard my wheels locked.

He woke up as calmly and as comfortably as a drunk, confused young man could. It took him a second to realize the situation, but when he did, he got out of my car without a word and headed inside. I watched him stumble to his front door, thinking about how he no idea of the stop-and-go game I just played with his body; of how much faith he and everyone else puts into their Uber drivers, and all the otherwise low-status jobs that seem replaceable when done well, but can actually fuck your life up pretty good when done poorly or maliciously—like a fast food worker who doesn't wash his hands, or the janitor who forgot to refill the bathroom stalls with toilet paper.

By the time I dropped him off, it was well after three in the morning. Bars in Pennsylvania close at two, and because I was in the middle of nowhere, I didn't think I'd get any more rides. At that point, I was fine with calling it a night, as there was only so much degeneracy

---

*Of course, I would say no. If he countered with an offer of a hefty tip, though... well, shoot, every man has his price. Before I know it, I'm jerking off my rider for ten grand (which would be my threshold, by the way) all because I didn't adhere to my principle of never touching strangers in my Uber.

I could take in one day, and I could feel its effect on my spirit. There's something that happens to you when you see nothing but moral deprivation for fifteen hours straight, when everyone you meet is acting on impulse, driven by their own selfish desires.

Driving home, I tried to decompress from what I witness as a driver: a sad reality that is exacerbated on a day like today. The world is full of people who live a life so stressed or unfulfilled that they spend their free time chasing their reality away with booze and sex and any other means of instant gratification they can get their hands on.

Seeing that every week in, week out, month after month, year after year, is the kind of thing that can lead you down a pretty depressing path. So as I wrestled with pointlessness of life, much to my surprise, I heard the ping of an Uber request. It was only a few minutes away.

The pickup point was at the end of a long, wide driveway. I could see a building and the dark outline of a silo against the night sky, and a man walking toward my car. He greets me with an unfamiliar clarity of sobriety. Turns out, he had just finished his shift at the Lehigh Valley Diary Farm.

He greeted me in a way that suggested he was in a good mood, which, at that time of night, was as rare as being sober. I didn't even think to ask what he did there because I had an urge to tell him what just occurred to me.

"You know, I've been driving since yesterday morning, and you are the first person I've picked up who hasn't been drinking." I shared with him a thought I have often but rarely said out loud, how driving Uber has shown me the endless cycle of emptiness and depression so many people live with. If I'm driving on a weekday morning, my passenger is most likely miserable, tired, and dreading going to work. In the afternoon, that same passenger isn't happy to be done work, but instead, relieved, and already mentally and emotionally prepping themselves to do it all again tomorrow. On the weekend, I drive that same person, picking them up from their house or apartment to take them to a bar or some other social gathering, and it's this brief window when they aren't stressed about work or life or whatever else that brings them down during the week. For this small period of time, I have happy people in my car, filled with the hope and excitement of an impending party. Then I pick them up after the party is over and the bars have closed, only to see they have drunk themselves into oblivion. It's as if the part of their life they look forward to most is the part where they get to forget about it. The mass of men may lead lives of quiet desperation, but when that desperation is seen and heard over and over again in my back seat, it becomes very loud and apparent to me.

Of course, with a five-star rating and a possible tip hanging in the balance, I gave him the lighter version of my dark and depressing outlook, telling him that "after seeing people indulge themselves all day, it's encouraging to see someone with a good attitude, out here, trying to make an honest buck. Makes me feel like I'm not the only one." Over the course of our conversation, he shared with me that he has worked every job under the sun, as he had a little girl he was trying to care of. He didn't mind working overnight at the dairy farm. He said the pay was good and the work wasn't bad, especially compared to some of the other jobs he's had.

He told me the worst job he ever had was at a repackaging plant. Not only was the work extremely tedious and boring, but he had a bit of a moral issue with what he was doing. His job entailed wiping off expiration dates from expired food, and as long as the food wasn't visibly old, smelly, or damaged, he would put on a new expiration date. Most of the time, he explained, the expiration date is only there for quality control, and there are so many preservatives in foods these days that they are still okay to eat for years, "as long as you are fine with putting those chemicals in your body." The frustrating part about the job, though, was that he was essentially encouraged to re-date everything. Something would have to be extremely un-buyable in order for his boss to be okay with him throwing it out.

They would then sort these re-dated items into different quality piles, with the lowest quality going to the discount grocery stores, and the higher quality going to the most expensive grocery stores, which were all owned by the same people anyway. He wasn't sure of the legality of a lot of what they did there but justified it by saying that his girlfriend had just gotten pregnant, he really needed the money, and it paid very well. But one day, his boss asked him to put new dates on old dog food, and he loves animals so much that it made him really question what he was doing there. He quit that week, and now lives his life eating as much natural, home-grown food that he can.

I didn't share with him how interesting I thought it was that it wasn't until he was forced to put animals at risk that he hit a tipping point. Like, *who cares about people? Just don't fuck with animals.* I didn't know how to phrase it without him thinking I was calling him an asshole, when in reality, one of my favorite things I learned in psychology was the way people treat animals is a huge indicator for social function, as those who are violent toward pets have a proclivity for psychopathic tendencies. I always figured that meant those who cared about animals were more empathetic.

When I dropped him off, I encouraged him to go get some well-deserved sleep, to which he said he could only do so for a couple of hours, as he promised to take his daughter out for pancakes that morning.

I watched him haul his toolbox up steps to his aged apartment building in the cold, early morning hours, and wondered why is it that a guy like that has to work his ass off just to make ends meet, when every weekend I drive scores of entitled assholes spending their time drinking and partying and lighting money on fire—money that most likely wasn't earned with as much difficulty as the dollar of the dairy farmer. I know that life's not fair, and I also know that I don't know all of the decisions the dairy farmer made to get to that point in life. But I just wish there was a way that people like him could be rewarded, that goodness and honesty and hard work was valued in a way that at least afforded this man the opportunity to get more than a couple hours of sleep before having pancakes with his daughter. Then again, maybe that is what makes it all worth it. Maybe the pancakes and time spent with his daughter is that much more valuable because of what it took to get there. Maybe that struggle, that purpose, is what keeps him out of the bars on Friday and Saturday night and what gives him a good attitude about work, despite how difficult an overnight farm job might look from the outside.

As I drove home, I kept thinking of the dairy farmer's situation and how it was so incredibly different than the majority of people I meet in my Uber. And like St. Patrick drove the snakes out of Ireland, this dairy farmer drove the negativity out of my thick Irish skull and reminded me of how much my worldview is influenced by my environment, be it what I do for work, to what I do in my free time, down to the content I mindlessly consume.

When I spend most of my time driving people complaining about having to go work, I'm going to think everyone hates their job. When I spend most of time driving people to and from the bar, I'm going to think the world is full of drunks. In reality, only my world is full of drunks. There are a lot of people who have the same attitude as that dairy farmer, I just don't see them as much. I wanted to make it a point to put myself in situations where I am reminded of that. Otherwise, it's like looking at the world through shaded glasses. After a while, it's easy to believe that everything is a lot darker than it actually is.

16
Santa Drops the N-Bomb

I was sitting in bumper-to-bumper traffic, when I heard the dreadful thud and clank against my car.

A delivery biker was weaving through the traffic and onto the sidewalk, and in doing so, nailed the rear side of my car with both his body and his bike.

Already pissed I was stuck in traffic, patience was not in my repertoire that day.

"What the hell, dude?" I yelled out my window.

"Fuck you."

"Fuck me? You just hit my car."

"What the fuck you gonna do about it?"

"You better hope there's no damage."

He was probably in his late teens or early twenties, long and athletic looking. He moved his bike to the side, squared his shoulders to me, and slowed down his speech for emphasis. "What the fuck are you gonna do about it?"

I'm sitting in my car, and not only is he directly outside of my driver's window, but he is on the sidewalk, elevated. I'm in a very disadvantageous position if I tried to get out and he took the implied route of the violence.

"How bout I call the fucking cops, how about that?"

"Call the fuckin cops. You think I care?"

"Better hope there's no damage, then we won't have to find out."

"Fuck you, pussy."

I think he knew I was bluffing about calling the cops, but he wasn't going to stick around to find out. He grabbed his bike and started moving down the sidewalk.

I popped out to inspect my car, and fortunately, no damage was done. But what made this otherwise typical Philly encounter memorable was what happened when the kid was walking away. A guy in a pickup truck, about five cars ahead, waved down the biker. "Hey, brother. You're okay by me. Ignore that asshole!" You read that right. I was the asshole in this situation. As pissed as I was that I was still stuck in traffic in a car that just got hit by some dumbass who put a nice little bow on the exchange by making me look and feel like a total punk, all of my anger turned to confusion when I heard that. *Why the hell would Pickup Truck Guy say that?* It bounced around my head for a while. It finally dawned on me: I'd bet dollars to donuts it's because the kid was black. And the driver who greeted him with that cringe-wannabe soulfulness of "hey brother" was white.

That driver had no idea what was going on between me and the kid. Because if he did, there is no way he would think it's okay to slam into someone else's vehicle and then strong arm their way out of it.

Instead, that guy in the pickup saw me, a white guy yelling at a black guy, and he took it as an opportunity to be the anti-racist superhero so many whites dream of being.

I admit, my analysis of the situation is purely speculative, but it's within reason. There was an article that made waves a couple years back titled "Being White in Philly." In the city proper, white people make up far less than half of the population, yet in the wealthy suburbs, far more. The author of that article talks about when wealthy whites encounter minorities, specifically black people, there is this weird "dance" that white people do. It's saying hello to a black person passing them on a sidewalk, when they wouldn't have said it to a white person. It's holding the door a little longer for a black guy, when they would have let it close on a white guy. It's going out of their way to make sure the black person knows, "I'm not a racist."

And on the surface, it's hard to argue that going out of your way to be extra nice is a bad thing. But treating someone nicer based on their skin color is still treating someone different based on their skin color. And I don't think you treat black people like that unless you feel like they don't belong. Put it this way: when there is a guest in my house, I go out of my way to make sure the guest feels welcome. When my roommate is home, I treat him like he belongs. There is a huge difference.

It has been my experience, working this job as a white man, often picking up people of different races, that the more I treat everyone the same, the more likely my actions or attitudes will be classified as racist. Of course, there are the one-off events of people calling me a racist to my face when a ride doesn't go their way. But what really bothers me is when that opinion comes from the social justice warriors who judge from a distance; people who I know would never dream of even driving through the neighborhoods I pick up people in. Perhaps that's why I constantly wrestle with the issue of race—something that is so simple to me but seems to be a never-ending issue for so many people in this country. And one weekday morning while driving for Uber, I saw one of the most confusing displays of its complexity unfold right in front of my car.

I had a passenger in my car, and we were in a nice Center City neighborhood where people lived, rather than worked, just south of Rittenhouse Square. For those of you unfamiliar with Philly, what matters here is that we were far enough from Center City that the big buildings had been replaced by row homes, but still close enough that there was a decent amount of foot traffic, at least for 10 a.m. on a weekday morning.* I had pulled up to a red light, stopping behind an absolute beater of a car, when a man on a bicycle passes me on my left. With impeccable timing, the woman driving the beater cuts her wheel to the left, punches the gas, and forced the man on the bike, who had an uncanny resemblance to Santa Claus, to veer toward the sidewalk, just to avoid getting hit. He tried to jump the curb, but he lost control, falling off of his bike and landing on the cement. I assumed it to be an accident, that is, until the woman in the beater put the car in reverse, positioned the vehicle so it was horizontal in the road (now blocking both lanes of traffic), and aimed directly at Santa Claus, laying on the sidewalk, trying to gather himself. It looked as though she was fixing to run her car up onto the sidewalk and into him, but there was a scuffle inside the beater. The young man in the passenger seat was wrestling the woman's hands off of the steering wheel and the shifter, screaming, "Mom, don't do this!"

I don't know if her son overpowered her, or if she realized running over a guy on the sidewalk was not a prudent course of action, but regardless, Mom got out of the car steaming. "You fucked with the wrong nigga! I'm a fuck yo pussy ass up!" Santa Claus, still seated on the sidewalk, checking his arms and legs for wounds, responded with a "fuck off." From the jumbled arguing that ensued, I pieced together that at some point prior to what occurred in front of me, Santa Claus had smacked the hood of the woman's car. He

---

* That's one thing I noticed very early on in my Uber career: once 9 a.m. hits, the normal people of society have gotten to where they need to be for the day. The kind of people I see out on the street after aren't typical. Myself most certainly included.

accused of her being in the bike lane, and she eloquently replied with a "fuck a bike lane, bitch!" No matter what actually transpired, when there is violence brewing, the details of right or wrong become trivial. She kept screaming variations of "you fucked with the wrong one, nigga!" and "Imma a fuck you up, nigga!" and was getting closer and closer to Santa Claus, who is now on his feet, holding his bike as a barrier in between the two. The woman's son, a skinny teenager wearing a white beater, mesh shorts, flip-flops, and a stocking cap, gets out of the car and runs to the woman, physically restraining her.

"Leave me the fuck alone!" Santa said. "You were driving like a maniac." At this, the teenager pulls his mom back, causing her to stumble, and steps to the man. "What the fuck did you call my mom?!" Santa Claus stands firm. "Get the fuck away from me!"

When Mom regains her balance, she jumps back into the scene, bear hugging her son, reversing the role of who was holding who back.

"Baby let me handle this. You got priors! It ain't worth it."

That comment proved effective, and he calmed down to a point where he didn't need to be restrained any longer, although he was still fired up. It was right about then that I felt warm air pulsing onto the back of my neck. I look over my shoulder to see my passenger leaned all the way forward, over the middle console, soaking in the show. When I looked at him, he realized he was a little too close and slid to the driver side of the back seat to get a better view.

"Sorry if this is holding you up," I said, as her car was still horizontal in the roadway, blocking any traffic from moving through.

"Oh, it's fine," he said, as if he was more than okay with bypassing the rest of his day to see how this unfolded. I couldn't blame him. We had front row seats to high-quality content.

Santa Claus had backed up across the entire sidewalk, his back now literally against the wall, and his requests of "get the fuck away" and "leave me the fuck alone" went ignored by the mother and son duo that kept getting louder and louder the closer to him they got. They continued shouting variations of "Nigga, how bout I fucking kill you," "Dickhead nigga," and "You a ho" for what felt like forever. Eventually, Santa Claus fell silent and decided to eat the shit they were spewing at him. The boy was behind the woman, but the woman kept getting closer with every insult and threat until she had a finger in his face. Santa Claus's demeanor changed to that of a man defeated, and he began pleading with them to stop.

Unfortunately, those pleas went ignored.

"You picked the wrong one, nigga." "You a stupid nigga! You piece of shit nigga."

Finally, realizing his pleas to stop would not work, Santa Claus exploded: "STOP CALLING ME A NIGGER!" Hard r and all.

I heard my passenger gasp in disbelief, and it was as if the busy city street full of passersby rubbernecking the event stopped in their tracks to see what would happen next. I don't think since the camera phone had been invented has a white person ever risked saying the N-word so loud and so clear and in such a public setting at all, let alone the fact that it was directed at a black person. Everyone within earshot was holding their breath, anticipating the repercussions.

Now this man was old, but you could tell he was sturdy. I wouldn't be surprised if he had been an athlete back in his day. There is something I always found quietly amusing when women threaten violence; it's almost endearing, like when a cute little puppy growls at older, bigger dogs. The thing is, when push comes to shove and a woman is faced with the consequences of her threats, her tune tends to change real quick. And I think the way Santa Claus exploded reminded her that even her teenage son with priors might have a hard time with this old guy if things escalated further.

Every set of eyes on that city block was locked onto that woman, waiting to see how she would respond to his demand of "Stop calling me a nigger." I can't speak on behalf of everyone there, but I am pretty sure we were all thinking the same thing: we are about to witness the murder of Santa Claus.

She composed herself, stepped back to her car, and said, "Well then stop acting like one!" She ordered her son to get back in the car. The light was red again, but she sped through the intersection anyway.

As my rider and I sat there in disbelief as to what we just witnessed, I kept trying to work out the situation.

She was repeatedly calling him the N-word, and of all the things happening, amidst jumping off his bike and the threats of violence, the thing that set this guy off was being called the N-word. And then, even though he didn't call her the N-word, he still broke societal norms by using that word in its full, unadulterated form. But what I couldn't decide is if this woman's response was genius or insane.

She simultaneously insulted the white guy by saying he is acting like a N-word, something he obviously does not desire, but by doing so, she validated the negative connotations associated with that word. Made me think of that Chris Rock joke, there's black people, and there's niggas. And the niggas are fucking it up for the rest of us.

As I was reading way too much into her response, my rider, a white guy in his thirties, said to no one in particular, "I still can't believe that guy said the N-word like that."

And then it dawned on me: Of all the things to take away from that debacle—it wasn't the attempted vehicular assault, or a senior citizen being flung off his bike, or the threats of violence that almost led to the death of Santa Claus in a Philadelphia street on a sunny Monday morning. The most shocking thing about that situation was a guy with less melanin using a word that is said every day by millions of people with more melanin.

I know people like to point to the N-word as evidence of how prevalent racism is in our country and the historical horrors that have come along with it. But I think they are looking at it all wrong. There is no way faster way for a white guy to lose his job than to say that word in any context; it doesn't even have to be maliciously. There isn't a single word in the entire English language that garners that level of restriction; that society will make an active effort to demonstrate it is an unacceptable word for white people to say. If that isn't a sign of an anti-racist society, I don't know what is.

But, then again, like the white man who holds the door a little longer for a black man... maybe it's the opposite.

17
The Explanation of Uber Pool

For chapters 18-21, you have to understand how Uber's service called "Pool" functions. (Lyft had a similar feature called Share). Here's how they work:

In its never-ending hunt to squeeze every penny out of the transportation industry, while simultaneously maintaining its loose relationship with the truth, Uber created a cheaper alternative known as Uber Pool. While a great idea in theory, it was most certainly made by someone who has never worked as an Uber driver, and has enough money that they would never actually use the service. In other words, it's poor people shit.

The idea behind Uber Pool, for those unfamiliar, is that you can carpool with people going the same direction as you for a cheaper price. Say Jack calls an Uber Pool to the airport, forty minutes away. On the way there, they pick up John, also going to the airport. Ideally, the riders get the same service for cheaper, and the driver gets paid more because he has two riders in his car.

In theory, it was a dream solution that saved riders money and helped drivers earn more. In reality, it was a nightmare for everyone.

The problem started with the fact that it was presented to the rider as a cheaper alternative, without being clear as to why. I can't tell you how many times Uber riders were confused, surprised, or even angry that we had to stop and pick someone else up. On one hand, I understand that it was a newer service and Uber seemed to intentionally make it unclear as to what would happen when they ordered an Uber Pool, leaving it to the driver to break the bad news. On the other hand, I sometimes wanted to scream at these passengers, especially when they were taking their anger out on me for a choice that they made. *I'm sorry sir, but why did you think this option was 50 percent cheaper? Was it your lucky day and Uber just decided to give you the same service for a much cheaper price? Are you God's gift to earth and you're being rewarded for it in the form of a cheap Uber? Didn't you think maybe there was a catch?*

After people get past the fact they are not God's gift and they'll be riding with a stranger, they then have to experience one of the most frustrating parts of driving for Uber: the waiting. Some people might take the full five minutes to come out to the car, which means if you're a passenger in an Uber pool, that's five minutes sitting in the car, with your Uber driver, waiting for a stranger. Even if you don't have somewhere to be, the awkwardness of that situation can make that five minutes feel like forever. And that could happen multiple times in a single trip.

To make matters worse, the way the algorithm worked was that if, as a rider, your destination was the furthest away out of everyone else in the pool, and the pool kept getting riders added to it, you could be in the car, essentially, forever. For example, if you are going to the airport on the edge of town, but on the way, Uber kept adding riders to the pool that were en route to the airport but never actually at the airport, as a driver, I'd be required to pick those people up. This would go on as long as the app kept adding riders, as drivers didn't even have the option to reject an added ride once a trip started. I always thought a more appropriate name for Uber Pool would have been Uber Orgy, because once it starts, nobody has any idea who is riding where and how long it's going to take, and by the time it's done, everyone is going to feel like they got fucked.

Speaking from personal experience as a rider, I once opted to save $15 at the end of the night and went with Uber Pool. What should have been a five-minute trip turned into a forty-five-minute trip, as the minivan we were in up kept picking up more and more people.

As a driver, I've seen quite a few riders miss their flights due to Uber Pool. They are presented with an acceptable estimated time of arrival when they order it, but then during the ride the ETA is pushed back because of additional pick-ups. One time, after informing a lone female passenger heading to the airport that we were going to have to take a detour and pick someone else up, she asked me to let her out on the highway in a last-ditch effort to call another Uber and catch her flight. I hinted at the idea that if she were to offer me the right amount of cash I'd sign off the app and just take her directly to the airport, but wasn't pushy about it, as it always feels a bit uncomfortable telling a rider that we should operate off the app, untracked, especially when it's a woman by herself. Regardless, I don't know if she was uncomfortable with the idea, or was too innocent to realize that for the right price, anyone will do just about anything, but either way, she didn't bite. I couldn't bring myself to leave her on the highway as she requested, and pulled off at the next exit to at least give her next driver a chance of finding her. I always wondered if she made it.

If it wasn't frustrating enough from the driver's end dealing with all of the added nonsense of picking up extra riders, being rerouted constantly, and having to explain to disgruntled passengers why someone else is getting in ("I'm sorry sir, I know you didn't realize you'd be sharing the ride but that's the reason it was so much cheaper"), earnings from Uber Pool fares were considerably lower than normal fares. Plus, the kind of people who typically order Uber Pool are not in a spot financially where they will be willing to tip. So your bottom line really took a dive.

When the pandemic hit, Uber was forced to shut the service down, and fortunately, has not brought it back, at least not in my market. In summation, Uber Pool was an absolute shit show.

But it did make for spectacular content. The following are stories that took place during an Uber Pool ride.

18
An Uber Pool through the Projects

La Salle University is a private Catholic school located in the heart of North Philadelphia. The tuition is $33,000 per year, and that's not including room and board. Meanwhile, in the neighborhood surrounding it, if you are earning $33k per year, you are in the top 1 percent of that district's earners (of course, that's not including drug dealers). I've always found it ironic the neighborhoods around colleges are usually kind of neighborhoods people go to college for so that they don't have to live in those kinds of neighborhoods as an adult.

That said, Uber does not discriminate as to who, what, or why someone needs a ride. It's always a crapshoot in a neighborhood like that: Am I getting a college kid going to the library, or a hood rat looking to do hood rat things with his hood rat friends?

On this particular Saturday night, it would turn out I was in for a little bit of everything. A previous ride had brought me from Center City to North Philadelphia, not far from La Salle University. At this point in my Uber career, I was still naive enough to believe in the idealistic approach of leaving my app on in these kinds of neighborhoods. I felt like I was being a good human, and that feeling outweighed the fact that the risk, coupled with the considerable knock in my earnings, was a clear indicator that it's actually a terrible approach. But that's a story for another time.

The first rider to enter this Uber Pool adventure was a young kid who got in my car talking on his phone. If I was making a bad movie, I could cast him as a D-boy, and portray him as a lot harder than he actually was. In reality, I got the impression that he was just a teenager trying to fit in. I think if he had D-boy kind of money, he wouldn't be calling an Uber Pool. He didn't hang up his phone call, but gave a kind greeting when he got in. If you haven't picked up on it by now, something as simple as "Hello, how are you doing?" from an Uber rider is not a given, and the fact that this guy would prioritize treating me like a human being over his phone call made him okay in my book. I confirmed the address, and we went on our way.

He was heading all the way to Southwest Philadelphia, so I was betting there would be other riders added to this Uber Pool. Sure enough, before long I was called to a woman holding a toddler and a bag of laundry. I never like taking kids without a car seat, but I always feel stuck between a rock and a hard place. I know if I leave them there, she's not going go and buy a car seat, she's just going call another Uber until she finds one that takes her. Meanwhile, you got this little kid outside in the cold, and a mom most likely struggling to make ends meet, and I'm supposed make her life harder? And if that wasn't enough pull on my heartstrings, I've always had a soft spot for anyone that has to Uber to the laundromat, which happens more often than you'd think. The first time I encountered the Uber laundry ride I couldn't help but think of that infamous Bernie Sanders quote that out-of-touch Republicans mocked him for, when he said, "it's expensive to be poor."

I've never lived in a building that didn't have a washer and dryer in it, and I never realized what a blessing that was until I saw the lengths that some people have to go to just to wash their clothes. When you don't have a washer and dryer in your dwelling, not only is it a huge time spend, but it seems like the poorer the neighborhood, the further away someone has to travel to find a laundromat. So these people call an Uber just to avoid taking three different buses to get to one.

With all that in mind, I popped my trunk, helped her load the laundry bag into it, and the two got in. I know that by taking a kid without a car seat, if something were to happen, doing the humane thing here would leave me totally screwed with my insurance. But how the fuck could I refuse a young mother and her child, standing in the cold with a trash bag full of dirty clothes, a four-block ride to the laundromat?

Not a D Boy continued his phone conversation throughout the entirety of the laundromat run. Soon after we dropped off mother and child, I got another request, this time at La Salle University. I let Not a D Boy know we had another rider to pick up, and a few minutes later we pulled up to what looked like a meme of a suburban dad. Windbreaker, golf club hat, khakis, and at the risk of sounding like I am making this up—white New Balance sneakers.

From the back seat, still talking into the phone, I hear, in a hushed tone. "Yo I gotta go. I think it's 5-0."

Now I don't know if you have picked up on this in my storytelling, but I don't like adding color to the story unless it's necessary. Color in terms of flowery language, in my Hemingway fandom, is almost always superfluous. Color in terms of race is almost always the same.

Except when it's not. And in this case, it's relevant. Not a D Boy was black, Laundry Girl was Latino, and I think it goes without saying that the Dad Meme was as white as a glass of milk on a paper plate in a snowstorm.

It has been my personal experience living and working in poor black neighborhoods that whiteness is almost always associated with law enforcement. If I had a dollar every time a black person asked me if I was a cop, and then another dollar for when they (incorrectly) reminded me that if I lie it's entrapment, then I wouldn't have to drive Uber. It makes sense if you think about it—if these poor, all-black neighborhoods are marginalized, and the only white people that come into that neighborhood are cops arresting them, of course they would get suspicious when they see a white person. Now I can't say for sure if Not a D Boy actually believed that Dad Meme was a cop, or just wanted to sound tough to whomever he was talking to on the phone. The way this ride would turn out, though, left me thinking he wasn't leaving anything to chance.

Even though Dad Meme sat in the front, Not a D Boy was shuffling about in the back seat. It was odd enough to stand out to me, but otherwise I didn't think too much of it. I confirmed with Dad Meme that he was heading to the airport, and he shared that he had come to Philly from Florida to see his daughter's field hockey game, who plays at La Salle. He said it was only his second time in Philadelphia, but he's loved everything he has seen so far.

What that translates to is he's only seen the tourist spots. Little did he know, he was about to get a real taste of the city of Brotherly Shove.

I had let Dad Meme know that we had to drop Not a D Boy off on the way, however, a few minutes into the ride we got yet another request. In a rare Uber Pool occurrence, this woman was actually heading to the airport too. She didn't say much, but by her all black uniform, non-slip shoes, and lack of luggage, my bet was that she worked in one of the terminals at a restaurant or fast food joint. Her addition to the Uber Pool would otherwise be forgettable except for the logistics of her pickup had her get in on the passenger side, forcing Not a D Boy to slide from the passenger side of the back seat to the driver's side. He was hesitant, but finally did so reluctantly.

After fifteen or so minutes of Dad Meme blabbering and silence from the other two passengers, it was finally time to drop Not a D Boy off. Thing is, Not a D Boy lived in one of the worst projects of Southwest Philadelphia. It was nighttime, and there was a good amount of people out, none of whom looked especially welcoming. There was a busted couch in the middle of the project courtyard, making the scene look like it could have been ripped from the *Wire*. Now I had been through there before, and I assumed the woman in the back was from Philly, as she seemed unfazed. I don't even think she looked up from her phone. Dad Meme, however, had a face that would make a deer in headlights look comfortable. You would've thought this man was looking at a battlefield. His eyes were as wide as saucers, in total shock. I don't know if I've ever seen a grown man so shook.

If the substance of his field-hockey-dad-from-Florida conversation wasn't enough to make Not a D boy realize that this man was certainly not 5-0, the fight-or-flight hormones that were pouring out of that front seat were. In retrospect, I think that revelation gave Not a D Boy enough courage, before getting out, to "accidentally" drop his phone onto the floor in front of the woman. The woman went to grab it, but Not a D Boy started digging around on the floor by the woman's feet for an uncomfortable amount of time. As if four strangers in a car together wasn't already awkward enough, whatever this kid was doing was making it ten times worse. The woman pushed her knees to the door to avoid getting her feet touched, meanwhile the Dad Meme was staving off a panic attack as he took in the surroundings. Not only were we in the middle of the housing project complex, but my headlights were beaming directly in the center of it, onto a large group of people. So there we were, a car full of passengers, two of whom being the only white people in a five-block radius, not moving for an extended period of time, as the entire project courtyard scoped us out, trying to figure if we were friend or foe. I almost felt bad for Dad Meme, since even I was getting uncomfortable with the situation.

Fortunately, I think Not a D Boy felt the same, because after all, it is one of those rare truths that transcend social class, race, and location: whether you a young man pulling up to the projects in Southwest Philly, or a pre-teen girl meeting up with friends at the mall in Beverly Hills: nobody wants to show up anywhere with a Dad Meme. I think Not a D Boy realized his risk of dork by association was getting higher every second he spent in this car, and eventually I heard him mutter, "Fuck it," in disappointment, and gets out.

"You get your phone?" I called after him, assuming the expletive meant that he didn't.

"Nah, I got it," he said, still oddly upset.

As we left the projects, I turned to Dad Meme to make sure there was blood returning to his face.

"I bet that's not a part of Philly they showed you on school visit."

"It was not."

I heard a chuckle from the back seat.

After I dropped them off, I thought about the different slices of life I get to experience as an Uber driver—the panorama of perspectives so few others get to see. The mother who has to juggle a baby and a bag of laundry and a commute to get her clothes clean. The juxtaposition of a guy who pays $33,000 for his daughter's tuition so she can play field hockey, sharing a ride with a woman his daughter's age heading to a job where she most likely earns less than that all year. Or the neighborhood in Southwest Philly that was so ratchet it almost gave a grown man a heart attack. It made me think, there should be a requirement that visitors of a city have to drive through the worst part of it, just to understand what your fellow humans are dealing with. But aside from that, I kept chewing on the inexplicable awkwardness of Not a D Boy's exit.

If he found his phone, why did he sound so disappointed?

On a hunch, I pulled over and started digging under the seat myself. My hunch was quickly proved correct.

This kid was so nervous that Dad Meme might be a cop that he threw a bag under the passenger seat. That's why he was being so weird about sliding over when the Airport Girl got in. His "accidental" dropping of the phone was his attempt to grab it back, and I guess at some point during the ride, the bag had slid so far toward the front he couldn't reach it.

On one hand, I felt like I lost my whiteness a bit, since it wasn't until he saw Dad Meme that he told his friend on the phone "I think it's 5-0" and I heard that shuffling, which I now know was him throwing that bag under the seat. Is my status as an Uber driver so low that it overrides my skin color? Am I ever going to be able to go to the hood again and have people ask me if I'm a cop?

On the other hand, I was pretty pumped I found myself a bag of several grams of the best kind of weed: the free kind.

19
Tits Out in the Uber

I like to think these stories that I'm sharing with you have deep-seated value, perhaps a moral or lesson buried somewhere within, that can help clarify the human existence and assist in your understanding and operating in this world. In this instance, however, I fear as though there is no overarching theme, no "Why does this story need to be told, and why now?" that can be answered sufficiently. In this instance, it is simply that there was a titty out in my Uber, and the child in me would kick my ass if I didn't share it. Plus, I am still questioning the morality of sharing this on YouTube, and a faceless medium like this makes me more comfortable in treating this story like the titty and exposing it.

The pickup request came in half an hour after the bars in this college town had closed, and two freshman girls stumbled out of a pizza shop. I recognize I may overuse the term "stumble" in describing the gait of my passengers, however, in this instance, one of the girls, Nelly, holding a large box of pizza, quite literally stumbled and fell into a tree. Her shoulder made contact with the trunk as if she was a running back, the pizza the football, and the tree the linebacker she was trying to plow through. It looked painful, but the silver lining was that it prevented her from face planting onto the sidewalk. Most importantly, she secured possession of the pizza box as any football coach would have hoped.

As Nelly struggled to regain her footing by the tree, the other girl, an attractive blonde, gets in the back seat, laughing at how drunk her friend is. We both watched Nelly wobble around the front of my car and open the passenger door, deciding to sit up front next to me. She was struggling to get in the car while keeping the pizza level, so I grabbed the box from her—it's a good thing I did, too, because almost immediately after, she completely wiped out. She fell forward, hitting the inside of the open car door, pushed off of it in an attempt to regain her balance, and sent herself flying backward. Fortunately, her fall was broken with a perfect landing on the front seat. Blondie finds this hilarious (which it was), however, being that we were in my car, I had concerns.

"You aren't going to throw up, are you?" I asked.

"You better not," Blondie immediately stopped laughing. "This is on my account."

"Immsooomadddrightnow." Nelly added. Neither her friend nor I knew what that meant. It was only a five-minute trip, so I said a quiet prayer to myself, and told her that if she needed to throw up to let me know so I can pull over. I figured it might take longer to assess the situation (and if need be, try to kick this woman out of my car) than it would to complete the trip, so I got moving.

As Nelly is mumbling nonsense, Blondie in the back is in high spirits. "I'm so glad I stopped drinking when I did," she said, looking at Nelly as all the evidence she needed to support that decision.

To add a wrinkle to the story, this was an Uber Pool. It was close to three in the morning, and the trip was short, so I was hoping I could get the girls to their dorm without getting any other requests. Unfortunately for all of us, that would not be the case. A new rider was added to the trip.

"Just so you know, we have someone to pick up." I always hated informing passengers of this. It's kind of like how people who drive drunk never expect to get pulled over—those who order Uber Pools never expect to have anyone else added to the ride… until they do.

"Oh great," Blondie said sarcastically. A moment passes, and then the implications of picking up someone this late at night set in. "Is it a boy or a girl?" she asked.

"Unless this is the first female Dave I've ever met, I think it's safe to say it's a boy." I was expecting disappointment, as most people don't like the idea of a strange man, most likely very drunk, getting into the back seat with them at this time of night. But her behavior seemed to indicate otherwise. She fixed her hair and adjusted her outfit. I wondered if she was the type to care about her presentation, or if perhaps she was looking for love in the back of an Uber Pool. *That would be a first,* I thought.

As Nelly is flopping about the front seat like a dying fish, an object I had never seen in my Uber caught my eye. Intermittently illuminated by each streetlight we passed, a dark cylinder protruded from a flesh-colored backdrop.

Is that… ? Yup. That my friend, is a titty. At some point in nailing the tree trunk, or falling to the front seat, or flopping about during the drive, the titty found its way out of her low-cut shirt. *Nelly's Nipple has entered the Uber Pool.*

Now I'm a grown man that grew up in the age of the internet. In other words, I have seen more tits than pretty much every man in history that lived before 1900, combined. Plus, I will die on the hill that boobs are most appealing when they are concealed or at a distance. The moment nothing is left to the imagination, and you are confronted with the flop of the breast, the bumps of the areola, and the wrinkled skin of a nipple that always reminded me of a dried cranberry, the body part loses its appeal. So don't get this twisted into some idea that there's this perverted Uber driver getting aroused by the sight of a nipple. What's happening here is the shock of seeing a titty on the job. I don't care if the titty belonged to a good-looking college girl or a wrinkly old grandma: when there's a titty gone rogue in the Uber, it's gonna raise my eyebrows.

Now if this had been a regular Uber, I would have probably ignored Nelly's Nipple, figuring she (or her friend) would notice it at some point. But there was a strange and most likely drunk man about to come into this car, and that seemed like a recipe for disaster. Nelly was so far gone there was little to no chance she'd comprehend what I was saying if I told her to fix herself, so I was faced with the daunting task of informing Blondie that I was staring at her friend's tits—but with innocent intentions.

"Yeah, so this guy is about to get in…" I started, uncomfortably, "and uh, I don't know how to say this. Like, with all due respect—she's kind of hanging out here."

"Yeah, she's not going to fix that," Blondie said, still teasing her own hair and making sure her shirt was as low as it could possibly be while keeping her puppies perky. I don't know if it was wrong of me to attribute her actions to that of an attention-seeking whore, but she seemed to have nothing on her mind except impressing this potential suitor, and clearly did not pick up what I was putting down. I guess she thought I was concerned about Nelly's appearance, perhaps thinking "hanging out" was a reference to her essentially lifeless body slumping about with every turn.

"Mehh?" Nelly said, a few seconds after I mentioned the hanging out. I wasn't sure if she was asking whether I was referring to her, or just making the nonsensical sounds of a blackout drunk. So I decided to continue to address Blondie instead.

"Aright, well. Uh. There's a guy that's about to get in the car, so you might want to cover—"

"That's alright," Blondie interrupted with a hopeful tone. "It only matters if I'm looking good."

I fucking knew it. I wasn't being a misogynist—I was being observant. She was looking for love in the in the back of an Uber Pool. But even though she might have been ok with leaving Nelly and her Nipple out to dry, but I had to at least try one more time to get my point across as we pulled up to Dave, who was waiting on the curb.

"No, I don't think you understand. She's like..." I make a circle motion around my own chest. "... out."

"Oh." She looked at Nelly's chest. "Oh, my God!" She reaches into the front seat and adjusts Nelly's shirt moments before Dave gets in the car. "Keep your shirt on, geez!"

It was ironic to hear the friend say that, because sure, Nelly accidentally had her nipple out, but Blondie's own top was closer to lingerie than something that could be considered clothing. If she had opted for a bikini top when getting dressed that night, it would have been more conservative than the unbuttoned button down she was wearing, exposing a cleavage exaggerated by a very skimpy, see-through bra that perfectly accentuated her very well-endowed chest. It was the kind of sight that makes you feel bad for blind men.

History has shown me that college dudes at this time of night are most likely going to be the hammered frat-boy type, squeezing every last minute out of the party. But I was pleasantly surprised to find that Dave was a little more *Half Baked* than he was *Animal House*, and got into the car with a polite greeting to all and a smile on his face when he saw that he hit the jackpot. He just found himself in the back seat of a car with a beautiful blonde girl advertising her tits like they were going out of business.

Dave threw out a line of flirtation to see if it would stick. And it sure did. Blondie was caught, hook, line, and sinker, and immediately started flirting back. It's not for me to speculate on either party's intentions, but it was clear they were both thoroughly enjoying each other's company. Touching, laughing, and joking about helping the girls eat the pizza, Dave was pulling out all the stops for this Hail Mary attempt at an Uber Pool hookup, and Blondie was loving every second of it. The chemistry was there, so much so that when we arrived at the girl's freshman dorm, the two in the back seat lingered. I didn't want to be the guy to break it up, but I couldn't sit there forever, especially with Nelly passed out in the front seat, a ticking time bomb of regurgitation.

As corny as this sounds, I was still in the beginning stages of my Uber and YouTube career, and I had a card with my information on it that I would give out to passengers. It's embarrassing to admit that now, as I quickly realized it is not an efficient marketing approach, but hey, you live and you learn. I only include this because it's relevant to the story, as I thought handing her my card would punctuate the end to our ride and get the girls moving. I think Dave knew what I was doing and wasn't letting this end without a fight. Sitting directly behind Nelly, he started playing with her long, brown hair that was spilling over the seat and into the back.

That was a huge red flag for me. To be clear, I don't think Dave was being a creep, instead, he was simply following the playful tone that Blondie had set, using Nelly as the butt of quite a few jokes during the ride. But when it comes to strangers in an Uber, I draw a hard line at physical touch, and in a situation where the girl in the front can't even form sentences, it's most certainly not the move. Again, to be clear, all of his actions came with Blondie laughing in encouragement. But as with most things of this nature, it can be a slippery slope, and this Uber was not about to be the start of that slide.

"Hey Dave, let's keep our hands to ourself here," I said in a Dad voice I didn't know I had. I was hoping I didn't come off as a douche, but instead, more of a reminder of "hey man... we are two dudes around a very drunk girl. Let's not fuck around too much." Fortunately, he picked up exactly what I was putting down, and snatched his hands back as if her hair was on fire.

I don't know if it served as a bit of a wake-up call to Blondie, or if she got a little jealous the more Dave played with Nelly's hair (my money's on the latter), but at this moment, Blondie decided she's had enough, saying, "Time to go Nelly!" before getting out of the car herself.

The problem was, Nelly wasn't budging.

"I'm not leaving until I get that yes," she said.

"What?" I asked.

"I want that yes."

"I don't know what you are saying."

"Nelly, let's go!" Her friend yelled as she walked around the car.

"No, fuck that, I want that yes."

"I don't know what that is."

"I want that yes!"

"She wants that dick!" Dave chimed in. Had I not been so apprehensive about whatever the hell was happening, I would've laughed. Immature and cliched, sure—but the timing and delivery were impeccable.

"A card? Do you want a card?" Blondie suggested. "Just give her a card."

"Oh, a business card? Sure." I reached for another one.

"No, I want that yes!"

"I'm sorry Nelly, I don't know what that is. But you got to go."

Blondie is standing next to the open passenger door, trying to coax her home. I get out and walk around the back of the car.

"Nelly! Get. Out!" she demanded. "Dave, you get out too," she said, with a much quieter tone—I assume she didn't want to come off too thirsty. I am sure Dave saw this invitation as his last chance for romance, and he opened his door right as I got to that side of the car. Without breaking stride, I caught the door as it was opening and closed it shut.

"I got this Dave, don't worry." I hated to be a cock block, but there was a whole lot of risk in that situation and the reward of a one night stand that I wasn't even going to be participating in was not worth it. Best case scenario is I'm stuck trying to get Nelly out of my car while Dave and Blondie have at each other... worst case scenario is the opening scene of a *Law and Order* SVU episode.

Again, Dave complied without protest, in another moment that seemed to remind him of what was actually happening here. Meanwhile, Nelly is still refusing to leave my car, repeating over and over again in her slurred speech some form of "I want that fucking yes!"

Dave is laughing.

"I want that yes."

Blondie is laughing.

"Give me that yes!"

I see no end to this.

"Give me that fucking yes!

I dropped my patient demeanor.

"There will be no yes for you Nelly! Nipple or no nipple, you're a drunk girl and I'm a grown man, so whatever it is that you want from me, you ain't getting it!" is what I wanted to say.

What I actually said, in a very firm tone, was, "Look, she needs to be out of my car. I don't want to touch her, so let me hold the pizza and you pull her out."

Blondie could tell I wasn't playing anymore. Her mood changed to match mine, handed me the pizza, and in a stern voice, said, "Nelly, let's go!" Blondie reached in and yanked her friend out as she was in the middle of repeating her request for the thousandth time. "I want that yee—whoaaaah!" Nelly yelled as she was extracted against her will.

"Get it together," her friend demanded. "You need to get in this dorm or you'll be sleeping on the street."

The two walk off, and I got back into the car with a dude I just cockblocked for everyone's own good. I was unsure if he was going to be upset, or grateful.

"*Yoooo*, that's crazy," he said, laughing. I breathed a sigh of relief. I silently thanked the Uber gods that I had this interaction recorded on a dash camera, just in case these girls' memories got a little hazy the next day, and more importantly, that Nelly had a friend with her. I don't know what I would have done if this girl was that drunk, and alone, and refusing to get out, all while that titty of hers refused to stay in.

20
Death Threats in the Uber Pool

I had just graduated high school and was spending the week at the beach with my friends, when I had the bright idea to schmooze the foreigners working at the pizza shop that was about to close to give me the pizza at a highly discounted rate. After all, my young drunk mind thought, "It's the end of the night and they are just going to throw it out anyway. What I'm offering is a win-win solution." I would get cheap pizza for me and my friends, and they make a couple bucks off of what is about to be trash.

Needless to say, my plan did not go well. No matter the logic, reason, or charm I was piling on this young man and woman who spoke broken English, they wouldn't budge. And why would they? It's not like their hourly wage changes depending on the amount of pizza they sell, let alone the fact they probably don't have the authority to make that call in the first place. Unfortunately, that is a retrospective I have now as a sober adult. The eighteen-year-old me, drunk off Banker's and Sprite, embarrassed in front of my friends that my genius plan didn't work, lashed out at these kids, who were probably about my age, telling them they don't know the first thing about business, that they need to learn English, and to "get the fuck out of my country."

Fortunately for me, these foreigners were the type that flood shore towns every summer —college students from Eastern Europe that come over here to work in resort towns as part of an exchange program. I share that because I want it to be clear: while I resorted to xenophobic attacks, there was not a hint of racism or classism in my anger. And I think we can all agree that on the list of *ism*s, if you had to pick one to be—I mean, gun to your head and you have to choose to be racist, sexist, homophobic, or whatever—I think going with xenophobia is the play. I'm not saying I'm proud of what I did, I'm just saying if my deplorable actions were caught on camera, I feel as though it's something that even a straight white male could recover from eventually.

And that's what is really fortunate for me about this situation: it wasn't caught on camera. This was in 2006, before the age of everyone and their mother having a hi-definition camera at all times and the ability to share whatever they want with the entire world. I often wonder how different my friends and I would have acted knowing that everything is recorded all the time. But then again, if I recall how much Banker's Club I put in that Sprite bottle, I'm not so sure that would've changed anything.

But that's not who I am. That was who I was in that moment. A young, dumb, drunk kid, acting out of frustration and embarrassment. To this day, I still cringe at my actions every time I pass by that pizza shop and mitigate that feeling with a quick prayer for those two workers, hoping they are doing okay, wherever life has taken them.

Thing is, I could fill an entire book of similar instances where I lost my patience, said something inappropriate, or was just a general asshole to someone for no good reason other than I wasn't in a good mood. Sure, alcohol was usually involved, but that is no excuse. And not because alcohol shows your true intentions. I know that to be bullshit, lest my true intentions on certain nights were to spend all of my money, throw up on my new sneakers, lose my phone and my friends, and as a result, be forced to take a long, lonely walk home, where I take a tumble—and instead of immediately getting back to my feet, think *this concrete sure is comfy* and decide this would be a good spot to rest my legs for a bit… only to wake up on a sidewalk with the sunrise a few hours later. Alcohol is not an excuse because I'm the one that chose to drink the alcohol.

I share this because it is my own shortcomings that weigh on my mind when I look at the hours and hours of footage of my Uber riders in their worst moments; videos I've collected as an ancillary haul of running a dash camera while Ubering for my own personal safety and security. I can't explain it logically, but life has shown me that you get back what you put out, and what kind of hypocrite would I be to expose these people in their worst moments, as if I wasn't a flawed human myself? The biggest difference between the people who look like assholes in a viral video and those who watch in judgment is that there happened to be a camera around.

That said, this story that I am about to share with you is one of the most meaningful things that has ever happened in my Uber. There are so many layers to this story that it would give tiramisu a complex. But what I found most revealing is what happened after the ride.

It was a rainy Sunday, and instead of opting to waste the day away watching football, I figured I go earn some cash. My first request was a dreaded Uber Pool, but it was close to my apartment, so I accepted. Before I even picked up the passenger, there was another rider added to the pool. A middle-aged man still in his clothes from last night gets in and sits directly behind me. A few blocks away, we picked up the second leg of the pool, a woman named Kelly and her friend. Kelly is a woman who I would guess is in her early or mid-twenties, and Kelly was talking on her cell phone, visibly upset. Kelly's friend sat in the back, responded to my greeting, while Kelly got into the front seat without acknowledging me. Though mid-conversation, it didn't take long to realize she was speaking to the father of her child, and that they weren't together.

"Jimmy... why you so angry? You so mad you don't even want to go get your son. That's dumb...." *Sounds like this will be a pleasant ride.* "What you mean?! Cuz you always be with girls that's dumb."

With new riders in the car, the dude behind me wanted to make sure we were heading the right direction and double checked the address with me. I think my response made it hard for Kelly to hear her child's father on the phone because this was the only time Kelly acknowledged my existence during the ride, and she did so with a stare that could cut glass. *So sorry to interrupt.* If I had the gall to share this video, there is no doubt in my mind that this moment would turn into the top gif result for "look of death."

"Why you so hype?" is where my unavoidable eavesdropping picked back up after confirming the address. "You hype as shit. You mad. You so angry," she said, not breaking her speech as she switched the phone to her other ear. "You're angry as shit, because your girlfriend is dumb."

Ah, a practitioner of the simple, yet repetitive insult approach.

"Oh, you're not going to go get [our son] because of me? Oh, wow. I'll make sure I let him know that. I'll make sure I let him know —" she paused for dramatic effect, with a smile on her face, excited to deliver the blow, "that every time your dad gets mad at mommy he doesn't come get you."

Dammit. I liked it better when she stuck with the childish insults—not when she brings the child into it. This is starting to make me feel bad.

"Cuz you're weird. You are weird as fuck."

Nice. Back to the schoolyard slander.

"You didn't see your son in two weeks."

Dammit. Leave the kid out of this!

Then she got even louder. "You didn't see your son in two weeks... now you see him for a few hours, and you're just like, fuck him, his mom made me mad. That's dumb. That is so dumb!"

It was odd to hear this argument as a spectator, with no bias or context. It was a perfect example of someone trying to win an argument, rather than resolve it, as it seemed like she was thoroughly enjoying pointing out all the flaws of her child's father. She spoke of him not being present in their son's life not with anger or sadness, but with a "gotcha" tone. A tone that was about to change.

"What?" she snapped, with a hint of fear in her voice. Whatever it was that he said, she was not expecting it.

"No... cu cuzz...who?" I could hear the panic set into her voice.

What the hell did he just say to her?!

"Goodbye. You can't take him."

Oh shit.

"You can't take him! You don't got none of his shit. You can't take 'em no fuckin where. You can't—Jimmy, that..." Her voice dropped. The fight or flight response was fully activated, and in her calmest tone yet, she said, "I'm gonna be honest with you—the day that you try to take my son is the day you will die. That's just real rap." It seemed that fight was the route she decided to take. "That's. Real. Rap."

There was nothing about this woman's tone that made me think she was joking, and I wondered the protocol for overhearing death threats in an Uber Pool. At the same time, I will admit: the fact that it was a female making these threats made me think she probably wouldn't go through with it. Is it sexist not to take murderous statements from women as seriously as if they came from a man?

I assume in the pause that followed, Jimmy called her out for the threat she made because she got defensive. "You're the one threatening me! You threatening to take my son! That's my whole entire life. I'll really kill you over that one." She said this so matter of factly, I had to chomp down on my tongue to keep myself from laughing.

"I do! I provide more than..." [*muffled voice on phone*] "Jimmy you just started providing for our son. Get the fuck out of here bro! You just started doing shit for our son; I've been doing shit for the whole two years, bro!" [*muffled voice on phone*] "Go 'head..." [*muffled voice on phone*] "Yo you just started doing stuff. You just started buying him sneakers, you just started buying him clothes..." [*muffled voice on phone*] "After everything I provided? Even at your house I provided everything he has, so stop it, stop it, stop it, stop it..." [*muffled voice on phone*] "because you sitting here trying to discredit me as a mother and you cannot do that. At all."

I felt like I was learning so much about this family, and I'd only met the mother. As if there wasn't enough character revelation occurring, after the next bit of muffled speech coming through the phone, she snapped, "I can't discredit your bitch when she got caught on Instagram twerking with my son? I can do that." [*muffled voice on phone*] "Yes she did! She put my son on fuckin' Instagram twerking with her, like a dummy!"

Okay, Kelly. While I still think the murder threat was a tad excessive, I'm starting to understand your frustration. "I don't care about your girlfriend Jimmy, she's fucking bummy. I don't care."

Come on now, Kelly. Don't lie. It would seem as though you care at least a little bit.

"Okay, make sure you tell your son you didn't come get him because you upset..." [*muffled voice on phone*] "Oh, I'mma tell him anyway. I'mma tell him anyway!"

Spectacular. Thanks for reminding me of how fucked this kid's life is.

"No. Because he missed his dad, because he ain't seen you in two weeks and then only because you got an attitude you don't want to go get him? That's dumb! Every time you get upset that's what you're gonna do to my son? I'm gonna make sure he remember that. Cause you weird."

Great. Using the kid as a pawn. Gotta love that.

"Jimmy I don't care about you and your dirty-ass bitches and what y'all be doing... I don't care. Wait, what?" She started laughing, but it wasn't a genuine laugh. It was the kind of laugh people force when they are trying to conceal an explosive anger, the kind of laugh that made me realize she got hung up on.

She immediately called someone else, and continuing to laugh as it rang. "He mad as shit," Kelly said to herself, through the veneer of a smile. "He's so angry."

Finally, I heard a female voice pick up her call and say, "Hello." Instead of starting this conversation with any sort of greeting, like a sane person would, Kelly forced a maniacal laugh into her phone for a full nine seconds. I am not exaggerating. I counted it out when I watched the video back. That's a long fucking time to fake a laugh at the start of a call. It was a new level of crazy she was showing, and I was starting to put more stock into this death threat.

"So Jimmy said he's not coming to get Mikey cause he mad at me."

"Why's he mad at you?" the woman on the phone asked.

"I—I don't know," Kelly said.

If I had water in my mouth, this would have deserved a spit-take. *Come on, girl. You don't have the slightest idea?*

"I didn't do anything..."

This sure was an interesting opportunity to see how information gets relayed. No wonder they say there are two sides to every story.

"I told him his girlfriend is dumb. And he mad," she continued to laugh. "What's he so mad for? She really is fuckin dumb. Then he said he was going to take Mikey, and I said the day he do that, is the day he die. Period. That's just what it is." It was a hell of a way to frame a death threat; starting her story playing innocent, and then slipping it in at the end as if she was speaking in hyperbole.

"Okay, let's three way him, how 'bout that. Hold on..."

That sounds like its a great idea, Kelly. What could possibly go wrong?

I don't know if the guy behind me is like Kelly, and is also not a believer in normal societal constraints, or if he was just tired of listening to Kelly's toxic conversation and needed a distraction. Either way, as Kelly tried to call back Dad on three way, the dude behind me decided to make a phone call as well. Through his conversation, I pieced together that he had gotten lucky last night, and I had picked him up from the home of his one night stand. Meanwhile, Kelly's Friend is sitting in the back, quiet as a mouse, looking out the window. As the stranger next to her is recounting his Saturday night conquest, and Kelly is in the front threatening the life of her child's father, Kelly's friend is enjoying the passing scenery as if this was a peaceful Sunday drive.

When Dad didn't pick up for the three way, Kelly exploded to her loudest yet. "He fuckin' mad as shit cuz I told him his girlfriend is dumb as shit and she's fuckin ugly. Which she is. Cuz she always fuckin talking about me... every time I come to that school my cousins told me she be saying shit about me..." [*muffled voice on phone*] "I don't got nothing..." [*muffled voice on phone*] "I don't care, I don't care, I don't say nothing to that girl. I don't care."

As Kelly ranted into the phone, and the man behind me started to describe the party where he met the girl, and Kelly's Friend continued to enjoy the view as if there was nothing abnormal about what was happening here, the ride came to halt at a red light. It was then that I slipped into a brief existential crisis. I stared into that red light, waiting for it to change, stuck confronting the fact that I am a sum of my life's choices, and in those thirty seconds, I contemplated every single choice I have ever made since the day I was born that brought me to this miserable point in time. I thought about the people who told me to chase my dreams. I thought about the people who said there is beauty in the struggle. I thought about the idea of getting back what you put out—and felt lied to. I thought I was making the responsible choice today: working instead of being lazy. And here I am, making next to nothing with these two shitty fares, getting an up-close and personal look at the insanity this world has to offer.

What did I do to deserve this?

An eternity later, both parties are out of my car, and as I drove to my next fare, I imagined the kind of turbulence that takes place in Kelly's household on the regular. It made me think about all the crazy people I've have met, not only in my Uber, but over the course of my entire life. I was reminded that the world is full of adult Mikeys who grew up after having that kind of behavior modeled to them during their formative years. Shoot, good chance that was the kind of behavior Kelly had modeled to her when she was Mikey's age. So who the fuck am I to judge the way someone acts, knowing full well that I might be just as fucked up as they are had I been in their shoes.*

But that perspective is one that I am often reminded of while driving Uber and getting glimpses into the dysfunctional lives of my rides, and it's not why I thought this story was worth sharing. The biggest mark this rider left on me happened a few months later.

Once again, I found myself on the Uber grind, and I got a request from a familiar name at a familiar address near my apartment. As I get closer to the pickup spot, I got a feeling of deja vu. When I saw my passenger come out, I realized it was because I had been there before. As sure as I was born, there was Kelly, coming toward my car. I flashed back to our trip, and not only did I recall the disrespect and negativity she brought into my car, I remembered that her trip brought me to a very shitty part of the city, and she didn't leave a tip. Granted, I didn't know if she would act like that again, but I thought, *Why risk it?* We locked eyes momentarily before I peeled the fuck out of there, and as I drove away I could see her in my rearview sprint across her lawn and into the street, waving her arms at me in frustration.

The problem was, as I weaved through her neighborhood, I learned the hard way that the only other exit was closed for

---

* To be clear, I'm not saying it makes it okay to be an asshole. I'm just saying I understand how the asshole is formed. I believe it was Socrates who said, "He who can understand the asshole, can deal with the asshole."

construction. In other words, in order to get out of there, I was going to have to turn around and pass by Killer Kelly's house again. I sat for a minute, letting the dust settle and giving her some time to either head back inside or get another Uber. Despite this, when I pulled back around and had Kelly's house in view, she was still outside. The moment she registered that it was me coming toward her, it was on.

Kelly jumps off her stoop and charges at the street, trying to get in front of my car before I pass so that she can block me in. I was afraid she was going to do that, so I was ready. Before she even took a second step, I punched the gas and beat her to the spot. It wasn't even close. I smiled a little bit as I blew past her, not even to the sidewalk yet.

"You fuckin' racist piece of shit!" she screamed, still running after me, as I rolled through the stop sign and got the fuck out of that neighborhood before she got anywhere close to my car. If she was willing to kill the father of her child, I didn't want to find out what she would do to an Uber driver's car.

But even days after this man vs. machine time trial, I kept thinking about what she said to me; how she called me racist. Not that I care (I never started the trip, so she couldn't report me on some bullshit), but what amazed me was her inclination to assume she was a victim. She didn't think maybe this Uber driver made a mistake, or had something else come up, or even consider that perhaps she contributed to the situation somehow. Nope. Her first thought was that she was being treated poorly because of a personal characteristic. She really thought I took the time to drive all the way to her house and then decided to opt out of making money because of the color of her skin.

What's ironic about that line of thinking is that she had a name that told me what color she was the moment I saw the request. I called her Kelly for the sake of this story because had I went with her real name, I know there are some ignorant people in this world that would attribute her behavior to the color of her skin, when reality, it's more of a reflection of the low-class, trashy environment she comes from. I know that because, if you remember, I live in the same neighborhood. Plus, being that we do live in the same neighborhood, I don't want to be the next person on her hit list if this story goes viral. Point is, if I was racist, I wouldn't have wasted my time driving to her house. I would've canceled the moment I saw her name.

What's always amazed me about being an Uber driver is how people can treat us as if we aren't even in the car with them, as if our eyes and our ears don't work, let alone that we exist outside of our

Uber. We are treated as if our only function in life is to drive people around: it's like we don't have memories or opinions—like we don't live in the same neighborhoods, go to the same gas station, or shop at the same grocery stores.

This woman quite literally lived a few blocks away from me. There was a good chance our paths had crossed before we met in my Uber, and a good chance they would cross after, whether we knew it or not. Of course, it would be unfair to expect this woman to recognize me the way I did her. After all, that would be antithetical to the idea that Uber drivers are forgettable creatures. But what I find so interesting about this event is her knee-jerk reaction of victimhood. And I fully understand I may sound like I'm overanalyzing this woman's actions in an otherwise trivial interaction—but that's not the point. What I learned from Kelly is that when shit goes wrong, it doesn't help to point the finger. Instead, I consider how I might have contributed to the situation. I don't always have an answer, but it sure helps to keep me from being an asshole to others.

And that's the irony of the whole thing. Since Kelly doesn't realize that it was her own behavior that caused me to treat her that way, she will continue that behavior—never realizing that her anger is the cause of the turbulence in her life, not the other way around.

21
Uber Cures Me of my Racism

Reader be warned: By the end of this story I may start to sound like that family member of yours that is kind of "out there"; you know, the one who sees the Thanksgiving dinner table as his own personal soapbox. So I apologize in advance, and by all means, feel free to skip ahead if this story—and what some may call the "rant" that comes with it—isn't one that interests you. But I have to get this off my chest. Not only is this one of the most frustrating things to happen to me as an Uber driver, I think it sheds light on a perspective that is never brought up in mainstream media, and that is the perspective of an average, working-class white guy when it comes to racial issues. And don't think I'm saying this perspective isn't shared because the average white man is oppressed, or that the average white guy isn't given the opportunity. This perspective is never shared because the average white man is smart enough not to risk saying something that could end up costing him his job.

Well, fortunately for you, I'm not that smart.

I was several blocks off of Temple University's campus—an area that has only a few student houses sprinkled in an otherwise terrible neighborhood—when I got stuck with a pool ride. Two young men, in their late teens or early twenties, come walking to my car, looking like the kind of people that "fit the description," even when they don't. They were waiting outside when I showed up, and they greeted me with a "Hello, sir. Appreciate you picking us up." Even more significant than appearance, I've learned that the initial interaction is the best predictor of how a ride is going to go, and there is nothing like an articulate and respectful greeting that lets me know you're probably not a piece of shit. Plus, the fact that they were ready to go when I pulled up only added to that conclusion. These might seem like trivial things, but when you give ride after ride to people who make you wait on cramped city streets with no place to park, getting honked at by other drivers and forced to circle the block multiple times until the passenger comes out, only for them to not even say hello, you end up really appreciating the riders who show the smallest sign of respect.

From what I gathered from their conversation, these two young men were a rap duo on their way to shoot a self-produced, low-budget music video. While I can't stand giving Uber Pool rides, I appreciated the fact that the Gen Z version of Method Man and Redman, currently plotting their aspirations in my back seat, were being mindful of their expenditures on their way up.

The next pickup on the pool ride was only two blocks away. They were not outside when I pulled up, so the waiting game began. I felt bad for the dudes in my car, wasting their time, but I had no choice but to wait until the timer ran out until I was able to cancel that part of the trip and move on. As we sat there, in my old stomping grounds, I made a bet with myself that these new riders who were making us wait were certainly from this very underserved neighborhood. As I'm sure any other Uber driver would attest, there is an undeniable correlation between riders being late and what tax bracket they are in: the closer to the extremes the longer they take. In other words, both the very rich and the very poor seem to take their sweet-ass time.

With only ten seconds to go before I could cancel, a guy who could have been mistaken for Steve Urkel comes strolling out, his girlfriend following, both taking their sweet-ass time to get to my car. I was reminded that there is one demographic more unwilling to consider other people's time than rich people or poor people, and that is the entitled college student. Over the course of the ride, I'd pick up that they were freshmen at Temple.

We left North Philly with a full car. WuTang Clan Z was getting dropped off in Southwest Philly, and then Urkel was heading to West Philly. There wasn't much talk during the longer-than-average trip, and I dropped off the first two guys without incident; they left with a friendly and respectful goodbye that matched their greeting.

So now it's me, Urkel, and his girlfriend leaving Southwest Philly and heading to West Philly, driving through a police district a friend of mine happens to work for. I'm in that area of the city a lot, and I always keep an eye out for him, hoping one day I finally catch my buddy in uniform just so I can ask him if he likes going to work dressed like he's going to invade Poland. So when I spotted a Philly Police cruiser heading the opposite direction, I thought today might be the day my wish came true, and I looked into the cop car driving by to see if it was my buddy behind the wheel.

It was not.

I kept driving, thinking nothing of it, until I see in the rearview the cop car make a U-turn in the middle of the street (an illegal U-turn, by the way, with no turn signal—shows you how important traffic laws really are) and turn on his blue and red lights.

Now if this was the suburbs, even though I was all but certain I didn't do anything wrong, I would have instantly thought there's a 50 percent chance this cop was coming to jam me up on whatever bullshit traffic infraction they felt like enforcing that day, because that's what my experience with cops in the suburbs has been. But I was in a city that tallies more murders every year than there are days in the year, so police don't usually waste their time with trivial traffic stops. So I slowed to the side of the road, giving the cop room so he could pass.

Why isn't this guy passing me? Wait… is he pulling me over?

The quick *whoop* of his siren answered that question.

While I was perplexed as to what I could have been pulled over for, Urkel, who was in the passenger seat, took it personally. "You've got to be kidding me," he said.

Still a little salty that he took his sweet ass time to come out to my car, I was confused as to why all of a sudden this guy who called an Uber Pool seemed to be in such a rush.

The cop comes to my car and told me I had a headlight out. He asked for my license and registration.

It didn't even occur to me that's why I would be pulled over. Not only was it still light enough out that most cars on the road didn't have their lights on at all, but we were in West Philly. All the King's horses and all the King's men couldn't find the time to address all the broken headlights and taillights and vehicle infractions in West Philly. Philly cops don't pull you over for bullshit unless they have ulterior motives, and this guy was obviously fishing for something.

I told him I had just been stopped the night before* about it, and he laughed at me condescendingly. "Well, you need to get it fixed."

"Thanks for the insight, asshole. I know you're just a beat cop, but I didn't think you needed to be a detective to piece together that it's a Sunday and I'm working Uber. You think maybe, just maybe, there's already enough shit on my plate that fixing a headlight that I don't need during the daytime isn't a priority?" is what I wanted to say.

---

* You may have seen the video of this previous stop on my YouTube channel—it was the one where my rider had a warrant out for her arrest.

"Ah, I know, I'm sorry," is what I actually said.

At this, there is a knock on the other window. Urkel jumped at the sound, because after all, who would ever expect a second individual (who's armed, by the way) to sneak up on you from the opposite side just to investigate a broken headlight?

I rolled down the passenger window, doing so only because I knew it's what that officer wanted. But I could feel my blood pressure rise, thinking about how this guy pulls me over for a "broken headlight" and then approaches my car with a gun and an armed partner, for *his* safety. Has it ever occurred to anyone that maybe the safest thing would be to not pull over people for benign things like a headlight out? Maybe, if he actually cared about the headlight and wanted to help, police could do the human thing, and roll down their window and say, "Hey buddy, just so you know, your headlight is out."

Instead, his eyes are trained on me as I go for my information. His partner shined his flashlight into my glove box when I opened it. I know the cult of the Thin Blue Line will say he was doing that for his safety, which I'm sure is a very small part of it. In reality, though, he's hoping he spots something he can use to jam me up, and make it seem like he was doing something productive during his shift today other than driving around and pulling people over at random.

I hand over my license and registration and they head back to their squad car. At this, Urkel says, "I'm just going to get out here and walk home."

We were still a twenty-minute walk away from his house. This kid either had terrible time management skills, or he was just trying to make a point. My money was on the latter, but regardless of the reason, this was one of the most awkward positions I've ever been put in in my life. On one hand, I'm this guy's Uber driver. What right to I have to tell him to stay in the car? That's quite literally kidnapping.

On the other hand, it doesn't take a genius to know it behooves oneself to avoid doing anything out of the ordinary during a traffic stop. I mean, we are dealing with a police force that sends two guys with guns and bulletproof vests to investigate a broken headlight; there is no need to add to their apprehension. And it doesn't take a rocket scientist to figure that getting out and walking away in the middle of a stop would do just that.

I struggled to find the politically correct words to keep this guy in my car; even more consequential than being his Uber driver who has no right to tell him to stay in the car, I'm a white man talking to a black guy about how to act around the police. Not a fun position to be in. If I say what I'm thinking—which is, *Why don't you keep your ass in my car until this thing is over with?*—not only do I sound like I'm keeping him against his will, but in my experience, the more I treat strangers of a different race as I would anyone else, the higher the risk of getting labeled a racist. Typically, I wouldn't care what he thought, as I know what I am and what I am not, but I didn't want him to report me to Uber and have to deal with whatever bullshit may come of it. I didn't know what those consequences were, but I knew that as white man with that charge levied against me, I'd be at the mercy of the powers that be.

On the other hand, if I *don't* say what I'm thinking and he gets out, there's a chance this situation escalates to the worst possible outcome. Next thing I know, I'm at the center of a nationwide protest featuring signs that read SAY URKEL'S NAME and URKEL'S LIFE MATTERS, with news media outlets labeling me as the idiot Uber driver that let his passenger out in the middle of a traffic stop.

As I fumbled over some *um*s and *ah*s, trying to figure out how to properly communicate the idea that he should keep his ass in my car until this thing is over with, the girl in the back shared some sense.

"Why don't we just wait?"

"Yeah," I quickly agreed. I was so glad she said it first. "It's just not a good look."

"Oh—" he was confused at first, but I could see his face changing as he connected the dots. "Oh, my God," he said through an uncomfortable and defeated laugh, as if there was a blatant injustice being done to him, a black man being targeted by police. I know that is presumptive of me, but given what happened after the ride, I'd bet dollars to donuts I was dead-on balls accurate.*

The cop came back pretty quickly because after all, he didn't give a fuck about the headlight, and once he realized I'm a Uber driver, the thought of adding a notch to his arrest record disappeared.

"Just make sure you get the headlight fixed," he said, handing me back my information.

"Yes sir, will do, thank you sir." Before he turned to walk away, I had to know: "You pulled me over because you saw me staring at you, didn't you?"

He smiled in a way that said he can't admit to the truth. "I pulled you over because of the headlight," and added a wink to boot.

You read that right. This motherfucker *winked* at me.

"I see. Well, a buddy of mine works in the eighteenth. I'm not sure if we are still in his district but I had my eye out for him."

---

* It's an industry term.

"Ah, na, we are a couple blocks away from the eighteenth."

The officer didn't know my buddy, and we parted ways. This is where the story should have ended, and if it did, it wouldn't have been worth telling. But of course, it gets worse.

It seems as though before we got stopped by the cops, the girl in the back seat requested another Uber to meet her at the point where I was dropping them off, timing it so that her Uber would be there when arrived. Because of the 3 minute and 17 second* delay of the traffic stop, the girl in the back missed her other Uber that she had called to meet her at the pickup spot.

Urkel's frustration had been rising since the moment we got pulled over, and I think his girlfriend missing her next ride sent him over the edge. He asked if he would get charged for the time spent at the stop. It was an ironic question, being that the entire model of an Uber Pool is to give you a cheaper, flat rate based on the fact that the rider has to be willing to make an indefinite amount of stops. Sure, being stopped by the police isn't part of the business model, but it's not like the stop added any more time to the trip than if we had picked someone else up. In fact, it added less time to the trip than I spent waiting for him to come out. Regardless, it was obvious he felt a certain way about what happened, and I would soon find out the lengths he would go to express that frustration.

Forgive me for getting a bit in the weeds about what would otherwise be trivial details—if not for the fact that the very next day I was notified by Uber that this rider reported me. According to them, I made the rider feel uncomfortable with racist remarks. Before I could even process this, the shock of it quickly turned to anger, as I was notified that I was suspended for three days and wouldn't be allowed to use the app until I took this online course about accepting different cultures or some shit.

I called. I emailed. I fought like hell to plead my case, telling multiple people at Uber that I have video evidence of the ride showing that I did nothing wrong. But Uber couldn't have cared less. I was pissed.

I was pissed at the cops for creating this situation under the guise of serving the community. I was pissed at Uber for leaving me high and dry. I was pissed at whatever Silicon Valley asshole who decided they would handle these situations with the bullshit diversity course I had to take, and I was pissed at Urkel for playing the race card

---

* I checked the time stamps on the dash cam. In other words, traffic stop or not, she probably wouldn't have gotten to that Uber in time.

over a few wasted minutes at a traffic stop and a $5 fee for missing an Uber: all at the expense of my livelihood.

As an antidote for my anger (read: instead of driving back to Urkel's house and pelting it with a carton full of eggs), like I try to do with any situation out of my control, I search for the humor in it, and I couldn't help but laugh at the absurdity of Uber's solution. For the sake of argument, let's say I actually was a racist, doing racist things as I chauffeured the very diverse Philadelphia clientele. When it is brought to Uber's attention that they have a racist driver on their hands, they solve that problem by giving me a three-day cleanse and an online class? And then what? Have I been cured of my racism? Who would have thought a couple of slides in a PowerPoint presentation was enough to exorcise the white supremacist demons inside of me, and why aren't they showing this thing in every school in the country right now? Forget revolutionizing the transportation industry, Uber has been holding the solution to America's four-hundred-year-old problem of race relations this whole time! And they are only sharing it with racist drivers like me? How incredibly selfish of them.

I don't know what's more pathetic, that C-suite executives approve of this woke corporate bullshit, or that there is actually a customer base that is satisfied by these PR antics.

The little bit of faith I have left in humanity likes to believe most people see through the farce of a three-day suspension and the diversity and inclusion class Uber forced on me, and recognize it for what it really is: Uber's way of covering their own ass as they continue in their hunt quest for the almighty dollar. But where that faith in humanity doesn't exist anymore is when it comes to the conversation about police.

It may come to a surprise to you, but I've never been black before. I wanted to be clear on that, and acknowledge that I understand my perspective is different because of it. But what drives me crazy about the conversation of policing in America is how people are so blinded by their own beliefs that they can't see any nuance, and instead choose to die on whatever hill they dug their heels into; be it the hill that says policing is a systemically racist institution and all cops are racists, or the hill that treats cops like infallible heroes that only get negative press because of a few bad apples.

It bothers me because in my experience, police do not discriminate: they are assholes to everybody. And the unwillingness of both sides to see the gray areas of this issue, and instead, try to "win the argument," is a *major* problem. For example, when statistics show that unarmed white people are actually more likely to be killed by cops than black people, the idiots in the Blue Lives Matter camp think they are scoring a talking point against the idiots in the Black Lives Matter camp; they don't realize that they are celebrating the fact that unarmed people are getting killed by police. So instead of looking at cops killing unarmed white people as a problem, it's used as a "gotcha" moment when someone says police target minorities. How fucking insane is that?

You think police target minorities? Well, guess what, you idiot, they kill more whites than anyone else! Isn't that great? It's like, nobody cares about the dangers of a police force that's undertrained and overworked, under-resourced yet over-militarized. But the second racism enters the chat, the debate dissolves into a discussion of what lives matter and whether or not you are an ally or a racist.

In reality, the issue isn't about what race cops treat worse: the issue is that police can abuse their power with little to no consequence as they protect the interests of the upper classes at the expense everyone else.

Thing is, I've been mistreated by the cops. I've been pulled over more than twenty times for mostly bullshit reasons. And I say "mostly" because, sure, before I turned eighteen I may have had a bit of a lead foot. But since then, I've been getting harassed because I don't look the way I'm supposed to look. I had a beat-up car in a decent neighborhood. I was driving late at night in neighborhoods I'm unfamiliar with. I've even had a cop pull a gun on me before. Now I know, this universe has a sample size of 1, so I can't say had I been black, that cop would've pulled the trigger on me. I can't say that if I had been black, maybe the cops would have pulled me over forty times instead of twenty, or maybe those twenty stops would have led to more drastic consequences.

I don't know. But unlike Urkel, my first thought when we were pulled over wasn't that it had anything to do with my skin color. Maybe this is my white privilege talking, but I don't think a Latino cop that works in a neighborhood that is at least 90 percent black, would stop me, a white guy, just because there was a black guy in my car.

When I relayed what happened to my friend the cop, he laughed. Before I could even finish the story, he told me why I got pulled over.

"We call it the 'felon stare'," he said. Apparently, felons have a tendency to stare at cops, or at least that is the thinking among police officers. I guess they attribute it to guilt, or worry, or awareness, or all of the above. Point is, when that cop caught me staring down his squad car looking to see if it was my friend, he attributed it to the felon stare.

How pathetic is that? Police are so distrustful of the people in their own district, and the people in his district have such little regard for police, that simple eye contact is enough to raise suspicion. And what a terrible cycle it creates. As I mentioned multiple times in this book, I learned the hard way that avoiding interactions with police is usually in my best interest, and now I'm encouraged to not even make eye contact with them because it will arouse suspicion?

Now to be fair to Urkel, I don't know if he actually thought I was racist. I don't know if this was just his way of getting a free ride because of the inconvenience, or make up for his girl missing hers. I wouldn't be surprised if he used that accusation as a convenient card to play for no other reason than because he knew he could. It's a card that I have seen played so many times, and every single time, despite this allegedly racist society we live in, no charge will carry more weight than when a black person accuses a white man of racism. Except, of course, a white woman who says she was assaulted—especially if that accusation is toward a black man (had to throw that in there before you think I'm an out-of-touch-with-reality race denier who thinks white people have it harder than others).

But if I had to put money on it, I would bet that Urkel made this claim because he genuinely felt an injustice. I say that because there was a time when I was an angry teenager myself, with a hatred of authority and a knack for taking things personal. And if I'm being honest with myself, when I get on a roll like this over something that happened years ago, I'm reminded that the angry teenager is still alive and well inside of me, ready to poke his head out at a moment's notice. Channeling that empathy I had toward this kid, trying to see the situation through his eyes, I wondered if my calm demeanor, and my yes-sirs and no-sirs were part of what pissed him off; part of what made him think that I get to interact with police different than he does.

I wish I could talk to him and tell him that I was just as pissed, if not more so, than he was, at the situation. After all, I was literally working a job where my time translates to money. But I've learned the hard way that police never have my best interests in mind, and I've experienced firsthand how badly their unchecked power can fuck up people's lives. I wish I could tell Urkel that the yes-sirs and no-sirs and the apologetic tone I put on make me feel like the bitch of the year. But it's a game I've learned to play after being harassed and mistreated by cops more times than I can count. I play that game, because if it's a good cop, he'll appreciate my attempt to make his job easier and show mercy. If it's a bad cop, the bootlicking will feed the desire for power that got him to sign up for this job in the first place. Either way, I've know that compliance will almost always get me a better result than if I was disrespectful to a guy with a gun he got from the government along with its blessing to use it whenever he sees fit.

But you know what really breaks my heart about this situation? It's that despite the outcome, I know better. I work and live and play with a demographic of people as diverse as a box of Crayola (the big one too, with the built-in crayon sharpener) and it's not because of some forced initiative of inclusion from a corporation or government. It's just the natural course of life for most people from Delco.

But what if I was different? What if I didn't realize Urkel was just an angry teenager trying to make sense of the world, and attributed the way he treated me to his skin color? What if Urkel was one of the few encounters I had with black people, and I took his accusation personally?

It's incredibly frustrating: here I am, chauffeuring around four black kids in a neighborhood where most drivers of all races avoid accepting rides entirely by turning their app off, only to get pulled over by a Latino police officer, all while driving a Japanese-made car, mind you—yet I get accused of being racist? And as a result, some fuckin' millionaire nerd in Silicon Valley who wouldn't dream of stepping foot in the neighborhoods I'm working in decides that I need diversity training, and on top of that, takes away my ability to put food on the table until I complete it?

Imagine if this happened to someone who didn't know better —someone who didn't have a lot of experience with different races. Imagine if this happened to someone who was brand new to driving Uber. You can see how an event like this can plant the seeds of a racist ideology, as it lends itself to an almost rational conclusion to avoid picking up people of different races.

Even though the overwhelming majority of minorities would never make such a superfluous accusation of racism, if it takes just one to pull the race card for me to get suspended, why put myself in that position? I could avoid that risk altogether by not driving in those neighborhoods.

Would that be fair to the overwhelming majority of good people in those neighborhoods? Absolutely not. Would that perpetuate this endless cycle? Absolutely. But what recourse do I have? I'm just a fucking Uber driver.

22
A Family Drama

It's no secret that men seem to have an easier time watching what they say in an argument than women do. What's not often acknowledged is why that is, and in my opinion, it comes down to the threat of violence. Every guy knows there is a line that is not to be crossed, and if it is, things can and will get physical. It's a natural restraint that most women don't live with, so they skip across that line with ease; raising the stakes until they cut a wound so deep it's hard to forget. It's a sad truth that the most damaging words can only come from the people you know and love the most—after all, you care what they think, and they know exactly what to say that would hurt the most.

It was the most beautiful time of the saddest day of the year: the golden hour of Labor Day down the Jersey Shore. The setting sun transforms the September sky above the bay into a canvas of warm and inviting colors, creating a scene that you want to remember, yet no camera can capture, all while signaling the unofficial end of summer. Perhaps it was that mixture of pleasure and pain, happiness and sadness, nostalgia and longing that created the angst of the characters involved in this story; but if I had to bet, I'd say alcohol played a bigger role. Nothing like a day drink to get a family drama brewing before dinner time.

Three good-looking women in their early twenties and a middle-aged woman piled into my car next to a beach bar. The cute doe-eyed girl in the front seat, obviously the youngest of the three, was holding a large pizza box. When Blondie sitting in the middle of the back seat asked her for a slice, I kindly asked if they could wait to eat until they get home. Had I known this simple request would have ignited World War III, I might have just let them eat.

Unprovoked, Redhead sitting behind me laid into Doe-Eyes in the front for being "such a slob that she would think to eat a slice of pizza in this man's car." Typically, I'm the one that gets pushback for asking riders not to eat in my car,* so I wasn't necessarily upset that Redhead came to my defense. But she did so in such a vicious manner I was inclined to believe this was about more than the pizza. I still didn't know how my riders were related yet, but it was clear by how raw and rude they were speaking to each other that they were good friends or family—you don't talk in that manner otherwise. Doe-Eyes snapped back, saying it was Blondie in the back that asked for a slice in the first place (which it was), and as if that was the sound of the opening *ding*, hell broke loose in the Uber.

As they hurled a volley of insults at each other, the middle-aged woman tried to squash it, yelling, "Stop picking on your little sister!" and "*Your* friend asked for the slice!" and "I raised you two better than this!" All of these pleas were ignored, but they weren't totally useless. It helped me, the innocent bystander, just trying to earn a few dollars working on the very holiday designated to give the working class a rest, understand the family drama invading my space. I was able to piece together that Doe-Eyes was Little Sister, Redhead was Big Sister, the woman was their mother, and Blondie was a friend. If I was going to be trapped in a car with these women for the next thirty minutes as they went for each other's throats, the least I could do is understand who's who and get some entertainment out of it.

The back and forth between the sisters continued for a short while, their words loaded with aggression but saying nothing of real consequence. Among the *fuck yous* and the *go fuck yourselfs* and even a *you're a fucking cunt*, it surprised me that what really set it off was when the Doe-Eyed Little Sister called the Redheaded Big Sister a "loser."

Redhead snapped back with "You have zero friends and no one wants to date you right now." Rather elementary, sure, but the delivery was on point, and even more importantly, I knew that statement would take this argument into new territory.

"Oh, what, because you have so many boyfriends?" Little Sister said in a desperate attempt to swing back.

Redheaded Big Sister was ready for it, though. Without hesitation, she responded, "Do you really want to play that game?"

Little Sister in the front shut her mouth so fast I knew Big Sister was holding one in the chamber. Part of me was praying that this stopped here, but another part of me that was curious as to what she was going to say. In retrospect, I wish my curiosity got left on read, because Big Sister followed through with "Didn't you date so many

---

* It's the catalyst for what almost gets me knocked out in chapter 23.

cool guys that were all cheating on you at the same time?" Mom tried to cover Big Sister's mouth, but Big Sister swatted her away—she wasn't finished: "Didn't you date that Muslim who beat the shit out of you?"

My eyebrows shot to the sky when I heard that. Sure, it's a fucked up thing to say, but I was more shocked by the amount of character revelation conveyed in that single sentence. Those few words hinted at so much: Little Sister's dating experience, her acceptance and openness to different cultures, and Big Sister's implied xenophobia and willingness to go for the jugular. Plus, the fact that she was comfortable enough to say it in front of Mom illuminated the family dynamic.

As messed up as it was for Big Red to call out her little sister's less-than-desirable dating history like that, it wasn't enough for me to interject myself into a situation with these women I met for the first time five minutes ago, and was going to be stuck with for another twenty-five, trapped together in a small car. It seemed like the argument would die on its own after that comment, and a few moments of silence enveloped the car. When I watched the scene back on dash cam, it was during this silence that Little Sister was trying her very best to keep it together, turning her head toward the window so no one could see what was happening. Her eyebrows started to furrow, then her lips started to quiver, and then finally, the sound of a whimper cut through. As I was driving, I was unsure of what that sound was at first, until that little whimper transformed into a very audible, full-blown sob. This doe-eyed, pretty young girl was having a meltdown in my front seat, and instead of condemning Big Sister for what she said, Mom scolded Little Sister for crying, grabbing hold of her shoulder and yelling, "Knock it off! Stop it!"

Like a lion spotting a wounded gazelle, Big Red saw the tears pouring out of her Little Sister's doe eyes as an opportunity to pounce, and began mocking her for being so emotional. Little Sister waves the white flag at this point and goes silent. Mom's orders for the insults to stop were met by Big Sister taunting back, "What are you gonna do about it?"

As if my eyebrows weren't already damn near touching the ceiling, this chick was now belittling her own mother? *Daayummm.*

When she responded in that way to the woman who raised her, I had a feeling I was going to need to get involved to keep this thing from spinning out of control. And what happened next only solidified that prediction.

Little Sister's crying continued, seemingly getting worse with each moment. The demands that Big Red "stop picking on her" devolved into pleas that unsurprisingly went ignored. What was surprising, though, was how Mom made sure to throw subtle jabs at Little Sister even while coming to her defense, saying that the reason Big Sister shouldn't pick on Little Sister is because Little Sister "isn't as tough as you" and "she can't handle it."

It was then that Big Sister laid down the most savage insult I ever heard in my Uber.

"Aw, she can't handle this? Maybe she should have been hit a little more then. Would have done her some good."

I'm not proud of it, but it was so unexpected that I couldn't help but smirk (and may or may not have bit my tongue to keep from laughing). Eventually, Little Sister's cries snapped me back to reality and reminded me how incredibly hurtful that must have been.

It was at that point I had to shut that shit down, raising my voice and saying everyone is going to ride in silence for the rest of this ride or I'll leave them on the parkway.

To be honest, I was surprised at how effective a little bit of volume and the threat of a consequence worked.

Now, I have no idea what it's like to be a parent, or a parent of two girls, or a parent of two girls *like that*. But as I drove, I couldn't help but wonder if they would have acted that same way if it had been Dad in the car rather than Mom. I'm not well-versed in the theories of the supernatural, but I know there is something to be said about feminine and masculine energy, and I wonder how much further that would've gone if I hadn't inserted myself and shut that shit down.

About ten minutes pass by, and Little Sister had finally calmed down and stopped crying. What she did next reminded me that there is always more to the story, and that she might not be this innocent victim that I felt for when those tears started flowing. She started reaching all around my middle console, and when I asked her, in a very kind tone, what she needed—despite that I was offering to help, and despite being the one who had saved her from Big Sister's attacks— she snapped at me like I was the villain.

"A charger!" she barked, as if I was inconveniencing her by offering to help.

Maybe she should've been a hit a little more, after all.

After the most uncomfortable ride, we finally arrive to a Bayfront mansion with a private dock and a big, beautiful boat to go with it. Despite the thousands of rides I've given to people with much more material wealth than me, it's rides like this that make it easy to keep from falling into jealousy. Time and time again, this ride has been replicated—passengers who on the exterior seem to have a life that anyone would want, and an inner turmoil that isn't to be envied. I'm only speculating what it must feel like to be rich and miserable, but if given the choice between being broke or broken-hearted, I'm going for broke every time. From where I'm sitting, I'd much rather spend my Labor Day working Uber, happy in my Honda, than ending up miserable in a mansion after a day of partying.

As the girls got out, I told them to enjoy their pizza—a joke that did not land. Mom stayed in the car, making the common mistake of believing her Uber fare was a therapy bill and my back seat, a couch.

I should have been clearer about the silence lasting until they were out of my car, I thought, as this grown woman unloaded her struggles on me: a freakin' Uber driver whose life is so unstable he has to work Labor Day to make ends meet. She talked about how hard it is for her to be a mom of adult children, how she feels bad for Little Sister, and doesn't know what to do with Big Sister who is "Too. Much." As she droned on and on, giving unnecessary details of the family dynamic and chalking the argument up to their drinking, I kept thinking to myself how I wanted to be more mindful of what I say to the people I know best, because the more you know someone, the more responsibility you have to use that knowledge for good.

She finally finished her complimentary therapy session, and before exiting my car, she thanked me for putting an end the argument during the ride. "I don't think I can tell my husband what happened," she said. "He'd freak."

23
Scummiest Thing a Rider Ever Did

Part 1

It wasn't their attitude, or their entitlement, or the insulting gesture directed my way. It wasn't even the forbidden word I was called after I went out of my way to return their forgotten cell phone. The scummiest thing a rider ever did to me occurred a full week after the ride happened.

It was another Labor Day weekend, the final hoorah of the season and once again, I found myself down the shore. This particular summer, I had been busting my ass. I decided this would be a final weekend of grinding before I gave myself a well-deserved week off from driving. It also happened to be the summer I started Uber Karaoke on my two-year-old YouTube channel, and I felt like I was on my way to stardom as I just broke a whopping 400 subscribers. As long as the Labor Day weekend was as lucrative as it usually was for Uber drivers, I'd have enough money to take a week off and focus solely on my content endeavors.

Fortunately, it was as busy as I hoped, and I was giving ride after ride throughout the entire weekend. Before I knew it, it was getting to the point when the bars were letting out on Sunday night, the final hours of the last night of the summer. I received a pickup request at the Wawa located right next to the bars in Sea Isle, which was a common place to pick people up. With two bars on the same block, and another two bars just another block away, it has to be the busiest convenience store on earth at that ungodly hour; full of young, drunk guys and girls rummaging through the aisles for food and drink to settle the alcohol they've filled their stomachs with.

As I looked into that madhouse, feeling for the associates that had to work that shift and wondering just how much shrinkage* Wawa endures on a night like tonight, two girls come walking up to my car. One is blonde, one is brunette, both in their mid-to-late twenties with hoagies in hand, eating as they walked.

"For Kim?"

"Indeed!" The brunette said. "And we have two more coming."

"Would you mind wrapping that hoagie up?"

"Oh... can we eat in the back?"

Oh, I didn't realize that back seats don't get stained by condiments, and the lettuce and crumbs that you'll leave in the car will magically disappear by the invisible smurf that lives in my trunk and moonlights as my car's janitor.

"Would you mind not? It always gets super messy."

"Okay," she said, so sad, plopping down into the car and taking one final, gigantic bite to tide her over. Shreds of lettuce spill everywhere, but she started wrapping it up, so I didn't say anything. It's moments like these where I wonder if I am being mature by letting things go, or if I'm being a shmuck by letting someone walk all over me.

"Okay, I wrapped it up." It was as if she acknowledged she just spilled a bunch of shit everywhere but wasn't going to spill any more.

"I appreciate that." That was my way of saying I'm glad we aren't making this bigger than it needs to be.

The other girl—Blondie—oafs down into the seat directly behind me. She sizes up her hoagie then stuffs her face like a kid who just got home from fat camp.

"Hey!" Kim said to her, laughing. "Not just me, everybody." But Blondie continued to eat.

"Listen, if you are going to eat in my car, I'm not going to drive you."

"No, we're not." Kim said. "I just wrapped it up."

Blondie, with her cheeks full of food and still chewing, covers her sandwich and holds it up at me like a disgruntled middle schooler showing the teacher she turned her cell phone off. I don't want to have an issue, so I don't respond.

---

*In case your unfamiliar, it's the retail industry's term for loss due to theft, fraud, damaged goods, etc. I figured I'd explain it to save you from googling "shrinkage." You're welcome.

The two other people that they asked me to wait for were still nowhere in sight, and I'm getting more frustrated by the second. Not only is it awkward having two people in the car that you obviously aren't getting along with, but this is the prime time of the night, and every second I waste waiting for them makes it less likely that I'll catch another ride during the window of the ridiculously high surge pricing.

Kim calls out to a guy named Matt, who I would find out later is her boyfriend, to get in the car, as Blondie's boyfriend sits in the front seat. He immediately starts blabbering about a conversation he heard about cankles. It was the kind of story I hear often in the Uber —the kind that the drunk storyteller finds wildly entertaining but to my sober ears is less interesting than the sound of paint drying. At least the paint allows me peace with my own thoughts.

As her boyfriend blabbers, Blondie sees this as an opportunity to sneak another bite. But no one pulls the wool over the eyes of Driver Ed. While I could take this opportunity to brag about my observational skills, which I do believe are far above average, in this particular situation we are talking about a drunk girl unwrapping crinkly hoagie paper and munching down on a crunchy sandwich. You can't think of a creature less stealthy.

So not only was she eating again, there was still one more person we had to wait for, and that was it for me. I figured I was going to have to wait God knows how much longer for this fourth person, and if they were this much of a problem now, what would happen later? I've learned the hard way that it's much easier to end a ride before it starts than to kick people out after the car is moving, so I thought it best that I nip this nonsense in the bud right then and there.

"Alright, listen," I said, interrupting the riveting cankle story. "I'm going to ask you guys to get out. I'm sorry."

Kim looked directly at her sister, still eating, after both her and I told her to stop eating, turned back to me, and says "Why?" As if she was completely clueless and innocent and I was insane. At this point, Matt finally showed up and got in the car.

"I'm sorry sir, could you guys just get out? Just get another Uber. Or the Jitney. I already told you not to eat in the car…"

"We're not eating!" Kim laughed like I'm an idiot.

"No one is eating!" Blondie said, her cheeks so full of sandwich she looked like a yellow-haired chipmunk.

"I saw you eating. It's alright. If you could just get out, that would be great."

"I'm not eating! No one is eating!" the chipmunk said again.

"Nobody is eating." Her sister backed up the blatant lie.

There is an element to liars that I could never relate to but almost have a weird respect for: how they can look you dead in the face, despite clear evidence to the contrary, and still stick to their story. I always wonder if they are consciously lying, or if they are so delusional that, by repeatedly saying it, they end up actually believing their own lie. The most interesting part about it is that if they recite their lie long enough, it usually makes an honest person question the truth—after all, an honest person can't fathom the idea of someone lying about something so obvious. It's like, if you tell me the sky is green long enough, I may never believe you, but I might go and get my eyes checked just to make sure. That's the long way of saying that after this all went down, when I replayed the story in my head, I had to check the dash cam just to make sure I wasn't crazy. And I wasn't.

"Guys, there's plenty of Ubers. It'll be totally fine," I said.

It's just the girls bitching at this point—the guys are silent. I'm really hoping they interject soon, and that they do so in my favor. I'm not looking to be understood here, I'm just hoping that they respect the decision that I made in my car and choose not to escalate the situation. A woman upset with you is similar to a child being upset with you: sure, they can say things, but the people who say "words hurt" are the kind of people that have never gotten punched in the face. And let's be honest, if these women decided to get physical, it's probably not gonna hurt, at least not to the point where I'd be justified in the court of public opinion to fight back. But if the guys in the car get involved, lord knows where that can lead.

"We'll get out," Kim started triumphantly, as if she was taking the moral high ground. "But *you* have to cancel it because we're not going to pay *FIVE* dollars for you being a dick," laying into *five* as if we were talking about a month's rent here.

"That's fine," I said, with no intention of canceling it. She just called me a dick, after all. It would only be right if I acted like one.

"No one is eating!" the Blonde Chipmunk was still sticking to her story.

"Okay," I said. "Could you just get another Uber? It'll be fine."

"Alright alright alright alright." Matt finally decided to quash the situation peacefully. *Thank God.* They start to get out.

"No one is fucking eating!" Chipmunk said again. She was really sticking to her story. You don't want to assume things about people based on singular experiences, but she was pretty hung up on something so obvious and so trivial. I'm going to go out on a limb here and say she's the type that has a really hard time admitting when she's wrong.

"There *are* plenty of Ubers... but—" Kim started. I was ready for some more choice words, but she bit her tongue and got out without saying anything else. Blondie, however, couldn't refrain.

"Well, you're a fucking dick," the Chipmunk said before getting out.

"Alright," I said.

"Here," Matt said, leaning in from the back seat. He was reaching into his back pocket.

"What's up?" I asked, wondering what he was reaching for. Could this be a redeeming moment of humanity? Could this man give me a glimpse of civility? This same mature individual who squashed the conflict and ordered his friends out—is he recognizing that this was all brought on by their own actions and is going to reward me for keeping my cool, despite the way I was treated? Did this guy realize how their shenanigans had drastically diminished my earnings, along with my faith in humanity, and wanted to offer an olive branch in the form of monetary compensation—a tip, if you will—for my troubles?

He finally found what he was searching for in his back pocket, pulled out his hand, and held up a stiff middle finger aimed directly at me. He laughed at his own joke.

"That's pretty good," I said.

I pulled away and around the corner, stopping not too far from the original pickup spot, since I had to stay close to them for another twenty seconds until the timer ran out and I was able to collect the cancellation fee, because I sure as hell was getting my *five* dollars. As I waited and watched, prepared to see her charging at my car when she realized I didn't cancel, I thought about how perturbed she was at the thought of me getting those *five* dollars, and how pissed she'll be when she realizes that she was charged. It always amazes how people have such an emotional connection with money. Covers to every bar on that entire island that night, on a holiday weekend, were $10 to $20. The cheapest drink you can find in any of those bars is at least $5, and by the sound and smell of things they had purchased plenty. A quick glance at their Wawa bag left me estimating at least $50 worth of food, and if I did drive them home, the Uber would have been more than $40 at that time of night. All that is to say, between the four of them, they easily spent $250 at the absolute minimum, yet she was concerned over a measly $5, because that measly $5 would have gone to *me*—the selfish prick who wouldn't let them dirty my back seat.

With a few seconds to go on the timer and no sign of them in sight, I thought this ride was over and my encounter with these assholes was finished. I could not have been more wrong. I checked the back seat, to see the damage done by the drunken eating, and to what to my wandering eyes do appear? It was Blonde Chipmunk's cellphone in the seat to my rear.

My, oh my, how the turn tables turn.

In all the dash camera footage I have seen of myself over the years, I've learned it is not uncommon for me to think out loud to an empty car, most likely the result of all the time I spend alone. In this particular instance, however, there was zero surprise when the replay showed me vocalizing my frustration when I reached for the phone.

"Dumb bitch," I said out loud to an empty car. I cannot explain how vindicated I felt in that moment. To put a cherry on top, her cell phone was in one of those wallet cases. So not only did I have her brand new iPhone, I had her license, credit cards, and whatever else was so important she carried around on a daily basis. And when I'm not being my best self, I'm the type of person that responds to insult or criticism by leaning into that insult and showing them what it would actually look like if I was being the way they were claiming I was.

As in, they want to call me a fucking dick? Well, I'm going show you what a fucking dick would do by chucking this goddamn phone and wallet into the ocean. That's what a dick would do, right?

But even before the angel appeared my shoulder to talk me out of it, the neutral voice of logistics started to reel me back in. As much as I wanted to indulge myself in that symbolic toss into the Atlantic, was I really going to take ten minutes away from the busiest time of the night to walk on the beach, all the way to the ocean, getting sand in my shoes, only to do something that they'll never know happened? Sure, she'll eventually realize her phone is missing, but she'll never know the lengths I took to put it with the fishes.

With that option out the window, there didn't seem to be any other choice that would be an adequate retaliation. When your first idea of vengeance is as beautiful and poetic as putting something your enemy needs on the ocean floor, anything else is just a pathetic let down. It was then that the dreaded angel on my shoulder showed up and started chirping in my ear.

Is it really necessary, Ed, for this girl to lose a cell phone over a few drunken words that she probably won't even remember saying?

"Ugh. No, I guess not."

I know you've said things you didn't mean when you were drinking, haven't you Ed?

"Yes, I have."

How would you feel if you lost your phone every time you said something mean?

"Alright, I get it. Geez, you never let me have any fun."

You know what you need to do.

"Okay, fine, I'm not going to destroy this girl's phone, but I'm not going out of my way to return it. That's on them."

So I started to dig through her phone and wallet in order to figure out a way to get it back to them. Her phone was locked, so I couldn't call any of her contacts. The address I found in the wallet was in Maryland. I assumed, being that it was Sunday of Labor Day, she was most likely heading back there tomorrow, and even if she wasn't, I knew I was heading back to Delco, an hour and a half away. It dawned on me that if I didn't get her this phone back tonight, it's only going cause a hassle for me tomorrow when she tries to track it down. I was reminded of one time, after a late night of working Uber, some asshole knocked on my door at six in the morning, causing my dog to go nuts and wake my whole house up. That asshole was some college kid I had driven the night before, who used the "find my iPhone" app to track down the phone he left in my car. That bastard couldn't wait until a normal hour? All that's to say, I knew the best option for all parties involved would be to get this thing back to her tonight.

After I canceled Chipmunk's ride, I had immediately gotten another request, not even two blocks away from where I kicked her and her entitled friends out. Ironically, I picked up the new riders at Drifters, another late night food spot. I explained to them the situation and asked them if they wouldn't mind if we just took a quick two-block detour to see if I could find my previous riders and return the phone.

Fortunately, the two girls I picked up where the type of people that make driving Uber fun. Despite it being the witching hour, they were not only agreeable and sympathetic to my situation, the one girl's gratitude toward the order of gravy fries she had in tow was enough to remind you of how it's the little things in this world that make life worth living. And for the record, they completely agreed with me that not eating in an Uber is a very reasonable request.

In no time, I was back to where I had kicked out Dumb Blonde Chipmunk and Co., and I kid you not, they were in the process of getting kicked out of another Uber. It was like the universe was reminding me the best punishment an asshole receives is that they have to live with themselves. I don't mean like they have to live with their guilt, I mean like they have to deal with the consequences of being a difficult person. Something as simple as ordering an Uber to get home caused turbulence for them, not once, but twice, in the span of ten minutes. That brought me great solace—because *fuck them*.

Now, before we get into the returning of the phone, there are two things you need to understand: First, I recognize I could have very easily just given the phone back. But, despite choosing to do the mature thing and return the phone, I was still pissed at the way they treated me and immaturely sought to have the last word with people that, in retrospect, I shouldn't care about. In the moment, though, I thought it would be vindicating.

Second, this is either going to sound very weird or very relatable—but there was this trend on TikTok of people talking about the "bits" they do in real life, things like asking a friend's toddler for a cigarette, saying "time to clear the weapon" when you have to pee, or offering to end an argument by challenging your opponent to a dance battle. It wasn't until I saw those TikToks that I realized other people had inside jokes with themselves, too. For me, I like to drop movie quotes into normal conversation—but they have to work well enough for the line to play even if nobody else gets the reference.* And there was a line from *My Cousin Vinny* that I had in the chamber, and it goes, "Excuse me, but I think a modicum of gratitude would not be out of line here." In retrospect, I wonder if part of the reason I decided to return the phone was not out of goodwill or morality but instead for the opportunity to finally use this iconic line in a situation perfect for it.

"Yo!" I yelled out to the Blonde Chipmunk and her boyfriend who were standing on the sidewalk, as Kim and Matt were still arguing with the other Uber driver that kicked them out. "Despite your asshole friend giving me the finger, I'm returning the phone that you left."

Chipmunk, the girl who's phone I had in my hand, shakes her head at me and shuffles her hand, as if to wave me to move along.

"I think you're gonna need this," I said.

"Oh, well, we didn't lose a phone," the cankle storyteller said, coming toward my car.

"This isn't yours?" *Did I get this wrong?* I started to wonder. *Maybe the phone was from the ride before Chipmunk and co. and I didn't see it.*

"Let me check." The dude is now at my passenger window while Chipmunk is still waving me away.

---

* There's even a few in this book you may have picked up on.

"If that's not hers then I'm not giving it back."

"I believe that's her phone."

"Is her phone missing?" The girl in the back seat asked. Even she was confused.

"Let me check," the boyfriend said.

"Is her phone missing?" I asked again. There was no way I was giving up the phone without confirmation. Not only would I lose all my leverage, but I'd miss my chance for vindication and, even worse, the opportunity to use the *My Cousin Vinny* line.

"Let me put in the code to see if it's her phone." Sticking his hand in my car as if there wasn't a woman sitting right there in the passenger seat. Total asshole.

"What's on her home screen?"

"Let me put in the code to see if it opens."

"Maybe it was the people before."

"Let me try the code!"

"What's her name? How 'bout that.

"Dumb Blonde Chipmunk."

I checked the license. Sure enough, it read "Dumb Blonde Chipmunk."

"Alright. There ya go," I said, handing over the phone, waiting for a "thank you" before I let go. It never came. This was my moment.

"Maybe a mortitude of graticum would not be out of order."

NOOO! I butchered the line!

As if I couldn't be any more unhappy with the situation, what this man said next took this to a level that actually pissed me off.

"No, you're a fucking cunt," he whined. "Go fuck yourself."

Now "cunt" is one of those words a man doesn't call another man unless he thinks he's not going to get punched in the face. So I took it as him questioning who I am as a man. It's not what he said that pissed me off, it's that he thought he could say it and I wasn't going to do anything about it. And after all, why would he? They treated me like shit from the jump, and I still went out of my way to return their phone like the little Uber slave that I was. Of course he'd assume I'd take that insult like a little bitch.

I saw red for a brief second. I wanted to put my car in park, get out, and charge. I don't give fuck if I got my ass beat two against one, I was too angry and too tired of getting walked all over by these fucking people. Not just tonight, but from the whole fucking summer. Night after night, week in and week out, getting disrespected and disregarded by entitled, selfish assholes when I'm just trying to earn an honest buck, this was the straw that broke the camel's back.

Fortunately, the gasp from the girl in the back seat after he said that was enough to keep me from overreacting, reminding me that there are other people in this world that don't think it's right to talk to someone like that, even if that someone is an Uber driver. I let out my frustration with that kind of crazy, forced laugh that angry people make when they are trying to conceal the fact that their head is going to explode,* and the wheezing sound that came out of my mouth indicated how very close I was to that exact thing happening.

"These fucking people," I said, before shaking my head and pulling away, apologizing to my riders for my language. That's when I knew I was fully back to earth. It's wild to think how much can change in an instant if one simple little decision is made differently.

"No, people like that," the girl in my back seat started, "bug me. Like you're doing something nice…"

And just like that, with a little bit of empathy and understanding from my riders, we changed the topic. I was fine putting that situation behind me as just another example of people treating Uber drivers like trash. The very next weekend, however, this story would unravel in a way I could have never imagined.

Part 2

A week later, I was celebrating a friend's thirtieth birthday in Philadelphia. He's a huge Penn State football fan, and his wife threw him a surprise party at a popular sports bar so he could watch the game. I actually remember telling him the story of the forgotten cell phone on the way to the bar; after all, it's not often that I am called a cunt by a grown man.

The basement section of the bar was rented out for his party, and there was only one bathroom available down there. At one point in the night, I had to go, and there were already a few people waiting, so I went upstairs to the main part of the bar to find another bathroom. I spot the sign for the men's room across the bar, and the couple sitting at a table on that side of the room caught my eye. It was one of those moments where I knew I recognized them but couldn't figure out where I knew them from. As I walked in their direction,

---

*In fact, very similar to Killer Kelly's laugh in chapter 20.

heading to the bathroom, I was racking my brains trying to place them, until I got close enough to get a good look and a light bulb went off. *Hold up… is that the couple from my Uber?* I was almost positive it was the girl who got her panties twisted over $5 because I "was a dick" and the dude who pulled a middle finger out of his back pocket. In other words, not the girl who lost her phone, and not the guy who called me a cunt.

In retrospect, I shouldn't have said anything. But it always bothers me how I am treated by people as if I don't exist outside of the Uber, as if I'm not a human being that lives and breathes and exists in the same world. So it's not often that I get an opportunity to prove my humanity. Plus, while I'm not the type to go looking for a fight, I *am* drawn to a good story. And the story that was sitting at the table in front of me was a story I've always wanted to hear: the story from the rider's perspective.

"Excuse me," I said to the couple. They were sitting with two other guys and another girl. "Where you in Sea Isle last weekend? I think I was your Uber driver."

"Oh, my God. That was you?"

"Wait…" the other girl said. "This is the guy that kicked you out?"

"I see my reputation precedes me," I said, with a smile on my face, and the entire table laughed. Not only did I have no idea about how they felt about me and our situation, but I also recognized that I was intruding on their little get together, so I figured I'd find out quick if this intrusion would be unwelcome—or if this was going to be a funny little cap to a story and the start of a new friendship.*

"I have to know, that other guy you were with—what's his deal?"

"That's my sister's boyfriend."

"You know he called me a cunt?"

"Well, you were being ridiculous."

"What?" This was the first thing that was said that moved my needle from friendly and toward frustration. She said it with a smile on her face, so I took it as playful, but I didn't expect them to lean into their behavior a week removed and relatively sober. A grown man called me a cunt, after all. It's the closest thing white men have to being called the N-word. If a white guy called a black guy the N-word,

---

* To be clear, I mean like, bar friends. Like maybe do a shot with them later that night kind of friends. Not like, actual friends. I love meeting new people, but I'm not delusional.

there is no circumstance where you would say to the black guy, "Well, you were being ridiculous." And you certainly wouldn't do that after the black guy went out of his way to return a lost cell phone when he didn't have to.

"What kind of person picks someone up at a Wawa and isn't okay with them eating in the car," Kim said. Before, I could respond, the girl at the table echoed the sentiment.

"Yeah, what did you expect. It's Wawa!"

"I can't control where I pick people up!" The logic was mind blowing. If I pick someone up at a hospital, should I be okay if they bleed all over my back seat?

"And then," Kim was cracking up, "we had to call him back." She imitated talking on the phone. "Hey, my sister left her purse in your car... could you bring it back?"

"False. That's not what happened." Now we were still laughing, and having fun, but the situation was going in a way I didn't expect from the jump. I had thought by now, they might've said sorry, or at least given me a simple thank you, and I could be reminded that the way people treat their Uber driver when they are hammered at two in the morning is not indicative of who they are as a person, and we could all go our merry ways.

So as they continued to poke fun at the way I handled the Uber situation, it occurred to me that maybe it's because they didn't understand what actually happened. After all, there is no fucking way they are this entitled and unappreciative of what I did for them, and did it despite the way they treated me.

So I filled them in on what actually happened, and just to show how things were still cordial at this point, in the middle of my retelling, Penn State scored and we all gave each other high fives. I wasn't even rooting for Penn State (as a Temple alum it's almost a duty to root against that godforsaken school), but I celebrated with them as I sign of peace. I didn't want any problems. But as I told the story, I could feel the table slowly turn against me. Perhaps I got a little too bogged down with the details, but I think the mood change had to do more with the truth they were being confronted with. In retrospect, it's probably not a good feeling to learn how poorly you treated a guy who was just trying to earn an honest buck and keep his back seat clean. I got my first whiff of that guilt when the dude said he didn't remember giving me the finger. But it wasn't until I got to the end of the story when things at that table went south.

"... So I asked Cankle guy to confirm the name... which he did, Dumb Blonde Chipmunk..." when I said her full name, Kim turned to Middle Finger Guy with a look so concerning that I had to address it.

"What? I got a memory." I don't get these fucking people. Obviously, it's a wild coincidence to lead us here to the same bar, seven days, and an entire state removed from where we first met, but I don't understand why people think Uber drivers don't exist outside of Ubering. Do they really think I can't retain information as simple as a name, especially one that was easy to remember? Who is going to forget Dumb Blonde Chipmunk? (For real though, the alliteration in her actual name made it roll off the tongue.) Plus, the name was crucial plot point to the most eventful ride of my weekend: What kind of master storyteller would I be if I couldn't remember such an important detail?

It always blows my mind when Uber riders treat me like shit when I am driving them to where they live. *Like, motherfucker, I know where to find you.* One time specifically, I remember a guy accidentally (or so he claimed) canceled the trip mid-ride. When he requested another Uber, he was paired with a different driver. I told him he could either get out and wait for the new driver, or just pay me $20 to take him the rest of the way. He agreed on the $20.

When we get to his very large house in a very wealthy neighborhood, he tells me he only has $7 in his pocket.

"Alright, *soooo* I'll guess I'll wait here and you can go get the rest." I needed that money, sure, but this was about more than that. I wasn't about to get hustled.

"Okay, sure." He said this in a way that had me thinking I knew exactly where this was going.

This middle-aged man, with his wife or girlfriend, were laughing and falling over each other all the way up their porch steps and to their door. After she opened it and walked through, he turns back to me and screams, "See ya!" Closing the door behind him and turning off the light.

So when I pulled out of his driveway, I thought it would be rude if I didn't take this opportunity to turn over the several flowerpots he had lining his driveway. Now I operate as if I am always being recorded when I'm out in public, and I took that into consideration. That's why after I flipped over the last one, I turned to the house, smiled and waved, before getting back into my car and leaving. I hoped to God he had some sort of doorbell camera and would see that it was me that did it. I wanted him to know that just because I'm an Uber driver doesn't mean I'm a little bitch. I've driven past that house multiple times in the years since I dropped him off, and I smile every time I see that the flowers have yet to be replaced.

"So anyway," I said to Kim and Middle Finger Guy, still shocked that I remembered her sister's memorable name, "I give the phone back, and then he called me a cunt!"

"You sound crazy right now, dude." Middle Finger Guy said.

"Yeah, well, I'm not the guy who flipped off an Uber driver from the back window." I was pissed. After hearing what happened, would it have been so hard to give a simple thank you? Or perhaps an apology? But the look of shame on his face when I called him out for flipping me off like a little bitch made the whole interaction worth it, at least up until that point. It reminded me that, yeah, he is a human. He does know what he did was wrong.

"What do you want?" he asked.

"What do I want?" This was my moment. "A modicum of gratitude would not be out of order!" I fucking nailed it.

"I think it's time for you to go," he said.

"What's the matter? Now that I'm standing in front of you, your middle finger don't work?"

"You got to go dude," he said again.

"If you want, we can continue this conversation outside."

"No, no, we aren't doing that," Kim interjected. He shook his head no.

"Yeah, that's what I thought," I said, triumphantly. "Fuckin pussy. All of ya. Bunch of pussies." I said, before storming off.

Look, I'm not proud of what I did there, and for the record, it was entirely a bluff. I hadn't been in a fight in a long while, and this dude was much bigger than me. I had no delusions of handling him if we got physical. On the small chance he'd take me up on the offer, my plan was to get loud enough around the bouncers that they notice, not be the one to swing first, and pray to God they intervene if he does. But calling him outside was my way of flipping the script on him. As helpless as I felt as an Uber driver being disrespected by drunk assholes, I put him in a similar situation. If he follows someone outside, who is much smaller than he is, to fight over some words that were said, well, it's not a good look for him. Little did I know just how bad he could have beat my ass, but I can assure you that he could, and he knew he could, which probably made it even more frustrating for him to listen to me run my mouth and not do anything about it. But more on that later.

After storming off, I went to the bathroom. On my way back to my friend's party, I got stopped by a waitress. "You got to go," she said, and called over the bouncers.

"What?"

"Weren't you harassing that table over there?"

Those rat-ass motherfuckers. They really are pussies.

"No."

"That wasn't you?"

"No, I'm with the private party downstairs."

"Oh. Okay then."

Still to this day, I can't believe that's all it took to get her off my case. Crazy how far a little bit of status can take you.

For the second time now, this is where the story should have ended. And if it did, I don't know if it would have made it into this book. It certainly wouldn't qualify as the scummiest thing a rider ever did to me. What happened next, however, still raises my blood pressure when I think about it.

The next day, when I engaged in the post-party ritual of recapping the night, I felt satisfied with the exchange with my Uber riders. I was shocked we crossed paths, and I wasn't proud of my actions, but I felt as though it brought equilibrium to the universe. They were assholes to me, I was annoying to them, and we both went on our way. Sure, I didn't need to ask that guy to step outside, and they didn't need to try to get me kicked out after I left them alone when they asked. But hey, it's all in a night of fun, right? I thought this episode was over, and the anger and frustration I felt previously had been vanquished.

That is, until that night when I got a message from Uber. "We received a claim that your rider felt uncomfortable on a recent trip because of an argument that felt threatening or intimidating during the ride." I was suspended from driving for seven days.

To say I felt angry would be the understatement of the year. I felt like a mat that got trampled on, and the ones who did the trampling reported me to my job because they didn't like the way I let them trample on me.

I had driven for Uber long enough to know how protesting this suspension would go. I tried anyway, saying it was false, telling them I had dash cam footage and offering to send it. I fought like hell, sending emails and making phone calls to get the suspension removed, not only because it was untrue, but I had just taken a week off of work. That meant I wasn't just planning to work the next week and weekend, but I *needed* to. I was furious. These assholes took away my ability to put food on my table, and they did so by lying about what happened. Talk about a cunt move.

I want to be clear, I know I probably shouldn't have gone up to them in the bar. And I definitely shouldn't have called them pussies and asked the dude to step outside. I wasn't right in doing that. Any of that. But not only was our interaction inconsequential, involving Uber was even more absurd because *it didn't happen while I was driving Uber.* So not only did they lie, but they came for my job as some sort of sick and twisted revenge.

It only reiterated the way I'm viewed as an Uber driver, like I have no other purpose in this world than to get you from point A to point B. Sure, the chances are slim that I would ever cross paths with my riders after our trip ends, but what if we do? What if you leave your fucking wallet in my car and have a memorable name? Does that make me intimidating because I remembered it? Or does that make you a narcissistic asshole because you think a guy working Uber is a doormat with a driver's license incapable of retaining information? *I'm a human being, dammit.*

The most fucked up part about this, and the fucked up thing about every instance of entitled assholes reporting gig workers over bullshit, is that it's no secret Uber drivers aren't working on the weekend because they have a bunch of extra cash to burn. We need money. And I needed this income. And these people are going to kick me when I'm down, getting me suspended because of something that didn't even happen during the Uber ride?

What if I were to get even with them by showing their bosses how they act when they aren't at work? And my story wouldn't even be a lie; I had dash cam footage that speaks for itself. What if I were to take that video of them being sloppy at 2 a.m., shoving food in their mouths and calling their Uber driver a fucking dick, flipping me the bird, and calling me a cunt, and send it to their place of work?

That sounds like something a cunt would do, right?

Well, I figured I would do just that. It would only be fair for me to do what they did, find where these people worked, and send them and their coworkers and their bosses the dash cam footage of their sloppy, drunken antics. While I'm at it, I'll be sure to let everyone know how they thanked the driver who went out of his way to return their lost cell phone, despite the way he was treated, by crying wolf to Uber and getting him suspended.

Will this video get *them* suspended from work? Definitely not. But will it make them uncomfortable? You're goddamn right it will.

Will it show their coworkers and their bosses how quick they are to lie over an inconsequential Uber ride, with no regard for how it might affect other people's lives? Absolutely. Will it make everyone they work with second guess them the next time push comes to shove? I could only hope. I uploaded the video to my computer and had the email written out and ready to go. Now all I had to do was find these people.

It was easy finding the girl who left her wallet, being that I had her name. Sure, her socials didn't have her government name Chipmunk, but instead, Chippy; but that wasn't hard to figure. Plus, she popped right up on the most slept on creeper site that exists: LinkedIn. Nobody thinks to look there, but it should be the first site you go to when trying to find someone. After all, people might want to keep their social life private and use nicknames or privacy filters for their Facebook and their Instagram, but people sign up for LinkedIn literally hoping to be found. Sure, they want to be found by potential employers, not disgruntled Uber drivers, but hey, the search engine works just the same.

As for the girl who reported me: I knew her first name, being that it was the name on the Uber request, and since she said at the bar Chipmunk is her sister, I could assume they have the same last name. It's often said that one shouldn't assume things, but the truth is, most times assumptions are correct. This was one of those times. When I found her on Linkedin, I was surprised to find out she was an actuary. You would think someone who works in risk management for a living would have accounted for the potential downsides of filing a bullshit report that could cost someone their job.

Now for the guy. That smug motherfucker at the bar. In the dash cam footage, the girl was calling him by his first name. In the selfie I took at the bar—because of course, when I saw them, and we were getting along, I asked for a selfie—I saw that he was wearing a school shirt that said BOXING on it. I googled "Matt Toolbag University Boxing" and just like that, I found him. Not only was he an actuary as well (how cute), but he was a fucking collegiate All-American boxer, with a fight weight of 174 pounds. In other words, had he stepped outside, he would have murdered me.

As I found out more information about this guy—where he went to school, where he works, where he lives—I almost became a little scared of the world that we live in. Anonymity does not exist anymore. You have to understand, I was equipped with nothing but his first name and a T-shirt he was wearing, and within minutes, I was watching a boxing match with him in it from six years ago on YouTube, trying to come up with a gameplan of what I would have done if we did come to blows.* That's why the craziest part of this story to me isn't the fact that I unknowingly picked a fight with an All-American boxer, or the insane coincidence of running into these strangers a week later, eighty miles away from where we first met (bet that wouldn't have shown up in any actuary tables), or that I was called a cunt by another grown man. The craziest part of this story to me is the fact that I was able to find all of this information about these people with nothing more than an internet connection and ten minutes of time.

And I'm just an Uber driver. Imagine what a more sophisticated entity could find.

As frustrated as I was with this situation, and how unfair it was that I would have to skip lunch for the next week, finding out that this guy not only took the higher road that night I saw him at the bar, but did so knowing that he could destroy me, brought me some peace. I felt like we did the same thing for each other. Him and his friends were total assholes in the Uber, but I showed them grace in returning that phone. Then I was an asshole and tried to escalate things in the bar, and he let did the mature thing and let it go.

And that realization was almost enough for me to think I shouldn't send this dash cam video to their coworkers and bosses (thanks again, LinkedIn).

But then I remembered I couldn't work for an entire week over a lie, and I don't think there is anything scummier you can do than take away a man's ability to earn a living. Plus, this was a clear example of the hypocrisy of cancel culture. After all, they had treated me much worse than I had treated them. Where was their week-long suspension?

Is it just because they are higher up on the totem pole? Because they work a corporate job, they are able—expected almost— to get sloppy every weekend and not be held accountable for it? But since I'm an Uber driver, and since Uber drivers come a dime a dozen, it's okay to cancel my life with an unfounded accusation because, fuck 'em—someone else will pick you up.

---

* Best case scenario, I shoot low, get a hold of his knee and drive him into the ground, hoping his hammer punches aren't strong enough to break my back, and as I hold onto his leg for dear life start praying to God the bouncers or anybody else comes to break it up. Worst case scenario, he connects as I'm going for the tackle, and I'm leaving in an ambulance and he's leaving in a cop car, because when street fights are that decisive, cops don't care about who was right and who was wrong— somebody's getting arrested. Long story short, if he did step outside with me, I would have been so fucked.

I kept thinking about how lucky I was that, at the time the situation unfolded, I was single, with no kids and no one to worry about except myself. I could deal with pinching pennies to get by. But I know that the typical driver isn't me—a single guy chasing a dream and using gig work when necessary to pay his bills. The typical driver is a married man with kids, in his forties or fifties, working Uber because he *needs* that money to take care of his family. I've seen the most heartbreaking messages on Uber driver forums from men and women who have sick parents they are taking care of, or kids they need to support, and unfair deactivations from Uber forced them into unsurmountable financial crisis. I kept thinking, if I had a kid, and these scumbags lied about something that cost me my job and prevented me from taking care of my child, I wouldn't hesitate to rain down hellfire on those motherfuckers. Looking at the dash cam footage that proved my innocence, I felt like I owed it to every Uber driver who got deactivated over some bullshit to remind people that just because we may have a low-status job, and we may get accused of things by higher-status people, doesn't mean we are guilty.

And I had these motherfuckers who were pointing the finger at me caught in 1080p looking like assholes. It was my turn for payback. Maybe that will teach Kim and Matt that they shouldn't fuck with people's livelihoods. Maybe it would prevent some other Kim and Matt in the future to think twice before spewing some bullshit and picking on the little guy. I got everyone's email and their place of employment—well, three out of the four, at least. Ironically, the one guy I couldn't find was the one who, in my opinion, made the most unnecessary escalation of this whole story and called me a cunt when I was returning the cell phone. I'm sure I could've found him if I spent some more time on it, but I figured one of the other three would share it with him.

I uploaded the video to YouTube, no faces blurred, with a commentary to go along with it to let everyone who watched it understand how petty and dishonest these people were, and how their lies affected me. I had every email address I needed to make sure that this YouTube link would wind up in the inbox of Kim, Matt, and the Dumb Blonde Chipmunk, as well as a few of their senior coworkers. And if you think I sound crazy—that I have too much time on my hands to do all this—need I remind you that because of these assholes, I couldn't work Uber all week? That freed up at least forty hours.

Just as I'm getting ready to put this video on the internet, that goddamn Good Angel appears on my shoulder and starts chirping in my ear again.

Oh, Eddie…

"No. Not this time."

Edward…

"What?"

What are you hoping to accomplish by doing this?

"I want people to know they shouldn't fuck with people's jobs."

And how are you doing that?

"By fucking with their job."

I know somebody else who likes to fight fire with fire.

Do it! Do it! I heard from my other shoulder.

Speak of the devil.

For the hundredth time, I'm not the devil. I only work for him.

Do the right thing Ed.

Yeah, do right thing and fight back.

Fighting does not make you strong.

That sounds like something a pussy would say.

Was Matt a pussy for not fighting you at the bar?

"Alright! Enough!"

I stepped away from my computer and went for a walk to try to clear my mind. I tried my best to let it go and convince myself to delete that video, but I was still so angry. As I walked, I realized I wasn't just mad at Kim and Matt, and it wasn't only over them lying. I was angry that I traded a holiday weekend for working from dusk 'til dawn, trying to earn an honest buck—only to get screwed by entitled assholes that spent that same weekend getting hammered. I was angry that society looked at them as "professionals" while they look at me as a pleb. I was angry at the idea that we are all just an email away from some asshole fucking up your life: an email in which truth isn't even required. And I was angry that I was an Uber driver. A lowly, forgettable, nobody-cares-to-hear-my-side-of-the-story, Uber driver. Cut 'em loose because who gives a fuck? There is money to be made, and Uber has a big corporate ass that needs to be covered, and as long as the world is spinning there will always be another working-class schlub that'll be there to pick you up because he needs the pennies this gig is offering.

But I figured even though I'm just a lowly Uber driver, the least I can do is not add to these sad realities. Though it would feel vindicating, posting this uncensored video wouldn't change the way people think about Uber drivers, at least not when compared to fancy corporate jobs like Mr. and Mrs. Actuary. It probably wouldn't even get on Uber's radar, and even if it did, it definitely wouldn't happen quick enough for them to lift my one-week suspension. The only thing exposing these people would do is add to the uneasiness we all live with in this digital age, scared to say or do even the most trivial things, worried our actions will be perceived as offensive or wrong. We now live in a world where even the smallest transgressions can be captured and broadcasted to the 4.9 billion people that have access to the internet, allowing any one of those people to criticize and judge those transgressions as if they never made a mistake in their life.

And as much as I wanted to beat Kim and Matt at their own game, I couldn't bring myself to click **Publish**. I deleted that uncensored video from my YouTube drafts, and I x'ed out of that email blast I had queued up.

I think I did the right thing. But why does doing the right thing with this gig always make me feel like such a sucker?

24
A Rich Man's Date Night

When you are living paycheck to paycheck, it's like your finances are a beach ball that you are trying to keep in the air, doing everything you can to keep that ball from hitting the ground. For me, there was nothing more indicative of how close that ball was to hitting the ground than when I had to work Uber on a weeknight. At times, the earnings were so low that after taking into account gas and wear and tear on the car, I was barely breaking even; but that didn't matter, because I could put those expenses on a credit card and pay them next month. I needed cash *now*.*

So during on a particularly tight month, I found myself working on a cold, rainy Tuesday night. I got an Uber request at a big house on a big piece of land in a wealthy Philadelphia suburb. A sophisticated-looking middle-aged man that we'll call Country Club hobbled to my car in a way that made me think he was either injured or drunk. It didn't take long to realize it was the latter.

"Get me the fuck out of here!" he said.

"Heading to Riddle Ale House?"

"Yeah, I'm just going to run in a grab a few beers. Would you be able to drop me off at my girlfriend's after? It's right up the street."

"Sorry man, if it's not in the app I can't take you anywhere else." This dance was all but too familiar with me at this point. This would be the part where he would offer me cash.

"It's right up the road. I'll throw you a couple extra bucks."

"Sounds good to me."

---

* Did you involuntarily hear the JG Wentworth jingle in your head when you read this, just like I did when I wrote it? If so, I apologize. If you have no idea what I'm talking about, I implore you, DO NOT YouTube "JG Wentworth Jingle," unless you want the catchiest song to play in your head every time you hear someone say they "need cash now."

"Thank God. First thing to go my way all night. Do you ever give out your number? That way in the future I can just pay you off the app?"

As I gave him my digits, we passed by an upscale Italian restaurant.

"You ever eat there?"

"I have not."

"I was just there tonight. The food was great. If I wasn't there with my wife, I might have actually enjoyed it."

I'm not sure if you, dear reader, picked up on what he just admitted, but as a driver, every little piece of information is retained and analyzed in hopes of understanding who the hell is sitting behind you. It's a never-ending, subconscious process of assessing the likelihood of that stranger stabbing you in the neck. It's a rare thing, especially after driving so long and seeing so many different walks of life, to be surprised by a rider's revelation, but I did not expect this out of a wealthy, put-together, older man with a beer belly. When I pieced together the disconnect of dinner with the wife, and drinks with the girlfriend, I tried my best to conceal my surprise but my eyebrows raised like a knee jerks when the doctor hits it with a hammer. Now, I'm not a sheltered man, I know how the world works. I know people do this every day, and I know I didn't know the whole story. The thing is, it wasn't the adultery that threw me off: it's that he was so nonchalant about it. I don't condone cheating, but if you are going to cheat, don't flaunt it in a way that reminds others of the sad realities of this world. Do it in silence and shame and with a crippling guilt like a respectable adult.

Fortunately, he was either too drunk or too excited to pick up on my discomfort.

"What's you're deal? You married? Kids?" he asked.

"Neither nor."

"Don't ever fucking do it. It's the end of your life."

"Thanks for the tip."

"When we get to the Ale House, end the trip there. I'll grab some beers, then she's, like, two minutes up the road. I'll throw you an extra $20."

"Alright."

"You got to end the trip when we get there though."

"Okay."

One of my favorite quotes is "a thief thinks everyone steals." That's to say, you see the world the way you operate in the world. And because I was operating under incredible financial stress, I assumed that he wanted me to end the trip because he didn't want to get keep getting charged on the Uber app when he was paying for the rest of the trip in cash. I thought it was just another example of how funny people can be with money. This guy just left a house that could cover a small city block, after eating a dinner that that cost more than what I would earn all night, and just offered me a five-minute job that translates to $240 an hour, and he's worried about what would be approximately $3 extra if I left the app on?

While irrational spending is certainly a common habit among us all, it turns out that when you aren't consumed with keeping that financial beach ball afloat, you see the world in ways that don't involve accounting for every nickel and dime. Before this ride was over, I would learn that turning off the app was one of the most rational requests I ever got from an Uber rider.

As Country Club lumbered out of the car and stumbled into the Ale House, I wondered if the ethical implications of this ride was enough for me to drive away, leaving him there stranded. In other words, is it wrong to bring a married man to his mistress? I know I'm not responsible for the actions of my riders, but at what point am I culpable? I mean, when I drive people to the bar, it's not my fault they get drunk, right? But what if I was driving a drunk guy to a parking garage to pick up his car so he could drive home? Should I try to dissuade him from making that choice, but ultimately leave the decision to him? Or should I physically prevent him from getting behind the wheel? I am inclined to say each person is entitled to make their own decisions, and it's not anyone else's place, especially a lowly Uber driver, to say what is right for them. *Shut up and drive* kind of thing.

But there is definitely an argument against that. Say I was driving two kids to high school, wearing trench coats and carrying duffel bags, and I overheard them discussing their sinister plans of what they wanted to do when they got to the school. I don't think it would be right for me to complete that trip, ya know? So we can all agree there is a line. But what is that line? Does it have to do with people getting hurt? I mean, I'm sure this guy's wife and kids would be hurt if they found out. But then again, that hurt comes from them finding out, not from me taking to him to his girlfriend.

I wondered how much of my internal debate was swayed by the fact that I simply didn't like the guy. He seemed like the kind of person that joins a country club just so he can tell people he belongs. I wondered how much of my personal dislike for this guy weighed in on this moral dilemma of finishing the trip, as I didn't want to be around him anymore, let alone help him do something that he enjoys and makes me feel bad.

But as much as I entertained the idea of leaving him at the Ale House, I knew it would do nothing but delay his conquest and hurt my much-needed bottom dollar. That's the thing about taking principled stands: the more money you have, the more morals you can afford. And I was not in a place financially where I could prioritize my morality over my bills.

The door swings open, and he stepped outside, stopping and smiling, holding up the twelve-pack of beer for me to see, as if we were buddies in this together. He moved toward my car, and I don't know if he was so drunk that he slipped, or forgot about the small steps that lead into the door he just came out of, but his foot kicked out from under him as if he was a cartoon character stepping on a banana peel. Foregoing his own personal safety, Country Club secured the beer first (clearly a man with priorities), tucking it like a football, before shooting his other arm out for the handrail in hopes of staying afoot. But it was too late. This well-groomed member of high society was going down, and going down hard. If it wasn't for the handrail he had bounced off of, he could have very well cracked his skull on the cement steps.

He rolled around for a moment on the ground, looking like a drunken seal in a sweater vest. I thought about getting out to help him, but once I knew he wasn't seriously injured, I let him fend for himself and chalked up his fall as karma. When he finally got up, he played it off with a goofy smile and shrug that made me incredibly embarrassed for him—and for myself, for being at a stage in my life where I needed his $20.

"It's freezing out there," he said when he got back in, not acknowledging his fall.

"You're going to have to let me know where to go."

"I got it right here. Hold on." He looked at his text. "123 West Second Street."

He wasn't kidding, it really was right up the street. I got out of that parking lot and fast. I was so ready to be done with this guy.

"You ended the trip on the app, right?"

"Sure did." *This guy and his fucking money,* I thought.

"Good. Sometimes the wife checks my Uber account."

I could feel the anger showing on my face, but I didn't even try to hide it this time. It pissed me off that this guy was using me to cheat on his wife. It pissed me off even more that he was bragging about it. But what pissed me off most was how naive I was to think he wanted me to end the trip to save a couple bucks.

Of course he didn't care about the money, Ed. I thought to myself. *That's only something a poor shmuck like you would stress about.*

We pulled into a driveway, and the lights in the house are all off.

"Is this it?" he asked.

"This is the address you gave me."

"Give me one second. Let me call her." I can hear it ringing.

"Sorry man, you got to go." It goes to voicemail.

"I've never actually been here before." He grabbed his beer. "Could you just hang here for a second, make sure I get in."

"Sorry man, I already have another request." I lied. I just wanted to get the fuck out of there. He looked at the house, and then back to me. "Alright," he said, and got out.

I was out of that driveway before he even got to the porch. Within a minute, though, he was calling me.

I should've never given him my number. I hit the decline button. I wanted to be done with this guy.

He called again. Declined again.

When he called a third time, I figured something had to be up, so I answered.

"Hello."

"You've got to help me." This grown-ass man said in a drunken whine. He sounded so desperate, I thought he was on the verge of tears. "I put the wrong address in. It's freezing out here. You have to come get me. Please. Please."

"I'm sorry, sir. I have another ride. You should just order another Uber."

"I can't."

Oh, that's right. You can't. My, oh my, how the turn tables turn.

"Please. I'm begging you."

In retrospect, I should've extorted this guy for all the cash in his wallet. But it's a weird thing, as badly as I needed money, and as much as I didn't like him, when you hear someone in physical and immediate pain, unless you are an actual psychopath, it changes things. And as much as I didn't like this guy and everything he stood for, it felt more wrong to let him freeze than to facilitate his cheating.

"Stay right there. I'll be there in a minute." I wasn't happy when I turned my car around, but the silver lining of it was that I was finally able to use my psychology degree in a real life scenario, applying

Maslow's Hierarchy of Needs to a moral dilemma I faced as I chauffeured wealthy adulterers from beer stores to their whores.

"Thank God," he said when he got back in. "It was freezing out there."

"So where are we heading?"

"I don't know. Let me try her again." He took out his phone, and though I wasn't able to hear her end of the following conversation, it seemed easy enough to fill in the blanks.

"Hey babe. I thought I was out front, but it wasn't your place..."

Muffled female voice on the phone

"I don't know, but they sure weren't happy when they answered the door."

Muffled female voice on the phone

"123 West Second Street."

Muffled female voice on the phone

"*Ohhh*, got it. Be there soon," he said, hanging up the phone. "It's *East* Second Street," he said to me. "Sorry about that. This is my first time at her place. She said she was tired of doing that hotel shit. Anyway, you think I can call you later for a ride home?"

There was no way I was going to subject myself to this guy and his shenanigans again, but there was no need to tell him that. Instead I said, "I doubt I'll be in this area, but you can try." I like to think I'm being mature by avoiding unnecessary confrontation, but there is a part of me that wonders if I'm too nice; so compliant that this guy I can't stand has every reason to think he is welcome to give me a call later for another ride. In other words, part of me feels like a little Uber bitch.

We pull up to her actual place in no time. It's a walk-up apartment on the backside of a residential house. It made me think it was the kind of place a divorcee would move to after her kids have moved out. She was waiting at the door with the light on, and opened it to wave when we pulled up. She looked like someone who was very good looking in high school and was fighting hard against father time with an arsenal of makeup, bleached blonde hair, and a very perky and very obvious addition.

"Check out those fucking tits," he said, as he peeled off a couple more bucks.

As I watched him walk into that house, I didn't wonder how he slept at night because I knew the answer. It was either in a huge house or next to some huge boobs. What I wondered was whether my approach to life has been wrong all along. Here I am, chasing down a dream, trying to live a life I can be proud of, and what had that gotten me? It got me stuck working on a Tuesday night just to keep that beach ball from hitting the ground. Meanwhile, this guy conducts himself like a total scumbag and the universe seems to reward him for it. Shoot, even the fact that he has a girlfriend speaks to the way the world works. After all, Ms. Lewinsky didn't get on her knees for the help.

I thought about all the dates I lost when they found out I drive for Uber, or the hundreds of snarky comments I've gotten from strangers and passengers for working such a shit job, and even the family and friends that judged me for my position in life. I wish they could have seen this interaction. Sure, I bet if life was a scoreboard, most of those people would put the Uber driver at zero and the guy with big house and fancy dinners far ahead. But here that guy was, creeping around, drunk at night, literally falling over himself, whining and crying and depending on me to save him.

So, who knows, maybe I am a sucker. Maybe I am behind on the scoreboard of life, and maybe I'll never get ahead. But at least I'm not *him*.

As I continued the grind of keeping that beach ball off the ground, I sat in the very real possibility that this life might not pan out for me the way I hoped, that my dreams would amount to nothing but a struggle to get by, and I wondered if I would be okay with that. I wondered if the benefit of enjoying what I do would outweigh the costs that came with it. I wondered how long I could last being looked at like I'm the irresponsible one, while witnessing first-hand the recklessness of people who meet society's standards of success. Seeing that disconnect is enough to drive a man to cynicism and bitterness, and that's not a fun way to go through life.

As I obsessed over these thoughts, one of my favorite songs came on the radio; a song by Zac Brown about how it's the simple things in life that mean the most. One line, specifically, stood out to me in a way that it never had before.

"There's no dollar sign, on a peace of mind, this I've come to know."

"I appreciate the sentiment, Zac," I thought out loud in an empty car. "But you got to be rich in the first place to come up with that shit."

25
10 AM Liquor Run

We arrived at the liquor store at 10:01 a.m., exactly one minute after it opened. It was impeccable timing, especially considering that if I didn't hit that one stoplight, my passenger would have been walking up to the door the moment the clerk unlocked it.

It was a Tuesday morning, and I was in an upper-middle-class suburb about an hour away from Philly. My passenger had gotten into my car and greeted me with a "How ya doin', brother?" in an accent that let me know he could work a plough or wrangle them horses or do whatever it is people in flyover states do. When I confirmed that his destination was a shopping center nearby, he said, "If it's okay with you, it's going to be a round trip. I just got to run into the store and you can *brang* me right back. I'll throw you some cash."

The ride there was in silence, and when we arrived, I was a little surprised at the destination, being that it was a weekday morning. But I had been driving for Uber long enough to know that the life of the average person is far from average. I had given up trying to put people in boxes based on superficial traits. What was impressive about this man, though, was that he went in and out of that liquor store so fast it was like they had the fifth of vodka waiting for him. With a bottle in hand, there seemed to be a weight lifted off his shoulders, and all of a sudden he was looking to chat.

"It never ceases to amaze me," he said, "how difficult y'all make it to get some liquor around here."

"What do you mean?"

"Back home, they sell at gas stations and corner stores all hours of the day. Around here you got to jump through hoops just to get a drink."

"Oh, right. They don't call it the Quaker State for nothing." It wasn't until I traveled outside of Pennsylvania that I realized how strict our alcohol laws are. Liquor and beer can't be sold in the same store, and up until recently, neither could be sold in any other place than state-designated stores that only sold beer or liquor.

He told me he was from the heart of Missouri, which I know to be as rural as rural can get, and that you can get your drinks from any gas station or grocery store "before the sun comes up."

"I came up here about three years ago, staying at my aunt's looking for work, and from what I heard Philly isn't the type of town you can mess around in."

"You heard correct."

"Well, what I got incorrect was that I thought out here, I was a lot closer to the city than I actually was."

"Oh yeah, this isn't anywhere close to Philly. This is one of the nicest suburbs in the area."

"Well, *shiiit*, that woulda been good to know before I went to the bar. I figured I'd bring my pistol, just a little .22, just because of all the shit I heard. Wouldn't you know, leaning over the bar to wave down the bartender, a woman sees the gun in my waistband and calls the cops?"

"Oh, no." I knew where this was going. This was the same area where I got pulled over for driving a beat up 1977 Cadillac late at night. And I don't mean pulled over like "Excuse me sir, can I see your license and registration?" I mean seven cop cars from multiple departments pulling me and my three friends out of the car and giving us a pat down. They told us my car matched the description of another that was involved in home robberies in the area, but I knew better. We were in a poor person's car in a rich neighborhood is all, and in a low-crime, wealthy area like this, that's enough to turn the whole department out. I could only imagine the kind of hell a call about a gun at a bar would raise.

"It was like the whole goddamn police force of Pennsylvania had nothing better to do than to come and get me. For a little .22!"

I had a feeling that for him, taking a pistol to a bar was similar to the way I bring a sweatshirt to spring baseball game. Better to have it and not need it, than need it and not have it. I had a friend from Missouri who told me that they literally checked their guns into their high school office during hunting season, and his school only did that for the appearance of responsibility. Other schools in the area would simply tell the kids to leave their weapons on their truck's gun rack in the parking lot, right there out in the open.

My rider goes on to tell me that the prosecutor wanted to charge him for every state line he crossed with that gun on the way from Missouri to Pennsylvania. He ended up spending some time in prison, and when he got out, he said, "Fuck Pennsylvania" and headed home to Missouri.

A couple years later, he was back in Pennsylvania over the holidays to visit family, and unfortunately, got a DUI. "I only had three beers before I ran out to get more," he said. "I was barely over the legal limit." Because he had a prior charge, this DUI came with some added penalties. Not only did he lose his license, but he was put on house arrest here in the Philly suburbs.

"My life is back in Missouri now, though, so I said fuck that." He explained how he worked out a deal where he can serve his house arrest at home, and make the sixteen-hour drive from Missouri to Pennsylvania once a month to meet with his probation officer. After he meets with his P.O., he stays for a few nights, drinking the days away until he is ready to make the sixteen-hour drive back home.

Before long, we were back at his house. I watched him walk down his driveway, bottle in hand, ready to drown his weekday morning away in booze. To be clear, this isn't my first rodeo dealing with someone going through the American criminal justice system. I'd bet dollars to donuts that there is more to the story, especially regarding the DUI and subsequent house arrest. I also recognize I am in no position to say if this 10 a.m. trip to the liquor store was something that he would've done before he had his troubles with Johnny Law, or if he is only doing it now as a result of it; though I am inclined to believe the adage that idle hands are the devil's workshop. I never understood what people expected those on house arrest to do.

As I drove away, I couldn't help but wonder how much being a Missourian in Pennsylvania contributed to his problems. I'm not saying drinking and driving is good, but flirting with the legal limit on an empty country road is a lot different than doing so on a busy suburban highway. And I don't have the first idea about solving the gun issue in this country, but I don't think I could have gotten a clearer picture of how different this man's relationship with guns is than my own. I couldn't get over how he thought the police were overreacting for having a gun at the bar, especially because it seemed a lot of his shock came from the fact that it was only a .22 that he was carrying. Meanwhile, I could've heard he had an airsoft gun and I would've thought, in the bar with no guns, the man with a smallest pistol is king, so it's a damn good thing the police turned out like they did. A guy with a gun in a place with alcohol in abundance is exactly the kind of situation we need police for. But in his mind, because of where he is from and how he was raised, he thinks his .22 is inconsequential, assuming there are several people in that same bar with much bigger guns, and that if he got out of order, they would make him ineffective real quick.

But what struck me most about this man's story is how it highlighted how big and different this country is. I'm not going to act like I have answers to the political questions that divide this country, and even if I did, I don't think I'd change anyone's mind. That's not how political takes usually go. It seems like the talking heads and political pundits are there to preach to the choir, or anger those who disagree. Hearing this guy's perspective, though, reminded me about one of my biggest lessons from driving Uber—how so many people come from so many different walks of life, and everyone's situation is unique and specific. It's impossible to say what works for one will work for another, let alone make laws mandating it. And that's a lesson I've learned from driving a mostly local clientele. Getting a snapshot of this Missourian's perspective was like hearing that lesson on steroids.

And so when I hear those talking heads and political pundits sounding off on the nightly news or see someone I know sounding off on a social media feed, before I even think about the content of what they are saying, I remind myself that anyone who thinks they have a blanket solution to a country of three hundred million people who live across 3.5-million square miles of land is certifiably insane.

Epilogue

"Excuse me sir, I have a question," she asked, from the middle of the back seat. She was one of four college-aged girls in my car. "Do you have a TikTok?"

"I do."

"Wait… are you the one that posts with your Grandma?"

"I am."

"YOU ARE?!" she screamed.

"*What?!* How did you know that?" Another girl asked.

"Me and my friend send each other your TikToks back and forth all the time."

It was November 2019, almost four years to the day I picked up my first Uber ride. I hadn't driven Uber in months—I had finally saved up enough money to devote the majority of my time to content creation. But it was the night before Thanksgiving, and I knew there was money to be made, so I had to turn that Uber app on. And I'm glad I did: It's a lonely endeavor creating content, and I've yet to see a number of likes or views that matches the feeling of an actual person telling you what your work means to them. And when that girl told me that, I got to experience that feeling for the first time.

A couple months prior, I had started uploading to TikTok, an app that, at the time, was slowly encroaching on the mainstream. Being one of the earlier adopters of it and the viral potential its algorithm allowed helped me to quickly build a following. It was almost fitting for a rider to recognize me that night while working Uber, as that same morning I crossed the milestone of 100,000 followers. That following eventually carried over to my YouTube channel, and over Covid is when my accounts really ballooned. I joke that it took a global pandemic and people being stuck in their houses for them to go through every other piece of content available on the internet before settling for mine, but in reality, I know that it had more to do with the years and years of beating on my craft; the patience and the persistence of showing up and getting a little better each day. In other words, I'm talking about practice.

As time went on, and my following has grown, the recognitions in the Uber, or on the street, or at the bar, have become more frequent. I don't share that because fame is the goal. If anything, it didn't take long being a Z-List celebrity to understand why actual celebrities go crazy. When I'm a few brews too deep, trying to get some food in my stomach at the end of the night, and a stranger yells across the Wawa, "Oh shit! You're the Uber guy!" my social anxiety skyrockets. I want to somehow express my gratitude to this person for the support, yet maintain an appearance of sobriety that I certainly don't possess in the moment—all the while, stressing that the alcohol in my system might facilitate me saying or doing something that can expedite the process of getting myself canceled. And I say "expedite" because I always figured my cancellation to be inevitable. I mean, you guys saw how many N-Words were in this book. If I self-narrate the audio version, it's only a matter of time.

The reason I share that I sometimes get recognized is because of how truly bizarre it all is: One minute I'm being told by a rider I've left them "starstruck," only for my very next rider to not even give me the respect of responding to my greeting, or goodbye. Once, after being told by a disgruntled passenger to "get a real job," I stopped to get gas and the attendant asked for a selfie. I've quite literally received letters from people in different countries telling me how my videos have helped them through some of the darkest days of their life, and then later that night I was referred to as a "retarded, worthless piece of shit" simply because I wouldn't let six people squeeze into my Uber. It's like I'm internationally known, yet still locally disrespected.

I once heard a movie star talking about how he likes being famous because whenever he meets people, they show him their best selves. I couldn't help but think how when I'm driving Uber, it's the complete opposite. Nobody is putting on any sort of pretense for a lowly, forgettable rideshare driver. As a result, day in and day out, I see people in their most human element, being their true selves as they argue with a significant other, complain about their job, or deal with terrible consequences that alcohol (almost always) seems to bring. At times, more often than you might imagine, I am treated like a therapist; riders feeling safe enough to share their deepest and darkest secrets due to the anonymity and assumed powerlessness of the Uber driver.

At other times, those same factors are what allows me to see one of the ugliest sides of human beings: the inclination to exploit even the tiniest smidgen of power any chance they get. It's an opportunity given to them by the very dynamic of an Uber ride—of rider to driver, boss to employee, master to servant; and it was only exacerbated when Uber tapped into that very human desire by advertising to new customers the idea that they could have their own personal driver at their beck and call for a few dollars.

I sometimes think of this one ride that occurred toward the beginning of my Uber career. A guy that looked to be around my age came to my car and asked me to wait for his friends who would be out shortly. We were making small talk, and when he asked me my age—I was twenty-nine at the time—he said, "What the fuck? You're tip just went down. I thought you were a kid. You're a grown ass man... what the fuck is your deal?" He told me I "better have the right story" as to why I found myself working Uber as a twenty-nine year old on a Saturday night.

After telling him to get the fuck out of my car, he tried to rectify the situation by recanting his threat, telling me he would tip me more. To be clear, I don't expect tips at all—it was knowing how this guy viewed me as a human being that made me want nothing to do with him, let alone provide a service for him. But alas, I was too broke to refuse free money and had to swallow my pride as I asked him how much he would pay if I drove him.

When we arrived at his destination and he counted out the money he owed me (read: that I extorted him for) I was embarrassed for him, struggling to find the right combination of bills to pony up his pathetic excuse for an apology. I was embarrassed for myself being in a position where I desperately needed this man's money. And above all else, I was fuming. This guy embodied the way so many people looked at me, and I wanted to explode.

He asked what I am doing out here: *I'm fucking trying, man. That's what I'm doing.* I don't know what kind of life you have or what kind of life you want for yourself, but this is what I decided I need to do right now in order to make my situation better.

I wanted to have the last word—actually, I wanted to punch this guy in the fucking face—but I thought the last word would be a more prudent course of action. As he was getting out, in one of the cringiest attempts at having a "gotcha" moment in my life, I blurted out, "You're going to see me on TV one day."

To be clear, what I actually meant was you're going to see a work of mine on TV one day. Ever since high school, my dream in life was to write a movie like *My Cousin Vinny*—the kind of movie that everyone knows; one that's quotable, funny, true, and no matter what point you turn it on, you can't look away. That dream has since changed, as I don't think the media landscape will allow us to ever see a movie like that again. But the point remains the same: I want to tell stories, great stories that resonate with a lot of people. Stories that help people learn, and think, and grow—and most importantly, laugh. I want to tell stories like the ones that shaped me when I was younger, and continue to shape me today.

I like to think part of what I'm doing trying to chase down this dream is being a counterargument to that douchebag who dangled a tip over my head because he thought his approval of my life mattered, and the so many others who think like him; who measure success by the kind of job you are working at a certain stage of your life. I like to think that there is someone else out there who sees what I am doing—quite literally broadcasting a part of my life that others think I should be ashamed of, and having fun doing it, and might be encouraged to remember that as long as you are trying your best, and you aren't hurting anyone else, you shouldn't get too wrapped up with what other people think.

Perhaps being treated so differently by so many people so often—valued by strangers on opposite ends of the social spectrum depending on what kind of work they know me for—helps me understand how meaningless the opinions of others are. Perhaps it helps remind me that just like they are making their assumptions based on whatever small glimpse they had of my life, I am doing the same to them. Maybe that's what gives me the patience to consider that their actions in my Uber aren't entirely indicative of who these people are.

It makes me think of one of the more popular videos on my channel titled "Worst Uber Ever." Four ornery and athletic young men got in my car after a night of drinking. From the moment I pulled up I could tell that they were looking for a fight. As we were driving through the empty dark roads of South Jersey, I requested they not smoke in my car, and that escalated the situation. I have never in my Uber career felt so close to having the ever-loving shit kicked out of me (or worse) by four guys, and had to swallow my pride and comply to their every request to avoid a beating. After I dropped them off, I could still hear them talking shit about me as they walked away, one of them specifically referring to me as "a lazy Uber driver."

I felt like the bitch of the year when it happened, being strong-armed into playing the role of a little Uber bitch boy, submitting to their every demand, in my own car, just to earn a few bucks. The entire ride was caught on my dash cam, and I had a hard time looking at the video. I don't know what's worse: getting walked all over like that, or *seeing myself* get walked all over like that. But I posted it anyway knowing that there are a lot of people out there that could learn from what I went through. I like to think it painted a picture of the true risks involved with driving Uber, and deterred people who aren't fit to handle that kind of situation with the patience (read: willingness to let entitled assholes trample all over you) required to make it out of a ride like that unscathed. The smallest amount of pushback in that kind of situation is how drivers end up getting hurt and riders end up in prison.

Even though I made it out of that ride without a scratch, it fucked me up pretty good. I didn't sleep that night because I was so pissed off—my natural Irish response to that familiar feeling of helplessness. On top of that, I didn't feel safe driving Uber for a long while after that, which really sucked, because I was still broke and had to keep working regardless.

Despite all of that though, when I posted the video of the ride, much to the dismay of many of my viewers, I chose to blur their faces out. I didn't feel right exposing them. First and foremost, they were white and used the N-word freely. That alone could prevent them from getting or keeping a job in the future. And if that wasn't enough, the drug use in the video and threats of violence sure wouldn't help their case. But aside from that, I didn't want to expose them on the belief (hope, really) that their actions did not represent who they were as people; that it was simply who they were at that moment in time. I didn't think it would be fair to show them in that light without giving them a chance to defend themselves, or at the very least, say sorry. Since that's not how the internet works, I thought it would only be right to conceal their identities.

I sometimes wonder if it's naive of me to think like this—if it's an overly optimistic view of people; that in reality, people like these four guys are scumbags through and through and having their true colors caught in 1080p and posted to YouTube is something they have coming to them. That people like me who try to show these guys compassion are only kicking the can down the road, causing others to experience their abusiveness, until one day someone finally exposes them for who they are. I'm not sure. But I do know that I would want to be given the benefit of the doubt if I had one of my worst moments caught on camera, and thought I'd act accordingly.

You can imagine my surprise when six months after posting the video, I got an email from one of the guys in the car. He took full accountability for his actions, was extremely apologetic, and even called me a "great man" as he thanked me for blurring their faces. He shared very personal information that he asked me to keep private, and I thought the fact that he would trust me to do so spoke volumes about his honesty. After all, at this point, the assumed powerlessness and anonymity of his Uber driver was gone—he was aware of the audience I had online, and it doesn't take a rocket scientist to piece together how I could use the revealing content of his email to my benefit and at his expense, especially with a comment section full of people calling to have their faces unblurred.

He reiterated multiple times that he wasn't sending this email as an excuse, but instead, to explain that his actions were not personal. He said that when he saw the video, he was disgusted with himself, and went into detail about the extenuating circumstances that caused him to act that way. What he said many times, in various ways, was that his actions in that video did not represent who he is as a person.

It was one of those things that I had believed in my heart—but was grateful to see evidence of. What really put the icing on the cake, though, was that he told me he was actually planning on driving Uber himself after he graduated. This was the very same guy I heard refer to me a "lazy Uber driver." I don't think I'm going out on a limb when I assume that he isn't going to be looking at himself as "lazy" when he takes up the side gig for himself. I thought it was a nice reminder that the things people say in the heat of the moment aren't things people necessarily believe.

That email is the most concrete piece of evidence I have that proves what I've come to learn about people: we aren't good, we aren't bad; we are a little bit of everything. Whether you see me at 3 a.m. behind the wheel of my Uber in sweatpants and a scruffy beard, giving the illusion of failure, or you come across my social media profile with a checkmark next to my name, giving the illusion of success, I'm the same person. Whether I meet someone in my Uber, drunk and out of their mind on a Saturday night, or calm and collected on a weekday ride to work, they are the same person. The guy who nearly assaulted me and the guy who was disgusted with himself for doing so are the same person.

In this book, I shared with you twenty-five stories that were snapshots of strangers' lives. These were twenty-five rides that I found extremely memorable, impactful, or just flat out hilarious. But it should be noted that in my rideshare career, I've given over five thousand rides, the majority of which weren't bad. They weren't necessarily good, but they weren't bad. Most people, whether they were rich or poor, black or white, male or female, and everyone in between, were just trying to get from point A to point B, too wrapped up in their own world to even make conversation with me, sometimes barely saying hello. But those twenty-five crazy ones will always outweigh the thousands of benign ones because that's how the human mind works. It's similar to how the news never reports on the millions of people who safely ride the subway every day—but the day someone gets stabbed, it's covered in a way that makes you think it's the rule and not the exception.

We are attracted to stories with conflict because those are the stories we learn from, that signal the danger we need to avoid. It has been programmed in us since the dawn of man, when two cavemen went out for a walk and only one came back with a story of what happened when his friend tried to pet a bear cub.

Unfortunately, I don't think our evolution has caught up (or will ever catch up) to a social media algorithm with the ability to tap into our desire for conflict, equipped with a never-ending supply of videos to fill that need. It's why my videos of bad Uber rides always get more clicks than the good ones. In perhaps the most telling example of this, I once posted a video titled "Great Conversation with Muhammad," where I picked up an Uber rider and we had, as the title suggested, a great conversation about a variety of sensitive topics, such as race and policing in America. It got less than 20,000 views over a span of half a year. Without altering anything else about the video, I changed the title of it to "Uncomfortable Conversation with a Black Man." The video exploded, getting half a million clicks in just a few months.

We live in a world that feigns a sense of connectivity, be it through social media, or apps like Uber that bring people together quicker and more efficiently than ever. But while these connections are vast, they are not deep. Instead, we get increasingly smaller snapshots of more and more people. And, be it consciously or subconsciously, we use these tiny snapshots to place people into boxes: rich or poor, liberal or conservative, too woke or not woke enough, lazy Uber driver or incredibly handsome and charming content creator, and the endless other value judgments we place on others. Really, these judgments are nothing but an attempt to take the limited information being presented to us about a person and use it to determine if that person can help us or hurt us. That why it's important to keep in mind that there is so much more to a human being than what we see of them in these snapshots—especially when that snapshot isn't one of their best moments.

With over five thousand rides under my belt, a conservative estimate would put the tally at over ten thousand strangers, from all walks of life, who have gotten in my car. And I truly believe that not a single one of them, even the rudest, most entitled, ignorant rider, treated me a certain way, good or bad, because of who I am as a person. Instead, their actions were a reflection of how they interact with the world—specifically, how they happened to be doing so in that moment. Acknowledging that creates patience and understanding, and even more importantly, allows for something that doesn't seem very fashionable these days, something that we all want at some point or another yet are always so reluctant to give: empathy and forgiveness.

That may seem out of place; a melodramatic call to action in response to the occasional entitled Uber rider. But similar to how spending too much time on social media, scrolling through the highlight reel of other people's lives, can give you a false sense of how good their life is and how much your life is lacking; working this job, seeing so many people who seem so unhappy, can create a sense of crushing pessimism that I have found to be common among other people who work so closely and so often with the public.

But at the same time, I have to acknowledge the fact that I still occasionally choose to drive Uber. At this point, the money is helpful, sure, but not as necessary as it was when I was living check to check to check to check to check. So the natural question is: *Why?* What is it about this bottom-rung, thankless job that keeps drawing me back?

Despite the entitlement, ungratefulness, and misery I see, there is something about this glimpse into people's actual lives, a view that isn't filtered through social media or framed by a thought-out caption. It's like a vulgar curiosity that keeps me wanting to find out who these people are that exist in this world with me, people I would probably otherwise never encounter. It's not always pretty. Sometimes, it's beyond frustrating—even to the point of demoralizing. But it's *real*. And there's something about encountering the "real" that is more satisfying than anything else.

This privileged look into the authentic lives of the strangers around me forces me to recognize that no matter what box I try to put people in; whether I pick them up from a mansion on the Main Line or in the slums of Southwest Philadelphia, I never really know who they are, or what I find most interesting: how happy they will be in that moment.

I keep driving because it's a constant reminder that no matter your station in life, it isn't always going to be peaches and cream. But the way you process the things that happen to you on a daily basis makes all the difference.

For More from the Author:

Books (available at eddiepdoyle.com):

I Hate You Jimmy - True Stories of Hanging Out with "That Guy in a Wheelchair"

YouTube Channels:

Eddie Doyle
Mondays With Mommom
Cheesesteaks Wit Eddie Doyle

Podcast:

Cheesesteaks with Eddie Doyle

Acknowledgements

I always had a weird annoyance with the Acknowledgment section of a book. It always felt like a jumbled, rushed way of fitting in as many people as possible, which I always imagined left those acknowledged a bit underwhelmed. I mean, these authors drop lines like "it couldn't have been done without you," and then rattle off five or six people in a row. You're telling me someone who was that crucial to the book's creation can't even get their own sentence? Plus, as a reader, I was always left confused and dissatisfied.

So I wanted to do something different. Head to my YouTube channel and search for a video titled "Internationally Known, Locally Disrespected Acknowledgements."

If you can see this part right here, it means you have one of the earliest versions of this book. Between you and me, though I know exactly who I want to Acknowledge in the aforementioned video, the video has yet to be made. I hope it turns out okay. If I miss the mark, oh well, I tried. But what I am going for is the idea that I need to acknowledge it all—the good rides and the bad rides, the people who love my channel and the people who hate watch it, those who have encouraged me and those who have done the opposite. This book was made possible by all of that. We have a tendency to think that the people who helped us are the ones who made us feel good while doing it. I think that's bullshit.

That said, I wanted to include this last little bit here in the earliest version for you. Because amongst all those people that have affected this book, it's people like you that are the first to buy the books, or the first to watch the videos, or the first to subscribe to a new channel of mine or the hundreds of other ways you guys show your support, that truly made this book possible.

So thank you.